D0706566

WORKS ISSUED BY

THE HAKLUYT SOCIETY

THE TRAVELS OF IBN BAṬṬŪṬA
A.D. 1325–1354

VOL. III

SECOND SERIES
No. 141

ISSUED FOR 1971

THE TRAVELS OF
IBN BAṬṬŪṬA

A.D. 1325 - 1354

Translated with revisions and notes from the Arabic text edited by

C. DEFRÉMERY and B. R. SANGUINETTI

by

H. A. R. GIBB

VOL. III

CAMBRIDGE

Published for the Hakluyt Society

AT THE UNIVERSITY PRESS

1971

PUBLISHED BY

THE SYNDICS OF THE CAMBRIDGE UNIVERSITY PRESS

Bentley House, 200 Euston Road, London N.W.1
American Branch: 32 East 57th Street, New York, N.Y. 10022

ISBN: 0 521 01033 0

Printed in Great Britain
by Robert MacLehose and Company Limited
at the University Press Glasgow

CONTENTS

PLATES

between pp. 622 and 623, photographs by J. Burton-Page

MAPS

FOREWORD TO VOLUME THREE

In the third volume of his travels Ibn Baṭṭūṭa visits the two large sectors of Islamic Society in the Central Asian and Indian zones. From Sarai which he visited at the end of volume II, he journeyed through the desert to Khwarizm and thence to Bukhara. Thereafter he moved southwards to the camp of the Sultan Ṭarmashīrīn at which he stayed for fifty-four days. There is very little in the fourteenth century chronicles which relates to Ṭarmashīrīn or to the events of his reign. The chroniclers put his reign at 1326–1334 with some uncertainty about the second date. He was the first sultan of his dynasty in Transoxiana to adopt the religion of Islam, but there seems to be some evidence that he was hostile to the rule of the Sultan of India.

Ibn Baṭṭūṭa then crossed the Oxus to Balkh in the territories of the Amir of Herāt and from there journeyed through the cities of Khurasan. It seems to be impossible that this journey could have been carried out in the time available. From Balkh he proceeded to Qundus for about forty days. Thereupon he crossed the Hindu Kush to the city of Ghazna. It is from this point that the crossing to the Indus valley is open to doubt. According to Ibn Baṭṭūṭa's statement he returned to Kabul and then crossed the mountains to the Indian side at Shashnagar and thence journeyed for fifteen days through the desert reaching the Indus at Janānī.

Janānī is no longer extant but is in the district of Sehwan. After some further excursions he moved up to Multān which was the capital of Sind.

He awaited there the Sultan's order to move to Delhi and incidentally takes the occasion to describe some of the trees and fruits of India. He left there for Delhi where he arrived on the 13th of Rajab 734, equal to 20th March 1334.

He first describes the city of Delhi and gives an account of the rulers of the capital and then describes Sultan Muḥammad ibn Tughluq.

It was probably a fortunate event that the seven years spent under the control of Muḥammad ibn Tughluq was the period when the Sultanate of Delhi was at its height and the vigour and endurance of the Sultan was at its peak. Under his rule the treasures of India were distributed to persons from all the old territories of Islam and Ibn Baṭṭūṭa takes full advantage of them.

The Sultan's personality has been debated by Indian writers of the period and most of the cruelties inflicted by him on both secular and religious individuals were carried out without mercy. Ibn Baṭṭūṭa himself came under the Sultan's displeasure and very nearly succumbed to his punishment. However, after a period when he resigned all his possessions he suddenly received a notice to attend the Sultan's court and was given the office of conducting an embassy to China.

My warm thanks are due to Professor Charles Beckingham for his kindness in assisting me to edit this volume, and in reading the proofs, to Mr John Burton-Page for the photographs of Delhi, and to my wife, to whose kindly encouragement this volume is indebted.

ABBREVIATIONS

BSOAS	*Bulletin of the School of Oriental and African Studies*, London.
Dozy	R. P. A. Dozy, *Supplément aux dictionnaires arabes.*
E.I.	*Encyclopaedia of Islam.*
E.I.[2]	*Ibid.*, second edition.
GJ	*Geographical Journal*, London
JA	*Journal Asiatique*, Paris.
JRAS	*Journal of the Royal Asiatic Society*, London.
R.C.É.A.	*Répertoire chronologique d'epigraphie arabe.*
Selections	*Ibn Baṭṭūṭa's Travels in Asia and Africa.* Translated and selected by H. A. R. Gibb.
Yāqūt	*Mu'jam al-Buldān.* By Yāqūt al-Rūmī.

CHAPTER IX

Turkestan and Khurasan

AFTER ten days' journey from al-Sarā we reached the city of Sarāchūq (*chūq* means 'little', so that it is as if they said 'little Sarā'), which lies on the bank of a great and swollen river called Ulūṣū, meaning 'the great stream'.[1] Over it is a bridge of boats, like the bridge of Baghdād.[2] At this city we reached the limit of the journey with the horses that draw the waggons. We sold them at the rate of four silver dinars per head, and even less, on account of their exhaustion and the cheapness of horses in this town, and hired camels to draw the waggons. In this city there is a hospice | belonging to a pious Turk of great age, who is called Aṭā, which means 'father'. He received us hospitably in it and called down a blessing on us. We were hospitably entertained also by the qāḍī of the town, but I do not know his name.

From this place we went on for thirty days by forced marches, halting only for two hours each day, one in the forenoon and the other at sunset. The length of the halt was just as long as the time needed to cook and sup *dūqī*,[3] and this is cooked with a single boiling. They would have with them [pieces of] dried meat,[4] which they put on top of this and they pour sour milk over the whole. Everybody eats and sleeps in his waggon while it is actually on the move, and I had in my waggon three slavegirls. It is the custom of travellers in this wilderness to use the utmost speed, because of the scarcity of herbage. Of the camels that cross it the majority

[1] Saraichiq, about 40 miles from the mouth of the Ural river, called in Turkish *ulu-ṣu*, 'Great River' and by the Arab geographers Yayik.

[2] See vol. II, p. 329.

[3] See vol. II, p. 474.

[4] Arabic *al-khalī'*, apparently a Maghribine term, described by Dozy as salted or marinated beef or mutton, soaked in oil and then sun-dried.

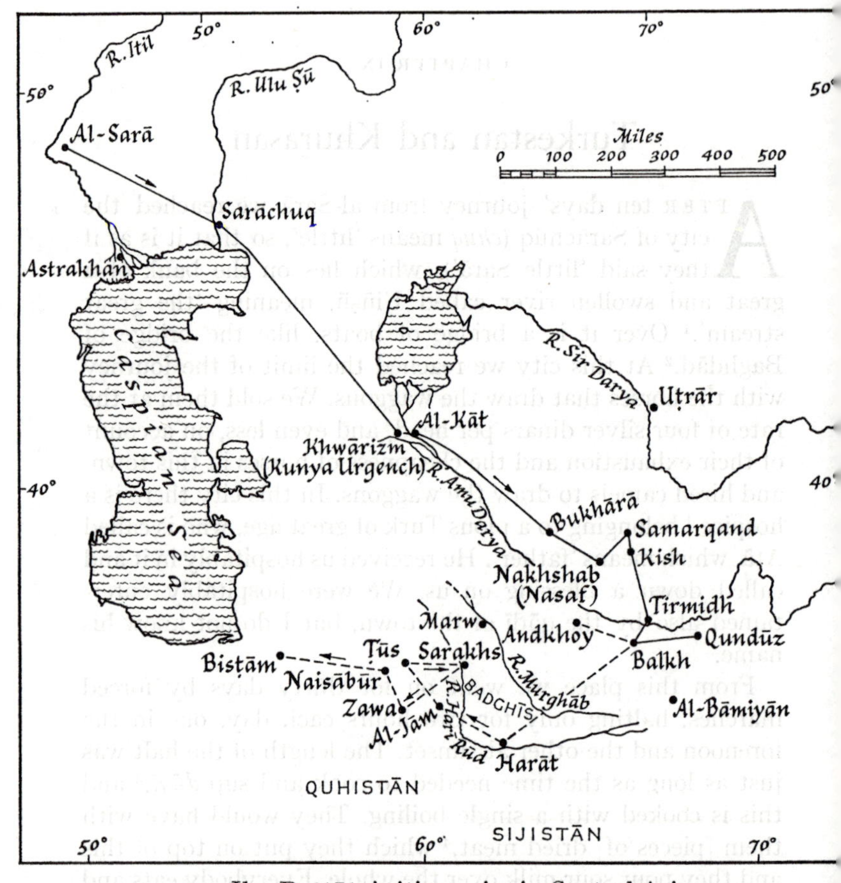

1. Ibn Baṭṭūṭa's itineraries in Central Asia

perish and the remainder are of no use except a year later, after they are fattened up. | The water in this desert is at certain known waterpoints, separated by two or three days' march, and is rainwater [in surface pools] and shallow wells under the sand.

3

After journeying through this desert and traversing it as we have described we arrived at Khwārizm,[5] which is the largest, greatest, most beautiful and most important city of the Turks. It has fine bazaars and broad streets, a great number of buildings and abundance of commodities; it shakes under the weight of its population, by reason of their multitude, and is agitated by them [in a manner resembling] the waves of the sea. I rode out one day on horseback and went into the bazaar, but when I got halfway through it and reached the densest pressure of the crowd at a point called al-Shawr,[6] I could not advance any further because of the multitude of the press, and when I tried to go back I was unable to do that either, because of the crowd of people. So I remained as I was, in perplexity, and only with great exertions did I manage to return. Some person told me | that that bazaar is much less crowded on Fridays, because [on that day] they close the Qaisārīya[7] and other bazaars, so I rode [again] on the Friday and went to the cathedral mosque and the college.

4

This city is in the dominions of the sultan Ūzbak, who is represented in it by a great amīr called Quṭlūdumūr.[8] It was he who built this college and the dependencies annexed to it. As for the mosque, it was built by his wife, the pious khātūn Turābak.[9] There is at Khwārizm a hospital, which has a

[5] I.B. does not indicate his pronunciation of this name. The traditional Arabic spelling (adopted here) aims at representing a native pronunciation somewhat like Khōrezm (see Yāqūt's *Geog. Dict.*, s.v.), but by Arabic speakers was commonly read Khuwārizm or Khuwārazm. This was properly the name of the region (Khorezmia), but often applied to its chief city, at this time (Kunya) Urgench, in the delta of the Amu Darya.

[6] Apparently a Khwarizmian name.

[7] See vol. I, p. 97, n. 115.

[8] Qutlugh-tömür (see n. 23 below) had taken the lead in securing the succession of Özbeg Khān to the throne in 1313, and was for a time the administrator of his empire, but was transferred in 1321 to the governorship of Khwārizm.

[9] Turābak is buried in the mausoleum at Urgench (see *Āthār al-Islām al-ta' rīkhīya fi 'l-Ittihād al-Sūfīyītī*, p. 27 and plate 18, undated).

Syrian doctor called al-Ṣahyūnī, after the town of Ṣahyūn in Syria.[10]

Never have I seen in all the lands of the world men more excellent in conduct than the Khwarizmians, more generous in soul, or more friendly to strangers. They have a praiseworthy custom in regard to [the observance of] prayer-services which I have not seen elsewhere, namely that each
5 of the muezzins in their mosques goes round | the houses of those persons neighbouring his mosque, giving them notice of the approaching hour of prayer.[11] Any person who absents himself from the communal prayers is beaten by the imām [who leads the prayers] in the presence of the congregation, and in every mosque there is a whip hung up for this purpose. He is also fined five dinars, which go towards the expenses of upkeep of the mosque, or of supplying food to the poor and the destitute. They say that this custom has been an uninterrupted tradition amongst them from ancient times.

Outside Khwārizm is the river Jaiḥūn, one of the four rivers which [flow] from Paradise.[12] It freezes over in the cold season in the same way as the river Itil freezes over,[13] and people walk upon it. It remains frozen for the space of five months,[14] and often they walk over it when it is beginning to melt and perish in consequence. It is navigable for ships in summer time as far as Tirmidh,[15] from which they import wheat and barley, the journey downstream taking ten days.

6 Outside | Khwārizm is a hospice built over the tomb of the shaikh Najm al-Dīn al-Kubrā, who was one of the great saints.[16] Food is supplied in it to all wayfarers, and its shaikh is the teacher at the college, Saif al-Dīn ibn 'Aṣaba, one of the principal citizens of Khwārizm. In the town also there is a

[10] See vol. I, p. 105.

[11] The other interpretation, 'warning them to attend the service', is grammatically possible, but *mu'lim* does not ordinarily convey this meaning.

[12] See vol. I, p. 49 and n. 152.

[13] See vol. II, p. 497.

[14] According to the geographer Yāqūt, it remained frozen over for two months.

[15] See p. 570 below.

[16] One of the major saints of the Suhrawardī order, killed in the Mongol capture of Gurganj in 1221; see his biography in *Fawa'iḥ al-Jamal*, ed. F. Meier (Wiesbaden, 1957).

hospice, whose shaikh is the pious 'sojourner'[17] Jalāl ad-Dīn al-Samarqandī, one of the most saintly of men. He received us hospitably in it. Outside the city again is the tomb of the most learned imām Abu'l-Qāsim Maḥmūd ibn 'Omar al-Zamakhsharī,[18] with a cupola over it. Zamakhshar is a village four miles distant from Khwārizm.

When I reached this city I encamped in its outskirts, and one of my companions went to visit the qāḍī, the *ṣadr*[19] Abū Ḥafṣ 'Omar al-Bakrī, whereupon he sent his substitute Nūr al-Islām to me. This man saluted me and then returned to him, and thereafter the qāḍī himself came with a group of his associates and greeted me. He was a man young in years but mature in welldoing. He has | two substitutes, one of them Nūr al-Islām, already mentioned, and the other Nūr al-Dīn al-Kirmānī, who is a great jurist, severe in his decisions and vigorous in [defence of] all that pertains to God Most High. 7

When my meeting with the qāḍī took place he said to me, 'This city is overcrowded, and you will have difficulty in entering it in the daytime. Nūr al-Islām will come to you to conduct you in towards the end of the night.' So we did as he suggested, and lodged in a newly-built college in which no one was living [as yet]. After the dawn prayer, the qāḍī above-mentioned visited us, and together with him a number of the principal men of the city, among them Mawlānā Humām al-Dīn, Mawlānā Zain al-Dīn al-Maqdisī, Mawlānā Raḍīy al-Dīn Yaḥyā, Mawlānā Faḍl Allāh al-Riḍawī, Mawlānā Jalāl al-Dīn al-'Imādī, and Mawlānā Shams al-Dīn al-Sinjarī, the imām of the governor. They are men | of generous nature and virtuous character, and the prevailing school of doctrine among them is the Mu'tazilite,[20] but they do not make open profession of it because Sultan Ūzbak and 8

[17] A 'sojourner' is a scholar or devotee who has spent one or more years at Mecca or al-Madīna; see vol. I, pp. 176, 221.

[18] Author of a celebrated grammatical commentary on the Qur'ān and other philological works, d. 1143.

[19] I.B. rarely, if ever, uses the current Egyptian form of abbreviation in which *al-Ṣadr* stands for Ṣadr al-Dīn. In Eastern Persia and Transoxiana it seems that the term *ṣadr* was regularly applied to the chief qāḍī; see Barthold, *Turkestan*, 353–5, and p. 549 below.

[20] The rationalizing school of Sunnī theologians; see vol. II, p. 416, n. 18.

Quṭlūdumūr, who is his governor over this city, are adherents of the [orthodox] Sunna.

During my stay there I used to attend the Friday prayers in company with the above-mentioned qāḍī Abū Ḥafṣ 'Omar in his own mosque, and on the conclusion of the service I went with him to his house, which is close to the mosque. I would then go with him into his reception hall, a most magnificent chamber, furnished with rich carpets, its walls hung with cloth, and a large number of arcaded niches in it, with vessels of silver-gilt and 'Irāqī glass in every niche. Such is the custom followed by the people of this country in [the adornment of] their houses. He would then produce a copious meal, being a man amply endowed with great wealth and landed property, and related by marriage to the amīr Quṭlūdumūr, the husband of the sister of his wife, | whose name is Jījā Aghā.[21]

9

In this city there are a number of admonitory preachers and revivalists,[22] the chief of whom is Mawlānā Zain al-Dīn al-Maqdisī. The khaṭīb at the Friday services is Mawlānā Ḥusām al-Dīn al-Mishāṭī, the eloquent orator, one of the four khaṭībs whom I have never heard surpassed in the whole world.

The Amīr of Khwārizm. He is the great amīr Quṭlūdumūr, and the meaning of his name is 'Blessed Iron', because *Quṭlū* is [in Turkish] 'blessed' and *dumūr* is 'iron'.[23] This amīr is the son of the maternal aunt of the exalted sultan Muḥammad Ūzbak and the greatest of his amīrs. He is the sultan's governor over Khurāsān, and his son Hārūn Bak is married to the daughter of this sultan; her mother is the queen Ṭaiṭughlī, who was mentioned earlier. His wife is the khātūn Turābak, whose name is associated with famous benefactions.

When the qāḍī came to greet me, as I have related, he said to me, 'The amīr | has learned of your arrival, but is still suffering from the effects of an illness, which prevent him

10

[21] For the title of *aghā* see vol. II, p. 434, n. 80.

[22] *Mudhakkirīn*, literally 'preachers who call men to remembrance', i.e. of the promises of reward and punishment in the Qur'ān.

[23] *Qutlugh* = 'fortunate' (Radloff, *Wörterbuch*, II, 996); *tömür* is a dialect form of the normal Turkish *tämür* = 'iron' (P. Pelliot, *Notes sur . . . la Horde d'Or* (Paris 1950), p. 61). *Qutlugh* is commonly rendered by *Quṭlu* or *Quṭluq* in Arabic transcriptions of Turkish names.

from coming to visit you,' so I rode with the qāḍī to visit him. On reaching his residence we entered a large audience-hall, most of the partitions[24] of which were of wood, and went into a small hall; this had a wooden cupola with ornamental embellishments, its walls hung with coloured woollen cloths and its ceiling with gold-embroidered silk. The amīr was [sitting] on a silk [carpet] spread for him, and had a cover over his legs on account of the gout with which they were affected, this being a malady very common among the Turks. I saluted him and he bade me sit beside him. The qāḍī and doctors of the law sat down [likewise]. He questioned me about his sultan, the king Muḥammad Ūzbak, and about the khātūn Bayalūn, and her father and the city of Constantinople. After I had replied to him on all these subjects, tables were brought in with food [of different kinds], roasted fowls, cranes, young pigeons, bread baked with butter, | which they call *kulījā*,[25] biscuits and sweetmeats. After these were brought other tables with fruit, seeded pomegranates in gold and silver vessels with gold spoons, and some in vessels of 'Irāqī glass with wooden spoons,[26] grapes and wonderful melons. 11

It is one of the regular practices of this amīr that the qāḍī comes daily to his audience-hall and sits in a place assigned to him, accompanied by the jurists and his clerks. Opposite him sits one of the great amīrs, accompanied by eight of the great amīrs and shaikhs of the Turks, who are called *arghujīs*.[27] The people bring their disputes to them for decision; those that come within the jurisdiction of the religious law[28] are decided by the qāḍī, and all others are decided by those amīrs. Their decisions are well-regulated and just, for they are free from suspicion of partiality and do not accept | bribes. 12

When we returned to the college after our session with the governor, he sent us rice, flour, sheep, butter, spices, and loads of firewood. In all of these countries [the use of] charcoal is unknown, and likewise in India, Khurāsān and Persia.

[24] Literally 'compartments'. [25] A Persian term.

[26] See vol. II, p. 442, n. 109.

[27] *Arghujī* is for *yarghujī*, the Eastern Turkish word for a person who decides such a lawsuit, from *yarju*, 'a lawsuit', in the language of Khwārizm.

[28] Generally those relating to marriage, inheritance and other matters of personal status.

As for China, there they kindle stones in which the fire blazes up as it does in charcoal; then when they turn to ash, the Chinese knead it with water, dry it in the sun, and it serves them as fuel for cooking again until it is entirely used up.[29]

Anecdote. A generous act of this qāḍī and of the governor. One Friday, after I had attended the service of prayers, according to my custom, in the mosque of the qāḍī Abū Ḥafṣ, he said to me, 'The amīr commanded that you be given five hundred dirhams, and ordered also that a banquet should be prepared in your honour at a cost of another five hundred dirhams, to be attended by the shaikhs, doctors of the law, 13 and principal citizens. When | he gave this order I said to him "O amīr, you are preparing a banquet at which those present will eat only a mouthful or two; if you were to give him all of the money it would be more useful[30] to him". He said "I shall do so", and has commanded that you should be given the entire thousand.' A little later the amīr sent this sum, accompanied by this imām Shams al-Dīn al-Sinjarī, in a purse borne by his page. Its value in Moroccan gold was three hundred dinars.[31] I had bought on the same day a black horse for thirty-five silver dinars and had ridden it on going to the mosque, and it was from that thousand and no other that I paid its price. Thereafter I became possessed of so many horses that they reached a number which I dare not mention lest some sceptic accuse me of lying, and my fortunes never ceased to expand up to the time when I entered the land of India. I had many horses, but I used to prefer this horse, give it special attention, and picket it in front of the 14 others. It remained with me up to the end | of three years, and when it died my affairs took a turn for the worse.

The khātūn Jījā Aghā, the wife of the qāḍī, sent me a hundred silver dinars, and her sister Turābak, the governor's wife, gave a banquet in my honour, for which she assembled the doctors of the law and the principal citizens. This was held in the hospice built by her, where food is supplied to all

[29] See Yule's *Marco Polo*, I, 442–3.

[30] The variant reading noted in the edition does not change the sense.

[31] A Moroccan dīnār weighed 4·722 grammes (as against the standard weight of 4·233 grammes in the East).

wayfarers [from her benefaction]. She sent a furred robe of sable and an excellent horse. She is one of the most virtuous, pious, and generous of women—God reward her with good.

Anecdote. When I left the banquet which this khātūn had given for me, and went out of the hospice, I found myself face to face with a woman in the gateway. She was wearing soiled garments, had a veil over her head, and was accompanied by several women—I do not know how many. She gave me the word of salutation, and I returned it, but did not stop with her nor give her any attention. Then when | I had gone out, 15 a certain person overtook me and said to me, 'The woman that saluted you is the khātūn.' I was covered with confusion on hearing this, and tried to go back to her, but I found that she had departed. So I sent my salutations to her through one of her attendants, together with my apologies for my action, the result of my having no acquaintance with her.

Account of the melons of Khwārizm. The melons of Khwārizm have no equal in any country of the world, East or West, except it may be the melons of Bukhārā, and next to them are the melons of Iṣfahān. Their rind is green, and the flesh is red, of extreme sweetness and firm texture. A remarkable thing is that they are cut into strips, dried in the sun, and packed in reed baskets, as is done in our country with dried figs and Malaga figs. They are exported from Khwārizm to the remotest parts of India and China, and of all the dried fruits there are none which excel them in sweetness. | During 16 my stay at Dihlī in India, whenever a party of travellers arrived, I used to send someone to buy sliced melon for me from them. The king of India, too, when any of it was brought to him, used to send it to me, knowing as he did my fondness for it. It was his way to give pleasure to the foreigners by sending to them the fruit of their own countries, and he used to give special attention to learning their desires and supplying them accordingly.

Anecdote. On my journey from the city of al-Sarā to Khwārizm I had been accompanied by a sharīf, an inhabitant of Karbalā named 'Alī ibn Manṣūr, who was [by profession] a merchant. I used to commission him to buy robes and other things for me, and he would buy a robe for me for ten dinars, but say 'I bought it for eight', and so charge me with only eight dinars and pay the other two dinars with his own money. I was in total ignorance of what he was doing until I learned of it from remarks made by other persons. Not only that, but he had also lent me a sum of dinars, and when I 17 received | the benefaction from the governor of Khwārizm, I repaid him what he had lent me and wished to make a gift to him over and above that in return for his good services, but he refused to accept it and swore that he would never do so. I proposed to make a gift to a slave-boy whom he had, called Kāfūr, but he adjured me not to do so. He was the most generous-hearted of all the 'Irāqīs whom I have met. He made up his mind to travel with me to India, but afterwards a company [of merchants] from his native town arrived at Khwārizm with the intention of proceeding to China, and he took the road with them. I remonstrated with him about this, but he replied 'These men, fellow-citizens of mine, will go back to my family and my kinsmen and will spread the story that I travelled to India to gain a livelihood by begging. This would be a disgrace for me. I shall not do it.' So he set out with them for China. I heard later on during my stay in India, that when he reached the city of Almaliq[32] which is 18 the last of the towns | in the province of Transoxiana and the first town in China, he stopped there and sent on a slave-boy of his with what he had of merchandise. The slave-boy was a long time in returning and in the meantime a certain merchant from his native town arrived and put up with him in the same caravanseray. The sharīf asked him to lend him some money until such time as his slave-boy should arrive. Not only did he refuse to do so but, not content with the vileness of his conduct in failing to succour the sharīf, he tried to bid against him for the lodging that he had in the caravanseray. When the sharīf heard of this he was so upset by it that he went into his room and cut his throat. He was found with a spark of life still in him, but he said to them 'Do not wrong him, it was I who did this by myself,' and expired the same day—God forgive him.[33]

The sharīf had in fact told me [a similar story] about

[32] Properly Almaligh, a town in the Ili valley, north-west of modern Kulja.

[33] Suicide is regarded as a sin, and is very rare in Islam.

himself. He had once received six thousand dirhams on loan from one of the merchants of Damascus. | This merchant met 19 him [one day] in the town of Ḥamāh, in Syria, and asked him for the money. He had sold on credit the merchandise that he bought with it, and was so ashamed at [his inability to repay] his creditor that he went into his room, tied his turban to the ceiling of the room, and intended to hang himself. But the appointed hour of his death was not yet come. He remembered a friend of his, a money-broker, went to him and told him his circumstances, and this man lent him some money which he paid to the merchant.

When I prepared to leave Khwārizm I hired camels and bought a double litter, the second side of which was occupied by 'Afīf al-Dīn al-Tūzarī. The servants rode some of the horses and we put horse-cloths on the rest because of the cold. [In this wise] we began our journey through the wilderness which lies between Khwārizm and Bukhārā, eighteen days' march in sands with no permanent settlement in them save one small township. I took leave of the amīr Quṭlūdumūr, and he presented me with a robe of honour; the qāḍī too gave | me another, and came out with the doctors of the law 20 to bid me farewell.

After travelling for four days we came to the city of al-Kāt,[34] the only settled place on this road, small and pretty. We encamped outside it, by a lake which was frozen over because of the cold, and the boys were playing on it and sliding over it. The qāḍī of al-Kāt heard of our arrival (he is called Ṣadr al-Sharī'a,[35] and I had already met him at the house of the qāḍī of Khwārizm), and came to greet me, together with the students of religion and the shaikh of the town, the pious and devout Maḥmūd al-Khīwaqī.[36] The qāḍī suggested that I should go to visit the governor of the town, but the shaikh Maḥmūd said to me 'It is the one that comes

[34] Kath, the ancient capital of Khorezmia, on the right bank of the Amu Darya, about 35 miles N.E. of Khīva. The old town was undermined by the river, and the new city described by I.B. was built on a canal some miles to the south-west of the present town.

[35] For the title of *ṣadr* see p. 543, n. 19 above.

[36] I.e. of Khīva, on the left bank of the Amu Darya and situated on a canal deriving from the river. The exact function of the 'shaikh' of the town is not clear.

who should be visited, and if this is a matter of concern to us let us go to the governor of the town and bring him.' They did so, and the amīr came after a while, accompanied by his officers and servants, and we saluted him. Our intention was 21 to press on with | our journey, but he begged us to stay and gave a banquet for which he assembled the jurists, the chief officers of the troops, and others, [and in the course of which] the poets stood up to declaim his praises.

We continued our journey on the road known as Sībāya.[37] Through that desert [it is] a journey of six nights without water, at the end of which we reached the town of Wabkana, one day's journey from Bukhārā.[38] It is a pretty town, with streams and fruit gardens. Its inhabitants preserve grapes from year to year, and they have there a fruit which they call '*allū*.[39] They dry it, and people carry the dried fruit to India and China. One steeps it in water and drinks the liquid. In its green state the fruit is sweet, but when dried it acquires a slight acidity, and it has a great deal of pulp. I have never 22 seen the like of it in al-Andalus, nor in the Maghrib | nor in Syria.

Thereafter we travelled for a whole day through contiguous orchards, with streams, trees and habitations, and arrived at the city of Bukhārā, from which is derived the name of the Imām of the Scholars in Tradition, Abū 'Abdallāh Muḥammad ibn Ismā'īl al-Bukhārī.[40] This city was formerly the capital of the lands beyond the river Jaiḥūn,[41] but was laid in ruins by the accursed Tankīz, the Tatar, the ancestor of the kings of al-'Irāq. So at the present time its mosques, colleges and bazaars are in ruins, all but a few, and its in-

[37] The term Sībāya does not seem to be found elsewhere. Yāqūt (s.v. Sabīrā) mentions a village Sibārā in the vicinity of Bukhārā. The variant reading Siyāsa is even more unhelpful.

[38] Wabkana or Wafkand, a suburb of Bukhārā three farsakhs north-west of the main city.

[39] Persian *ālū*, 'plum'. The yellow plums of Bukhārā were especially celebrated.

[40] See vol. I, p. 154, n. 319, and p. 554, n. 57 below.

[41] I.e. the Oxus (Amu Darya). 'Transoxiana' reproduces the Arabic name of this province, 'What lies beyond the River.' Bukhārā was the capital of the flourishing Sāmānid kingdom (900–999). Although sacked by Chingiz Khān in 1220, it soon recovered, and its ruinous condition at this time was due to its later destruction by the Mongol Īl-khāns of Persia in 1273 and 1316.

habitants are looked down upon and their evidence [in legal cases] is not accepted in Khwārizm or elsewhere, because of their reputation for factionalism, and making false claims, and denial of the truth. There is not one person in it today who possesses any religious learning or who shows any concern for acquiring it.

Narrative of the Origin of the Tatars and of their devastation of Bukhārā and other cities. Tankīz Khān[42] | was a blacksmith 23 in the land of al-Khaṭā, and he was a man of generous soul, and strength, and well-developed body. He used to assemble the people and supply them with food.[43] After a while a company [of warriors] gathered around him and appointed him as their commander. He gained the mastery in his own country, grew in strength and power of attack and became a formidable figure. He subdued the king of al-Khaṭā and then the king of China, his armies became immense in size, and he conquered the lands of al-Khutan, Kāshkhar, and Almaliq.[44] Jalāl al-Dīn Sanjar, son of Khwārizm Shah,[45] the king of Khwārizm, Khurāsān, and Transoxiana, [however], possessed great power and military strength, so Tankīz stood in awe of him, kept out of his [territories], and avoided any conflict with him.

[42] Tankīz is an Arabic transcription of Old Turkish *täŋiz*, 'ocean' (Radloff, *Wörterbuch,* col. III, 1045), of which Chingiz (*chiŋgiz*) is probably a Mongol dialect form. Tankīz (probably pronounced *teŋgiz*) frequently appears as the name of Turkish mamlūk amīrs; cf. vol. I, p. 78.

[43] One MS. reads 'and stir up their ambitions'. A somewhat similar account of Chingiz Khān's origins is given by William of Rubruck (see M. Komroff, *Contemporaries of Marco Polo*, p. 94), and apparently reflects a popular story based on his original personal name of Temüjin (Turkish for 'blacksmith').

[44] Khaṭā or Khiṭāy ('Cathay') was the name given to the northern and north-western provinces of China, which constituted a separate kingdom under the Khitan or Liao dynasty (see E. Bretschneider, *Mediaeval Researches from Eastern Asiatic Sources*, London, 1910, I, 208–9). Pekin, the capital of the Chin dynasty in China proper, was captured in 1215. Kāshghar and Khotān (both in Sinkiang) and Almaligh (in Semiryechye; see n. 32 above) were occupied in 1218.

[45] This again reflects popular legend, in which Jalāl al-Dīn, the son of Muḥammad Khwārizm-Shāh, has eclipsed the figure of his father, owing to his exploits against the Mongol invaders and later adventurous career in Persia and Azerbaijan; see *Histoire du Sultan Djelāl ed-Dīn* of al-Nasawī, tr. O. Houdas, Paris, 1895. The episode of Uṭrār (on the Jaxartes or Sir Darya, 100 miles north of Tashkent), however, is historical; see Barthold, *Turkestan*, 396–9.

It happened that Tankīz sent a party of merchants with the wares of China and al-Khaṭā, such as silk fabrics etc., to the town of Uṭrār, which was the last place in the government of Jalāl al-Dīn. His governor in the town sent a message to 24 him, informing him of this event, | and enquiring of him what action he should take in regard to them. Jalāl al-Dīn wrote to him, commanding him to seize their goods, mutilate them, cut off their limbs and send them back to their country—[displaying thereby], because of what God Most High willed to inflict of distress and suffering for their faith upon the peoples of the Eastern lands, weak judgement and a bad and ill-omened management of affairs. So, when he carried out this action, Tankīz made ready to set out in person with an army of uncountable numbers to invade the lands of Islām. When the governor of Uṭrār heard of his advance he sent spies to bring back a report about him, and the story goes that one of them went into the *maḥalla* of one of the amīrs of Tankīz, disguised as a beggar. He found nobody to give him food, and took up a position beside one of their men, but he neither saw any provisions with him nor did the man give him anything to eat. In the evening the man brought out some dry intestines that he had with him, moistened them with water, opened a vein of his horse, filled the intestines with its blood, tied them up and cooked them on a fire; this 25 was his food. So the spy returned to Uṭrār, | reported on them to the governor, and told him that no one had the power to fight against them. The governor then asked his king, Jalāl al-Dīn, for reinforcements, and the latter sent him a force of sixty thousand men, over and above the troops who were already with him. When the battle was joined, Tankīz defeated them, forced his way into the city of Uṭrār by the sword, killed the men, and enslaved the children. Jalāl al-Dīn [then] came out in person to engage him, and there took place between them battles such as were never known in the history of Islām.[46]

The final result of the matter was that Tankīz gained

[46] Jalāl al-Dīn defeated the Mongol army at Parwān (see p. 589, n. 199 below), but was pursued by Chingiz Khān, hemmed in against the Indus river, and escaped with his life only by swimming across it into Sind: see Barthold, *Turkestan*, 445–6.

possession of Transoxiana, laid waste Bukhārā, Samarqand and Tirmidh, crossed the River [i.e. the river of Jaiḥūn] to the city of Balkh and captured it, then [advanced] to al-Bāmiyān,[47] conquered it, and penetrated far into the lands of Khurāsān and 'Irāq al-'Ajam.[48] The Muslims in Balkh and Transoxiana then revolted against him, so he turned back to deal with them, entered Balkh by the sword and left it 'fallen down upon its roofs'.[49] He went on to do | the same at Tirmidh; it was laid waste and never afterwards repopulated, but a [new] city was built two miles distant from it, which is nowadays called Tirmidh. He slew the population of al-Bāmiyān[50] and destroyed it completely, except for the minaret of its mosque. He pardoned the inhabitants of Bukhārā and Samarqand, and returned thereafter to al-'Irāq. The advance of the Tatars continued to the point that finally they entered Baghdād, the capital of Islām and seat of the Caliphate, by the sword and slaughtered the Caliph al-Musta'ṣim billāh, the 'Abbāsid (God's mercy on him).[51] 26

Ibn Juzayy remarks: Our Shaikh, the Grand Qāḍī Abu'l-Barakāt ibn al-Ḥājj[52] (God exalt him), related to us that he had heard the *khaṭīb* Abū 'Abdallāh ibn Rashīd say: 'I met in Mecca Nūr al-Dīn b. al-Zajjāj, one of the scholars of al-'Irāq, who had with him a son of a brother of his. We engaged in conversation, and he said to me, "There perished in the Tatar massacre in al-'Irāq | twenty-four thousand men of the 27

[47] Transoxiana and Khwārizm were conquered in 1220, Balkh and Bāmiyān (at that time the capital of northern Afghanistan) in 1221.

[48] The expedition into Khurāsān in 1221 was commanded by Tuluy, the youngest son of Chingiz Khān, and the cities of Merv and Nīshāpūr were totally destroyed; see Barthold, *Turkestan*, 447–9. An expeditionary force under Mongol generals marched in 1220 through Azerbaijan and Transcaucasia into southern Russia.

[49] A revolt of the Muslim refugees at Merv and consequent destruction of the cities of eastern Khurāsān is related by Ibn al-Athīr (*Kāmil*, XII, 255–6). Juvainī (I, 130–1), although he places the destruction of Balkh on its first capture, also speaks of a second devastation of the city. The quotation is from Qur'ān, ii, 261.

[50] The destruction of Bāmiyān was in revenge for the death of one of his grandsons in the siege of the city: Barthold, *Turkestan*, 443.

[51] I.B. here combines two separate campaigns. Chingiz Khān did not 'return to al-'Irāq', but to Mongolia; the capture of Baghdād was the culmination of an expedition under his grandson Hulagu in 1256–8; see vol. II, p. 334.

[52] Not mentioned elsewhere.

class of scholars, and not one of them is left except me and that one", pointing to his brother's son.'

(To return.) We lodged in Bukhārā in its suburb called Fatḥ Abād,[53] where there is the tomb of the learned shaikh and pious ascetic Saif al-Dīn al-Bākharzī.[54] He was one of the great saints. This hospice where we lodged, to which the name of this shaikh has been given, is a large institution with vast endowments from which food is supplied to all comers, and its superior is a descendant of the shaikh's, namely the much-travelled pilgrim Yaḥyā al-Bākharzī.[55] This shaikh hospitably entertained me in his residence, and invited all the leading men of the city. The Qur'ān-readers recited with beautiful modulations, the homiletic preacher delivered an address, they then sang melodiously in Turkish and Persian, and [altogether] we passed there an exquisite and most delightful night. | I met on this occasion the learned and virtuous jurist Ṣadr al-Sharī'a; he had come from Harāt, and is a pious and excellent man.[56] I visited at Bukhārā also the tomb of the learned Imām Abū 'Abdallāh al-Bukhārī, compiler of *al-Jāmi' al-Ṣaḥīḥ*, the Shaikh of the Muslims (God be pleased with him), and over it is inscribed: 'This is the grave of Muḥammad b. Ismā'īl al-Bukhārī, who composed such-and-such books.'[57] In the same manner, the tombs of the learned men of Bukhārā are inscribed with their names and the titles of their writings. I had copied a great many of these, but they were lost along with all that I lost when the Indian infidels robbed me at sea.[58]

28

[53] The suburb beyond the Eastern (Qarshī) gate of Bukhārā, still called by the same name.

[54] Abu'l Ma'ālī Sa'īd b. al-Muṭahhar, d. 1261, one of the principal disciples of Najm al-Dīn Kubrā (see p. 542, n. 16 above); see *E.I.* s.v. Saif al-Dīn Bākharzī. The hospice or madrasa by his tomb was founded by the mother of the Great Khans Möngke and Qubilai, although she herself was a Christian (Juvainī, tr. J. A. Boyle, II, 552). The tomb is still in existence; see G. A. Pugachenkova & L. E. Rempel, *Vydayushchiyesya Pamyatniki Arkhitektury Uzbekistana*, Tashkent, 1958, pp. 72–3 and plates 11, 12.

[55] One manuscript repeats here, 'He was one of the great saints.'

[56] Presumably Fakhr al-Dīn Khīsār (or Khītār), entitled Ṣadr al-Dīn, whose appointment and diploma as qāḍī of Herāt in 1314/15 is cited at length in *Ta'rīkh Nāma-i Harāt*, Calcutta, 1944, 609–14.

[57] For al-Bukhārī (d. 870), celebrated as the compiler of the *Ṣaḥīḥ*, see vol. I, p. 154, n. 319. According to the early biographers he was buried in the village of Khartang, near Samarqand (*Ta'rīkh Baghdād*, Cairo, 1931, II, 34).

[58] In 1346; see *Selections*, p. 265 (vol. IV, 206 Arabic).

We resumed our journey from Bukhārā, making for the camp of the pious and exalted sultan 'Alā al-Dīn Ṭarmashīrīn, of whom we shall speak presently. We went by way of Nakhshab, the town from which the shaikh Abū Turāb al-Nakhshabī derives his place-name;[59] it is small and surrounded by gardens and streams. We lodged outside it, in a house that belonged to its governor. I had with me a slave-girl, who | was close to the time of her delivery, and I had intended to transport her to Samarqand, so that she might have the child there. It happened that she was inside a litter; the litter was put on a camel and our associates set off during the night, taking her with them, as well as the provisions and other effects of mine. For myself, I remained behind, in order to travel in the daytime, along with some of those who were with me, but the first party went by one road, while I went by another. So we arrived at this sultan's camp late in the evening, very hungry, and alighted at some distance from the bazaar. One of our party bought enough food to stave off our hunger, and one of the merchants lent us a tent in which we spent that night. Our companions set off next morning to look for the camels and the rest of the party, found them in the evening, and returned with them. 29

The sultan was absent from the *maḥalla* on a hunting party, so I met his deputy, the amīr Taqbughā, who assigned me a camping ground close to his mosque, and gave me | a *kharqa*—this is a kind of tent, a description of which we have given previously.[60] I put the slave-girl into this *kharqa*, and she gave birth to a child that same night. They told me that it was a male child, although it was not so, but after the [ceremony of the] '*aqīqa*[61] one of my companions informed me 30

[59] Nakhshab or Nasaf, about 100 miles S.E. of Bukhārā, and a main station on the old route through the Iron Gate to Tirmidh and Balkh; already coming to be called by its later name, Qarshī (Mongol = 'palace'), from the palace built there by Ṭarmashīrīn's predecessor Kebek Khān. Abū Turāb 'Askar b. Ḥusain (d. 859) was a celebrated early ṣūfī (al-Iṣfahānī, *Ḥilyat al-Awliyā'*, Cairo, 1938, XII, 45–51, and al-Sulamī, *Ṭabaqāt al-Ṣūfīya*, Leiden, 1960, 136–40).

[60] See vol. II, p. 440 and n. 103.

[61] A ceremony on the seventh day after the birth of a child, when it is given a name, and a ram or he-goat (according to the Mālikite rite) is sacrificed. The shorn hair of the child is weighed and an equal weight of gold or silver given in alms; see *E.I.*, s.v.

that the child was a girl. So I summoned the slave-girls and questioned them, and they confirmed the statement. This girl was born under a lucky star, and I experienced everything to give me joy and satisfaction from the time of her birth. She died two months after my arrival in India, as will be related in the sequel.

In this *maḥalla* I met the devout shaikh and doctor of the law Mawlānā Ḥusām al-Dīn al-Yāghī (which in Turkish means 'the rebel'), who is a man of Uṭrār, and the shaikh Ḥasan, who is related to the sultan by marriage. |

31 *Account of the Sultan of Transoxiana.* He is the exalted sultan 'Alā al-Dīn Ṭarmashīrīn, a man of great distinction, possessed of numerous troops and regiments of cavalry, a vast kingdom and immense power, and just in his government. His territories lie between four of the great kings of the earth, namely the king of China, the king of India, the king of al-'Irāq, and the king Ūzbak, all of whom send him gifts and hold him in high respect and honour. He succeeded to the kingdom after his brother al-Chagaṭay. This al-Chagaṭay was an infidel and succeeded his elder brother Kabak, who was an infidel also, but was just in government, showing equity to the oppressed and favour and respect to the Muslims.[62] |

32 *Anecdote.* It is related that this king Kabak, in a conversation on one occasion with Badr al-Dīn al-Maidānī, the jurist and homiletic preacher, said to him: 'You assert that God has mentioned everything in His exalted Book?' 'Yes' said Badr al-Dīn. Then said Kabak 'Where is my name in it?' to which he replied 'It is in His word (most High is He) *In whatsoever form He would He hath composed thee* (*rakkabak*).' This reply pleased him, he said *Yakhshī* (which means in Turkish 'good') and showed great favour to him and increased respect for the Muslims.

Anecdote. Among the judgements of Kabak it is related that a woman laid a complaint before him against one of the amīrs. She stated that she was a poor woman, with children

[62] Kebek (1309–26), Iljigadai (1326), and Ṭarmashīrīn (1326–34/5) were all descendants of Chingiz Khān's son Jaghatai in the fifth generation. The fame of Kebek's justice is attested also by the '*Anonym of Iskandar*', pp. 110–11.

to support, that she had some milk [for sale] with the price of which she could procure food for them, and that this amīr had taken it from her by force, and drunk it. He said to her, 'I shall cut him in two; if | the milk comes out of his belly, he has gone to his fate, but if not I shall cut you in two after him'. The woman said, '[No,] I release him from the obligation, and will make no demand on him.' But Kabak gave the order, the man was cut in two, and the milk came out of his stomach.[63] 33

To return to the account of the sultan Ṭarmashīrīn: after I had stayed for some days in the *maḥalla* (which they call the *urdū*),[64] I went one day to the dawn prayer in the mosque, following my usual practice and when I finished the prayer one of those present mentioned to me that the sultan was in the mosque. Accordingly, when he rose up from his prayer carpet, I went forward to salute him. The shaikh Ḥasan and the legist Ḥusām al-Dīn al-Yāghī came up, and told him about me and my arrival some days before. Then he said to me in Turkish *Khush mīsin, yakhshī mīsin, quṭlū ayūsin. Khush mīsin* means 'are you in good health?', *yakhshī mīsin* 'are you well?' and *quṭlū ayūsin* means 'blessed is your arrival'.[65] The sultan was dressed at that time | in a cloak of green Jerusalem stuff, and had a cap like it on his head. 34

He then returned to his audience hall, and [as he did so] people kept presenting themselves to him with their complaints, and he would stop to [listen to] each petitioner, small or great, male or female. He then sent for me, and when I came I found him in a tent, outside of which there were men ranged to right and left, the amīrs among them [seated] on chairs, with their attendants standing behind and before them. The rest of the troops [too] had sat down in parade order, each man with his weapons in front of him. These were the detachment on duty, who would sit there until the hour of afternoon prayer, when another detachment would come and sit until the end of the night, and there had

[63] A similar story has already been related by I.B. concerning a former governor of Tripoli in Syria; see vol. I, p. 89.

[64] See vol. II, p. 482, n. 254.

[65] Literally 'You are very fortune-bringing', *quṭlū* (*qutlugh*) meaning 'fortunate' (see p. 544, n. 23 above), and *ayū* (*ayugh*) being a strengthening particle.

been rigged up for them there awnings made of cotton fabrics. When I entered the king's presence, inside the tent, I found him seated on a chair, resembling a mosque-pulpit and covered with silk embroidered in gold. | The interior of the tent was lined with silken cloth of gold, and a crown set with jewels and precious stones was suspended over the sultan's head at the height of a cubit. The principal amīrs were [ranged] on chairs to right and left of him, and in front of him were the sons of the kings[66] holding fly-whisks in their hands. At the doorway of the tent were the [sultan's] deputy, the vizier, the chamberlain, and the keeper of the sign-manual, whom they call *al ṭamghā* (*al* meaning 'red' and *ṭamghā* meaning 'sign').[67] The four of them rose up to meet me when I entered, and went in with me. After I had saluted him, he questioned me (the keeper of the sign-manual acting as interpreter between us) about Mecca and al-Madīna, Jerusalem (God ennoble her) and [Hebron] the city of al-Khalīl (upon whom be peace), Damascus and Cairo, al-Malik al-Nāṣir, the two 'Irāqs and their king, and the lands of the non-Arabs.[68] The muezzin then made the call to the midday prayer | so we withdrew.

We continued to attend the prayer-services in his company —this was during the period of intense and perishing cold, yet he would never fail to attend the dawn and evening prayers with the congregation. He used to sit reciting a litany[69] in Turkish after the dawn prayer until sunrise, and all those in the mosque would come up to him and he would take each one by the hand and press with his own hand upon his. They used to do the same thing at the time of the afternoon prayer. When he was brought a present of dried grapes or dates (for dates are rare in their country and are regarded by them as conveying a blessing), he would give some of them with his own hand to everyone who was in the mosque.

[66] I.e. the scions of the royal house; see vol. II, p. 484, n. 258.

[67] The Red Seal, embodying the ruler's name, was traced or stamped on all official documents to authenticate them; the keeper or the *ṭamgha* was thus a kind of secretary of state; cf. vol. II, p. 307, n. 120. (The Arabic text has 'whom', not 'which'.)

[68] Presumably including Anatolia and southern Russia as well as Persia in this context.

[69] Literally 'for the *dhikr*'; see vol. I, p. 44, n. 133.

Anecdote. [The following is] an instance of the virtues of this king. One day I attended the afternoon prayer [in the mosque]. The sultan had not yet come, but one of his pages came in with a prayer-rug and spread it in front of the miḥrāb, where it was his custom to pray, saying to the imām Ḥusām | al-Dīn al-Yāghī, 'Our master desires you to hold back the prayer for him a moment while he performs his ablutions.' The imām rose up and said [in Persian] *Namāz* (which means 'the prayer') *birāyi Khudā aw birāyi Ṭarmashīrīn,* that is to say, 'Is prayer for God or for Ṭarmashīrīn?' He then ordered the muezzin to recite the second call for the prayer.[70] The sultan arrived when two bowings had already been completed, and he made the two latter bowings where the ranks ended, that is at the place where peoples' shoes are left near the door of the mosque. He then performed the bowings that he had missed and went up laughing to the imām to shake his hand, and after sitting down opposite to the miḥrāb with the shaikh (that is, the imām) beside him, and I alongside the imām, he said to me 'When you return to your country, tell how a Persian mendicant behaved like this towards the sultan of the Turks.'

37

This shaikh used to preach to the congregation every Friday, exhorting the sultan to act righteously and forbidding him from evil and tyrannical acts, | addressing him in the harshest terms while the sultan listened to him in silence and wept. He would never accept any gift or stipend[71] from the sultan, nor eat of any food of his nor wear any robe from him. This shaikh was indeed one of God's saintly servants. I used often to see him wearing a cotton cloak, lined and quilted with cotton, which was worn out and in shreds, and on his head a bonnet of felt, such as would be worth one qīrāṭ,[72] and with no turban round it. I said to him one day, 'Master, what is this cloak that you are wearing? It is not fit to be worn', and he replied 'My son, this cloak does not belong to me but to my daughter.' So I begged him to accept one of my robes,

38

[70] The call to prayer (*adhān*) is repeated with slight variations inside the mosque when the worshippers have arranged themselves in rows. This is called the *iqāma*, 'summons to rise', i.e. to begin the prayer.

[71] The term *'aṭā'* has the double sense.

[72] The *qīrāṭ* ('carat') was 1/24th of the gold *mithqāl* or 1/16th of the silver *dirham*.

but he said to me, 'I made a vow to God fifty years ago never to accept anything from anyone, but if I were to accept [something] from anyone it would be from you.'

39 When I resolved to proceed on my journey after | staying at this sultan's camp for fifty-four days,[73] the sultan gave me seven hundred silver dinars and a sable coat worth a hundred dinars. I had asked him for this on account of the cold weather, and when I mentioned it to him he took hold of my sleeves and kissed his hand after touching them,[74] with his natural humility, generosity and goodness of character. He gave me two horses and two camels also. When I wished to take leave of him, I encountered him in the midst of his way to his hunting-ground. The day was a bitterly cold one, and I swear that I could not utter a single word owing to the severity of the cold, but he understood this, and laughed and gave me his hand, and so I departed.

Two years after my arrival in India, the news reached us that the assembly[75] of his subjects and his amīrs had met in the most remote part of his territories, adjoining China, where the greater part of his troops were [stationed]. They swore allegiance to a paternal cousin of his called Būzun Ughlī (everyone who is of the sons of the kings is called by 40 them *ughlī*),[76] | who was a Muslim, but tainted in faith and evil in conduct. The reason for their [transference of] allegiance to him and deposition of Ṭarmashīrīn was that the latter had contravened the laws of their ancestor, the accursed Tankīz, he who, as related above, devastated the lands of Islām. Now Tankīz had compiled a book on his laws, which is called by them the *Yasāq*,[77] and they hold that if

[73] Probably from mid-March to early May, 1333.

[74] This, which is the alternative rendering of the French editors (see p. 455 of the edition) for 'kissed them with his hand', corresponds to the traditional phrase and action of 'kissing the ground'.

[75] *Al-mala'*, a Qur'ānic term for 'council' (i.e. assembly of shaikhs of clans), seems to be used here for the Mongol term *quriltai*.

[76] For Turkish *ughul* + *i*, meaning 'son of'. I.B.'s statement is confirmed by the usage of the Persian chronicler of the Mongols; see Juvainī, *Ta'rīkh-i Jahāngushā*, II (Leyden–London, 1916), Introduction, p. 9 (s.v. *pisar*). Būzun was the son of Duwā Timūr, another brother of Ṭarmashīrīn.

[77] For the codification of the 'Great Yasa' of Chingiz Khān see Barthold, *Turkestan*, 41; G. Vernadsky, 'The Scope and Contents of Chingis Khan's *Yasa*' in *Harvard Journal of Asiatic Studies*, III (1938), 337–60. The form *yasāq* is used also by the author of the '*Anonym of Iskandar*'.

any [of the princes] contravenes the laws contained in this book his deposition is obligatory. One of its prescriptions is that they shall assemble on one day in each year, which they call the *ṭūy* (meaning the day of the banquet).[78] The descendants of Tankīz and the amīrs come from all quarters, and the khātūns and superior officers of the army also attend. If their sultan should have changed any one of those laws their chiefs will rise up before him and say to him, 'You have changed this and changed that, | and you have acted in such- 41 and-such a manner and it is now obligatory to depose you.' They take him by his hand, cause him to rise from the throne of the kingship, and set upon it another of the descendants of Tankīz. If one of the great amīrs should have committed an offence in his territory, they pronounce judgement against him as he deserves.

Now the sultan Ṭarmashīrīn had abrogated the law relating to this day and abolished its practice, and they most violently disapproved of his action; furthermore, they resented his staying for four years in that part of his territories which borders on Khurāsān without ever coming to the region which adjoins China. It was customary for the king to visit that district every year, to investigate its conditions and the state of the troops in it, because it was the cradle of their kingdom, and their seat of kingship is the city of Almāliq.[79]

When the amīrs transferred their allegiance to Būzun, he advanced with a powerful army, and Ṭarmashīrīn, fearing an attempt on his life by his amīrs and not trusting them, rode out with a company | of fifteen horsemen, making for the 42 district of Ghazna. This was included in his provinces, and its governor was the chief of his amīrs and his close confidant, Burunṭaih.[80] This amīr, a lover of Islām and of the Muslims, had constructed in his province about forty hospices in which food was supplied to travellers, and had under his command

[78] *Ṭuy* is a variant form of *toi* (Ottoman Turkish *doy*), the common Turkish term for 'feast': Radloff, *Wörterbuch*, III, coll. 1423, 1141.

[79] See p. 548 above. The original *ulus* of Chagatai and his successors was in the vicinity of Almaligh. After the expansion of the Chagatai khanate over Transoxiana, the eastern provinces centred on Almaligh were called Moghulistān or (more popularly) Jatah.

[80] Apparently (like Borodai) a modification of the Mongol name Boroldai, 'the grey'; see P. Pelliot, *Notes sur . . . la Horde d'Or*, p. 63.

many regiments of troops. I have never, among all the human beings that I have seen in all the lands in the world, seen a man of more prodigious stature. When Ṭarmashīrīn had crossed the river Jaiḥūn and taken the road to Balkh, he was seen by a certain Turk in the service of Yanqī, the son of his brother Kabak. Now this sultan Ṭarmashīrīn had killed his brother Kabak,[81] whom we have mentioned above, and the latter's son Yanqī had remained in Balkh. So, when the Turk reported to him that he had seen Ṭarmashīrīn, he said 'He must have taken flight only because of something that has happened to his disadvantage', and he rode out with his officers, seized him and imprisoned him. When Būzun reached Samarqand and Bukhārā and received the allegiance 43 of their inhabitants, | Yanqī came to him, bringing Ṭarmashīrīn. It is said that when the latter arrived in Nasaf, which is outside Samarqand, he was killed and buried there,[82] and the shaikh Shams al-Dīn Gardan Burīdā was made guardian of his tomb. But it is said also that he was not killed, as we shall relate [shortly]. *Gardan* means 'neck' [in Persian] and *burīdā* means 'cut', and he was called by this name because of a slash he had on his neck. I saw him, in fact, in the land of India, and the story of [this encounter with] him will be told later.

When Būzun became king, the son of the sultan Ṭarmashīrīn, who was Bashāy Ughlī,[83] fled, together with his sister and her husband Fīrūz, to the king of India. He received them as distinguished guests and lodged them magnificently, on account of the friendship and the exchange of letters and gifts which had existed between himself and Ṭarmashīrīn, whom he used to address [in his letters] as 'brother'. Some time later, there came a man from the land[84] of Sind, claim-44 ing | to be Ṭarmashīrīn himself. Different opinions were expressed about him, and when this came to the ears of 'Imād

[81] According to Mu'īn al-Dīn Naṭanzī (*'Anonym of Iskandar'*, p. 111), Kebek died a natural death.

[82] I.B. seems to be unaware that Nasaf is the same place as Nakhshab, which he had mentioned a few pages earlier (p. 555 above). Mu'īn al-Dīn (*loc. cit.*) also places Ṭarmashīrīn's death at Nakhshab. MS. 2289 reads: 'he [Yanqī] killed him'.

[83] So, correctly, here in MS. 2289, against the reading *Ughl* of the other MSS and below.

[84] MS. 908 reads 'people'.

al-Mulk Sartīz, the slave of the king of India and governor of the land of Sind[85] (he is called also *Malik 'Arḍ*, because it is before him that the armies of India are paraded for review and he has general supervision over them,[86] and his residence is in Multān) he sent some Turks who were acquainted with Ṭarmashīrīn to see him. On their return they told him that he really was Ṭarmashīrīn, so he ordered a *sarācha* (that is to say, an *āfrāg*[87]) to be prepared for him, and it was put up outside the city. He also performed the ceremonial duties in the style proper to one of his rank, went out to receive him, dismounted before him, saluted him, and came to the *sarācha* in attendance on him, while the man entered it on horseback, in the usual manner of kings. No one doubted that it was in fact he. Sartīz sent a despatch about him to the king of India, who sent a group of amīrs to meet him and to welcome him with the [customary] ceremonies of hospitality.

There was in the service of the king of India a physician who had formerly been in the service of Ṭarmashīrīn, | and was now chief of the physicians in India. This man said to the king 'I shall go myself to see him and find out the truth of his claim, for I once treated him for a boil under his knee, and since the scar remained I can recognize him by that.' So this doctor went to meet him and welcome him along with the amīrs; he went into his quarters and was constantly beside him, because of his former relations with him. [At an appropriate moment] he took occasion to feel his legs and uncovered the scar, whereupon the man scolded him violently, saying, 'Do you want to see the boil that you healed? Well, here it is,' and showed him the mark of it. The physician was assured that it was he, returned to the king of India, and made his report to him. 45

Sometime later the vizier Khwāja Jahān Aḥmad b. Aiyās[88] and the Chief of the Amīrs, Quṭlūkhān, who had been the

[85] See p. 593 below.

[86] *Malik 'Arḍ*, 'King of Review', is Indian magniloquence for *'āriḍ*, the officer whose function it was to review the troops from time to time, examine their equipment, numbers and efficiency, and in some instances issue their pay. The French translation, 'il en avait le commandement', although possible, does not agree with the usage.

[87] I.e., a royal tent with an enclosure; see vol. II, p. 476.

[88] See pp. 617–18, 654–5 below.

sultan's tutor in his youth, came before the king of India and said to him, 'O Master of the world, here is the sultan Ṭarmashīrīn who has | arrived, and it is established that it is really he. There are here of his tribesmen about forty thousand[89] as well as his son and his son-in-law. Have you thought what might happen if they should combine with him?' These words made a powerful impression on the king and he commanded that Ṭarmashīrīn should be fetched at once. When the latter entered his presence, he was ordered to do homage, like all other visitors, treated without respect, and the sultan said to him '*Yā mādhar kānī* (which is a hideous insult),[90] how dare you lie, claiming to be Ṭarmashīrīn when Ṭarmashīrīn has been killed and here with us is the keeper of his tomb? By God, were it not for incurring disgrace[91] I would kill you. However, give him five thousand[92] dinars, take him to the house of Bashāy Ughul and his sister, the children of Ṭarmashīrīn, and say to them "This liar claims to be your father.'" So he came to their house and saw them, and they recognized him; he spent the night with them under the surveillance of guards, and was taken away the next day. They were afraid that they might be killed | because of him, and therefore disowned him. He was exiled from India and Sind, and travelled by way of Kīj and Makrān,[93] being received by the people of the land [everywhere] with respect, hospitality and gifts. He came [finally] to Shīrāz whose sultan Abū Isḥāq received him honourably and furnished him with an income sufficient for his needs. When on my return journey from India I entered Shīrāz, I was told that he was still living there. I tried to meet him but could not do so, because he was in a house which no one might enter to visit him, except by permission of the sultan Abū Isḥāq. I was afraid of the suspicions that might be aroused by [asking for] this, but afterwards I regretted not having met him.

[89] Ṭarmashīrīn had sent a number of Mongol chiefs, presumably with their followers, to enter the service of Sultan Muḥammad: see Mahdi Husain, *The Rise and Fall of Muḥammad bin Tughluq*, London, 1938, p. 107. Out of this there grew up a legend that Ṭarmashīrīn had invaded India and imposed a humiliating peace on Sultan Muḥammad: ibid. 100–5.

[90] Literally, 'O [son of a] prostitute mother' (*kānī* for Persian *gānī*).

[91] By killing a person who had sought his protection.

[92] MS 2289 reads 'three thousand'.

[93] See vol. II, p. 342, n. 238 (to p. 341).

Our narrative now returns to Būzun, namely that when he became king, he treated the Muslims harshly, oppressed the subjects, and allowed the Christians and Jews to rebuild their churches. The Muslims were aggrieved | by this, and 'waited in readiness for the turns of fortune against him'.[94] The report of this reached Khalīl, son of the sultan al-Yasaur, who had been defeated in [the attempt to seize] Khurāsān.[95] He approached the king of Harāt, the sultan Ḥusain, son of the sultan Ghiyāth al-Dīn al-Ghūrī,[96] told him what was in his mind, and asked him for assistance in troops and money on the condition that he, Khalīl, would give half of his kingdom to him when it was firmly under his control. The king Ḥusain thereupon sent a large force of troops with him, the distance between Harāt and al-Tirmidh being nine days' [journey]. When the Muslim amīrs[97] heard of Khalīl's arrival they received him with tokens of submission and of desire to engage in *jihād* against the enemy.[98] The first man to join him was 'Alā al-Mulk Khudhāwand-zāda, the lord of Tirmidh; he was a great amīr, a sharīf by descent from Ḥusain, and he came to Khalīl with four thousand Muslim [troops]. Khalīl was filled with joy at his adhesion, appointed him as his vizier and confided to him the management of his affairs. He was a man of great courage. [Other] amīrs too arrived from every quarter and assembled around Khalīl. When he engaged | Būzun in battle, the troops passed over to Khalīl, brought along Būzun as a prisoner, and delivered him up, whereupon Khalīl executed him by strangulation with bow-strings, it being a custom among them never to put any of the sons of the kings to death except by strangulation.

48

49

Khalīl was now firmly established in his kingship,[99] and

[94] An allusion to Qur'ān, ix, 99.

[95] Yasavur invaded Khurāsān in 1314 and again in 1319; after his second failure he was pursued by a force of Chagatai troops under Iljigadai (see p. 556, n. 62 above) and killed in 1320.

[96] See vol. II, p. 341, n. 237.

[97] The phrase used is 'the amīrs of al-Islām', apparently referring to those of the Mongol leaders who had become Muslims; cf. 'the troops of al-Islām' on p. 567 for the Muslim troops.

[98] I.e. the pagan khān and his followers.

[99] This account of Khalīl and his reign may be fantastic history, but it seems that a Turkish *faqīr* named Khalīl did succeed in establishing his rule in Bukhārā about 1340; see W. Barthold, *Histoire des Turcs d'Asie centrale*, Paris, 1945, pp. 159–60.

held a review of his troops at Samarqand. They amounted to eighty thousand men, clad, both they and their horses, in armour.[100] He discharged the troops that he had brought with him from Harāt, and marched toward the land of Almāliq. The Tatars appointed one of their own number as their commander, and met him at a distance of three nights' journey from Almāliq, in the vicinity of Ṭarāz.[101] The battle grew fierce and both parties stood firm, when the amīr Khudhāwand-zāda, Khalīl's vizier, with twenty thousand Muslim troops led a charge before which the Tatars could not stand their ground, but were driven in flight and slaughtered in great numbers. Khalīl stayed in Almāliq for three nights, 50 then went out to extirpate all that remained of | the Tatars. They submitted to him, and he crossed to the frontiers of al-Khaṭā and China and captured the city of Qarāqurum and the city of Bishbāligh.[102] The sultan of al-Khaṭā sent troops against him, but eventually peace was made between them. Khalīl became so powerful that the kings stood in awe of him; he showed himself a just ruler, established a body of troops in Almāliq, leaving there [as his deputy] his vizier Khudhāwand-zāda, and returned to Samarqand and Bukhārā.

Somewhat later, the Turks, seeking to stir up disorder, calumniated this vizier to Khalīl, asserting that he was planning to revolt and that he claimed that he had a better title to the royal power, by reason of his relationship to the Prophet (God bless him and give him peace), his generosity, and his bravery. Khalīl then sent a governor to Almāliq to replace him, and ordered him to come and present himself at the court with a small body of his associates. Then when he presented himself, Khalīl executed him as soon as he arrived, without further investigation. But this became the cause of

[100] Literally 'in breastplates', but the term seems to be used here in a general sense. On the armour for men and horses in the Mongol army see Plano Carpini, cap. xv, in M. Komroff, *Contemporaries of Marco Polo*, p. 25, and B. Spuler, *Die Mongolen in Iran*², Berlin, 1955, 410 ff.

[101] The text has Aṭrāz, possibly by confusion with Uṭrār. Taraz, on the river Talas, in the vicinity of the modern Aulié-Ata, was about 150 m. east of Uṭrār and some 300 miles west of Almaligh.

[102] I.e. the original centres of Mongol rule, on the Orkhon river and in the vicinity of Turfan. There was no sultanate of Cathay at this time, these territories being incorporated in the Mongol empire of China.

the ruin of his kingdom. When Khalīl became so powerful, he had acted in an insolent manner towards | the lord of Harāt, 51 who had caused him to inherit the kingship and furnished him with troops and money; he wrote to him demanding that the *khuṭba* should be recited in his territories in Khalīl's name,[103] and that his name should be struck on the dīnārs and dirhams. The king Ḥusain was enraged at this and indignantly replied to him in the rudest of terms, whereupon Khalīl made preparations for war with him. But the Muslim troops refused to support him, and regarded him as an aggressor against the king of Harāt. When the report of this reached the king Ḥusain, he despatched troops under the command of his paternal cousin Malik Warnā. The two armies met, and Khalīl was routed and brought as a captive before the king Ḥusain. He spared Khalīl's life, assigned him a residence, gave him a slave-girl and made him a regular allowance for his upkeep. It was in this condition that I left Khalīl [still residing] with him, at the end of the year 47, when I returned from India.[104]

Let us now return to where we were. When I took leave of the sultan Ṭarmashīrīn I journeyed to the city of Samarqand, which is | one of the greatest and finest of cities, and most 52 perfect of them in beauty. It is built on the bank of the river called Wādi'l-Qaṣṣārīn,[105] along which there are norias to supply water to the orchards. The population of the town gather there after the 'aṣr prayer to divert themselves and to promenade. Benches and seats are provided for them to sit on alongside the river, and there are booths in which fruit and other edibles are sold. There were formerly great palaces on its bank, and constructions which bear witness to the lofty aspirations of the townsfolk, but most of this is obliterated, and most of the city itself has also fallen into ruin. It has no city wall, and no gates, and there are gardens inside it. The

[103] The traditional form of public recognition of suzerainty; see vol. I, pp. 232–3.

[104] Since I.B. did not visit Herāt in 747/1347, this sentence must be taken to mean 'When I left India in 747, Khalīl was still in captivity in Herāt.' Ḥusain died in 1370–1.

[105] Samarqand was situated on a mound on the west (left) bank of the Zarafshān river. I.B. has confused its name with that of the river which flows by Nakhshab and Kish, literally 'The Fullers' stream'.

inhabitants of Samarqand possess generous qualities; they are affectionate towards the stranger and are better than the people of Bukhārā.

In the outskirts of Samarqand is the tomb of Qutham, son of Al-ʿAbbās b. ʿAbd al-Muṭṭalib (God be pleased with both al-ʿAbbās and his son), who met a martyr's death at the time 53 of its conquest.[106] | The people of Samarqand go out to visit it on the eve of every Tuesday and Friday,[107] and the Tatars too come to visit it, and make large votive offerings to it, bringing to it cattle, sheep, dirhams and dinars, [all of] which is devoted to expenditure for the maintenance of travellers and the servitors of the hospice and the blessed tomb. The latter is surmounted by a dome resting on four pilasters, each of which is combined with two marble columns, green, black, white and red. The walls of the [cell beneath the] cupola are of marble inlaid with different colours[108] and decorated with gold, and its roof is made of lead. The tomb itself is covered with planks of ebony inlaid [with gold and jewels][109] and with silver corner-pieces; above it are three silver lamps. The hangings of the dome[110] are of wool and cotton. Outside it is a large canal, which traverses the hospice at that place, and has on both its banks trees, grape-vines, and jasmine. In the 54 hospice there are chambers | for the lodging of travellers. The Tatars, in the time of their infidelity, did not injure in any way the condition of this blessed site; on the contrary, they used to visit it to gain blessing as the result of the miraculous signs which they witnessed on its behalf.

[106] The report of Qutham's death in 676, when the Arab general Saʿīd b. ʿOthmān is said to have besieged and forced the surrender of Samarqand, is attested at a fairly early date (Ibn Saʿd, *Ṭabaqāt*, VII/1, p. 101). But it is very doubtful whether Saʿīd did besiege Samarqand, and evident on the other hand that the cult of Qutham was promoted by the ʿAbbāsid caliphs after 750: cf. Barthold, *Turkestan*, 91.

[107] I.e., every Monday and Thursday night. It is strictly the saint himself, not his tomb, which is the object of visitation.

[108] *mujazzaʿ*, see vol. I, p. 195, n. 30.

[109] *muraṣṣaʿ*, see vol. II, p. 477, n. 237.

[110] The term *farsh* seems here to apply to the fabrics suspended over and around the tomb rather than to the floor coverings. This monument, known also as Mazārshāh, and now called Shāh Zindeh, is still one of the principal antiquities of Samarqand; see Pugachenkova-Rempel, *Pamyatniki Uzbekis-* antiquities of Samarqand; see Pugachenkova and Rempel, *Pamyatniki Uzbekistana*, 108 ff. and plates 63–74, and *Athār al-Islām al taʾrīkhīya fi 'l-lttihād al-Sufīyītī*, plate 21.

The superintendent of everything to do with[111] this blessed sepulchre and the adjoining buildings at the time of our lodging there was the amīr Ghiyāth al-Dīn Muḥammad b. ʿAbd al-Qādir b. ʿAbd al-ʿAzīz b. Yūsuf, son of the ʿAbbāsid Caliph al-Mustanṣir billāh. He was appointed to this office by the sultan Ṭarmashīrīn, when he came to his court from al-ʿIrāq, but is now in the service of the king of India, and we shall speak of him later.[112] I met at Samarqand its qāḍī, who was known among them by the title of Ṣadr al-Jahān,[113] and was a worthy and generous man. He made the journey to India after I went there, but was overtaken by death in the city of Multān, the capital of the land of Sind. |

Anecdote. When this qāḍī died at Multān, the intelligence officer sent a report about him to the king of India, stating that he had come with the object of presenting himself at the court[114] but had been cut off before doing so. When this report reached the king, he commanded that there be sent to his sons a sum which I cannot now recall of some thousands of dinars, and that there be given to his associates what he would have given them if they had arrived in his company during his lifetime. The king of India maintains in every one of his towns an intelligence officer, who writes to him to report everything that happens in that town, and about every traveller that arrives in it. When a traveller comes, they record from what land he has come, his name, description, clothes, companions, horses, servants, his manner of sitting and of eating, and all of his affairs and activities, and what may be remarked about him in the way of good qualities or the opposite. In this way no new arrival comes to the king | without his being advised of everything about him, so that his generosity may be proportioned to the newcomer's merits.

55

56

We set out from Samarqand and came in passing to the township of Nasaf, from which comes the ethnic of Abū Ḥafṣ ʿOmar al-Nasafī, the author of the book of rhyming verses on

[111] MS. 2289 vocalizes *ḥāli*. The superintendent (*nāẓir*) is the controller of the revenues from the endowments affected to a mosque or other institution.

[112] See pp. 679–85 below.

[113] For the title of *ṣadr* applied to chief qāḍīs in this region see p. 543, n. 19 above. *Ṣadr al-Jahān* thus means 'Chief Judge of the World', and was apparently the traditional title of the Grand Qāḍī of Samarqand.

[114] *Birasmi bābihi.*

the points of difference between the four jurists [who were the founders of the four Sunni schools of law] (God be pleased with them).[115]

We then came to the city of Tirmidh, from which comes the ethnic of the Imām Abū ʻĪsā Muḥammad b. ʻĪsā b. Sūra al-Tirmidhī, composer of the 'Great Collection' on the Tradition of the Prophet.[116] It is a large city with fine buildings and bazaars, traversed by canals, and with many gardens. It abounds in grapes and quinces of exquisite flavour, as well as in flesh-meats and milk of all kinds. Its inhabitants wash their heads in the bath-house with milk instead of fuller's earth; the proprietor of every bath-house has large jars filled with milk, and each man as he enters the establishment takes 57 some of it in a small jug, and then washes his head. | It makes the hair fresh and glossy. The Indians put oil of sesame (which they call *sīrāj*)[117] on their heads and afterwards wash their hair with fuller's earth. This gives a smoothness to the body and makes the hair glossy and long, and that is the reason why the Indians and those who live among them have long beards.

The old city of Tirmidh was built on the bank of the Jaiḥūn, and when it was laid in ruins by Tankīz[118] this new city was built two miles from the river. Our lodging there was in the hospice of the pious shaikh ʻAzīzān, one of the great and most generous shaikhs, who possesses great wealth and house property and orchards and spends of his wealth to [supply the needs of] travellers. Before arriving in this city, I had met its ruler, ʻAlā al-Mulk Khudhāwand-Zāda,[119] who sent in writing an order to the city for my entertainment as a guest, and every day during our stay in it provisions were

[115] Rhyming couplets (*rajaz*) were a favourite medium for the composition of college textbooks on subjects of all sorts, in order to facilitate their memorization. This poem of al-Nasafī (d. 1142) contained 2700 verses. The road from Samarqand to Tirmidh, however, does not pass through Nasaf, but through Kish (later called Shahr-i Sabz), over 100 miles east of Nasaf and on the higher reaches of the same river. I suspect that Ibn Baṭṭūṭa has confused the two cities; hence his distinction between Nasaf and Nakhshab, see p. 562, n. 82 above.

[116] One of the six 'canonical' collections of Prophetic Tradition, second in repute only to the *Ṣaḥīḥ* of al-Bukhārī. Al-Tirmidhī d. 892.

[117] Arabic *sīraj* or *shairaj*, 'sesame-oil'.

[118] See p. 553 above.

[119] See p. 565 above.

brought to us. I met | also its qāḍī, Qiwām al-Dīn, who was on his way to see the sultan Ṭarmashīrīn and to ask for his permission to him to travel to India. The story of my meeting with him thereafter, and with his brothers Ḍiyā al-Dīn and Burhān al-Dīn, at Multān and of our journey together to India will follow later.[120] [We shall relate also] the story of his two brothers 'Imād al-Dīn and Saif al-Dīn, and my meeting with them at the court of the king of India, as well as of his two sons, their coming to the king of India after the killing of their father, and their marriage to the two daughters of the vizier Khwāja Jahān and all that happened in that connection, if God Most High will.[121] 58

Next we crossed the river Jaiḥūn into the land of Khurāsān, and marched for a day and a half after leaving Tirmidh and crossing the river through uninhabited desert and sands to the city of Balkh. It is completely dilapidated and uninhabited, but anyone | seeing it would think it to be inhabited because of the solidity of its construction (for it was a vast and important city), and its mosques and colleges preserve their outward appearance even now, with the inscriptions on their buildings incised[122] with lapis-blue paints. People generally attribute the lapis-stone[123] to Khurāsān, but in reality it is imported from the mountains of [the province of] Badakhshān, which has given its name also to the ruby called *badakhshī* (pronounced by the vulgar *balakhshī*),[124] and which will be mentioned later, if God will. 59

The accursed Tankīz devastated this city[125] and pulled down about a third of its mosque because of a treasure which he was told lay under one of its columns.[126] It is one of the finest and most spacious mosques in the world; the mosque of Ribāṭ al-Fatḥ in the Maghrib resembles it in the size of its

[120] See pp. 606–7 below.

[121] See pp. 692, 735 below.

[122] Arabic *mudkhala*, which seems to imply something put into another thing, but I have found no example of its use as a technical term.

[123] Lapis-lazuli, Arabic *lāzward*. The mines are in the upper valley of the Kokcha river; see Yule's *Marco Polo*, I, 162.

[124] Cf. Marco Polo on the *balas* rubies and azure-stone: Yule, I, 161. I.B. has apparently forgotten his own 'vulgar' pronunciation in an earlier passage.

[125] See p. 553 above.

[126] Ibn al-Athīr (*Kāmil*, XII, 256) accuses the Tatars of digging up graves in search of treasure.

columns,[127] but the mosque of Balkh is more beautiful than it in all other respects.

Anecdote. I was told by a certain historian that the mosque 60 at Balkh was built by a woman | whose husband was governor of Balkh for the 'Abbāsid [Caliphs], and was called Dā'ūd b. 'Alī.[128] It happened that the Caliph on one occasion, in a fit of anger against the people of Balkh for some rebellious act on their part, sent an agent to them to exact a crushing indemnity from them. On his arrival at Balkh, the women and the children of the city came to this woman who had built the mosque i.e. the wife of their governor, and complained of their situation and [the suffering which] they had to endure because of this indemnity. Thereupon she sent to the amīr who had come to levy this tax on them a garment of her own, embroidered with jewels and of a value greater than the indemnity that he had been ordered to collect, [with a message] to him, saying 'Take this robe to the Caliph, for I give it to him as alms on behalf of the people of Balkh, in view of their poverty.' So he went off with it to the Caliph, laid the robe before him, and related the story to him. The Caliph was covered with shame and exclaiming 'Shall the woman be more generous than we?' commanded him to annul the indem- 61 nity extracted from the inhabitants | of Balkh, and to return there to restore the woman's robe to her. He also remitted one year's taxes to the people of Balkh. When the amīr returned to Balkh, he went to the woman's dwelling, related to her what the Caliph had said, and gave the robe back to her. Then she said to him, 'Did the Caliph's eye light upon this robe?' He said 'Yes'. She said, 'I shall not wear a robe upon which there has lighted the eye of any man other than those within the forbidden degrees of relationship to me.'[129] She ordered the robe to be sold and built with its price the mosque, the hospice, and a convent [for ṣūfī devotees]

[127] The great mosque of Rabat in Morocco called the Mosque of Ḥassān, begun by the Almohad caliph Abū Yūsuf Ya'qūb (1189–99) but apparently never completed; see J. Caillé, *La Mosquée de Hassan à Rabāt*, Paris, 1954, 2 vols.

[128] This story, which I have not traced in any other source, apparently refers to Dā'ūd b. al-'Abbās, a descendant of one of the local princely families, d.c. 871; see J. Marquart, *Ērānšahr*, Berlin, 1901, p. 301.

[129] I.e., those male relatives with whom marriage is forbidden (father, brother, son, and other ascendants and descendants).

opposite it, the latter built of tufa[130] and still in habitable condition today. [After the buildings were completed] there remained of the [price of the] robe as much as one-third, and the story goes that she ordered it to be buried under one of the columns of the mosque, that it might be available and come to light[131] if it should be needed. This tradition was related to Tankīz, who gave orders in consequence to pull down the columns in the mosque. After about a third had been pulled down without | finding anything, he left the rest as they were. 62

Outside [the city of] Balkh is a tomb said to be that of ʻOkkāsha ibn Miḥṣan of the tribe of Asad, the Companion of the Apostle of God (God bless him and give him peace) who will enter Paradise without a reckoning [on the Day of Judgement].[132] Over it is a splendid hospice in which we had our lodging. Outside of this is a wonderful pool of water, beside which there is an immense walnut tree, under whose shade travellers alight during the summer. The shaikh of this hospice is known as al-Ḥājj Khurd[133] (which means [in Persian] 'the little'), a worthy man, who rode with us and showed us the places in this city. Among them is the tomb of the prophet Ḥizkīl[134] (upon whom be peace), over which there is a fine dome. We visited there also many tombs of saintly men, which I cannot recall now. We stopped by the house of Ibrāhīm b. Adham[135] (God be pleased with him), which is a vast edifice constructed of white stone which resembles tufa. It was used as a storehouse for the grain belonging to the hospice [from its endowed lands] | and was barricaded [to prevent access] to it, so we did not go into it. It is in the vicinity of the cathedral mosque. 63

We resumed our journey from the city of Balkh, and travelled for seven days through the mountains of Qūh

[130] *Kadhdhān*, see R. Dozy, *Supplément aux dictionnaires arabes*, s.v.

[131] *Kharaja* is so vocalized in MS. 2289.

[132] The tradition is an early one (see Ibn Qutaiba, *Kitāb al-Maʻārif*, Göttingen, 1850, p. 139), although not mentioned by Ibn Saʻd. ʻOkkāsha was killed in the tribal war in Arabia in 632.

[133] MS. 2289 reads *Fard*, obviously in error.

[134] I.e. Ezekiel. The more celebrated tomb is in the vicinity of al-Ḥilla (see vol. II, p. 324, n. 173), but is not mentioned by I.B. in that context.

[135] See vol. I, p. 110, n. 160. According to the legend his father was a king in or near Balkh.

Istān.[136] These [contain] many inhabited villages, in which there are running streams and leafy trees, most of them fig-trees, and many hospices inhabited by pious devotees consecrated to the service of God Most High. Thereafter we arrived at the city of Harāt, the largest of the inhabited cities in Khurāsān. The great cities of Khurāsān are four; two of them are inhabited, namely Harāt and Naisābūr, and two are in ruins, namely Balkh and Marw.[137] The city of Harāt is very extensive and has a large population. Its inhabitants are men of rectitude, abstention from unlawful pleasures, and sincerity in religion; they follow the school of the Imām Abū Ḥanīfa (God be pleased with him), and their city is [kept] pure of all vice. |

64 *Account of the Sultan of Harāt.* He is the exalted sultan Ḥusain, son of the sultan Ghiyāth al-Dīn al-Ghūrī,[138] a man of notorious bravery and favoured by divine aid and felicity. That which was manifested to him of aid and succour by God Most High on two fields of battle[139] is of a nature to excite astonishment. The first of these was when his army engaged the sultan Khalīl, who had behaved insolently towards him and who ended by becoming a captive in the hands of the sultan Ḥusain.[140] The second occasion was when he engaged in person Mas'ūd, the sultan of the Rāfiḍīs; this ended for the latter with the dispersal of his troops, his own flight, and the loss of his kingdom. The sultan Ḥusain succeeded to the kingship after his brother called al-Ḥāfiẓ, this brother having succeeded his father Ghiyāth al-Dīn.

Account of the Rāfiḍīs. There were in Khurāsān two men,

[136] As a geographical term Quhistan ('mountain land') was the province lying to the *west* of Balkh. The main road from Balkh to Herāt did not touch this province, but ran via Merv ar-Rūd (now Bala Murghab), the total length being 109 or 117 farsakhs (320 or 350 miles, by alternative roads): Mustawfī, tr. Le Strange, 169, 171–2.

[137] For Naisābūr (Nīshāpūr) see pp. 583–4 below. Merv was totally destroyed by the Mongols under Chingiz Khān: Barthold, *Turkestan*, 446–9.

[138] See vol. II, p. 339, n. 223. Mu'izz al-Dīn Ḥusain (1332–70) was the third son of Ghiyāth al-Dīn to succeed to the throne of Herāt. *Ghūrī* is the usual vocalization, derived from their habitat in the Ghōr (Ghūr) mountains in south-western Afghanistan, but I.B. evidently pronounced it Ghawrī (see p. 576 below).

[139] Arabic *mawṭinain*; perhaps a better rendering would be 'notable occasions'.

[140] See pp. 565–7 above.

one of them called Mas'ūd | and the other called Muḥammad. 65
These two had five associates [desperadoes who go by the name] of *futtāk*, known in al-'Irāq as *shuṭṭār*, in Khurāsān as *sarbadālān*, and in the Maghrib as *ṣuqūra*.[141] The seven of them made a compact to engage in disorder, highway robbery, and pillaging of goods and properties, and their exploits became known far and wide. They took up their abode in an impregnable mountain near the city of Baihaq (which is called also Sabzār);[142] they would remain in hiding by day, and at nightfall or later they would come out and make sudden raids upon the villages, engage in highway robbery, and seize people's goods. There poured in to join them a horde of men like themselves, doers of evil and creators of disorder; thus their numbers increased, their power of attack was strengthened, and they became a terror to men. After capturing the city of Baihaq by a sudden assault, they went on to seize other cities, and acquired revenues [with which] they enrolled troops and mounted a corps of cavalry. Mas'ūd [now] took the title | of Sultan. 66
Slaves used to escape from their master to join him; to each of these fugitive slaves he would give a horse and money, and if the man showed himself courageous he made him commander of a section. So his army grew mightily, and he became a serious menace. The entire body of them made a profession of Shī'ism, and aspired to root out the followers of the Sunna in Khurāsān and convert it wholly to the Rāfiḍī cause.

There was in Mashhad Ṭūs[143] a Rāfiḍī shaikh called Ḥasan, who was held by them to be a saint. He supported them in this enterprise and they gave him the title of Caliph. He bade them observe the principles of justice, and they did indeed

[141] All of these are terms for the leaders and participants in popular movements against local authorities; *futtāk* = 'assassins', *shuṭṭār* = 'vagabonds', *ṣuqūra* = 'hawks'. I.B.'s account of the Serbedārs (= 'desperadoes', literally 'head-on-the-gallows') is extremely confused in parts; their first leader was a certain 'Abd al-Razzāq; he was murdered by his brother Mas'ūd, under whose leadership (1338–44) the movement reached its peak: see *E.I.*, s.v. Serbedārs. The form Sarbadāl is, however, used also by the local chronicler Naṭanzī (*'Anonym of Iskandar'*, 158–9, 231–2).

[142] Sābzawār (colloquially pronounce Sabzūr, according to Yāqūt, s.v. Baihaq), 64 miles west of Nīshāpūr, was the chief city of the district of Baihaq. It was captured by the Serbedārs in 1337/8.

[143] The modern Meshed, see p. 582 below. The shaikh referred to by I.B. was Shaikh Ḥasan Jūrī, a noted Shī'ite leader.

exhibit it to such a degree that dirhams and dinars would fall to the ground in their camp and not one person would pick them up until their owner came and took them. They captured Naisābūr, and when the sultan Ṭughaitumūr[144] sent troops against them, they routed them. He then sent against 67 them his deputy, Arghūn Shāh, and they routed him too | and captured him, but spared his life. After this Ṭughaitumūr mounted an expedition against them in person, at the head of fifty thousand Tatars, but they routed him, took possession of the province, and captured Sarakhs, al-Zāwa, and Ṭūs, which are among the principal towns of Khurāsān. They established their caliph in Mashhad ʿAlī al-Riḍā, son of Mūsā,[145] captured the city of al-Jām, and encamped outside it [with the intention of] advancing to the city of Harāt, at a distance of six nights' journey from there.

When the report of this reached the king Ḥusain, he assembled the amīrs, the troops and the citizens, and asked their advice whether they should await the arrival of these folk or march out towards them and engage them in battle, and the general agreement was for going out to meet them. [The men of Harāt] all belong to a single tribe called the Ghawrīya, and are said to derive both their name and their origin from the Ghawr of Syria.[146] So they prepared for the expedition en masse, and assembled from all parts of the region, for they are settled in the villages and in the open 68 country of Badghīs,[147] which extends over a journey of | four nights. Its herbage always remains green and serves as pasture for their cattle and horses; most of its trees are pistachios, which are exported from it to the land of al-ʿIrāq. The troops of Harāt were reinforced by the men of Simnān,[148]

[144] See vol. II, p. 341, n. 236.

[145] I.e. Mashhad Ṭūs (see p. 582, n. 166). For al-Jām see p. 580 below.

[146] For the Ghawr of Syria see vol. I, p. 82. I.B.'s confusion of the Ghōr (see n. 138 above) with the Ghawr is due to the similarity of the Arabic spelling. The supposed origin of the Ghūrids from Syria is, of course, fictitious.

[147] The region between the Harī Rūd and the upper Murghāb, to the north of Herāt. In all MSS the name is spelled Marghīs.

[148] Simnān, 100 miles east of Tehrān (see P. Schwarz, *Iran im Mittelalter*, pt. VI, Leipzig, 1929, 819–20), was occupied after the break-up of the Ilkhanate by the hereditary prince of Māzenderān, Jalāl al-Dawla Iskandar b. Ziyār (1334–60). The Serbedār Masʿūd was killed in battle with him in 1344.

and they set out in a body to meet the Rāfiḍīs, twenty-four thousand of them, counting both footsoldiers and horse men, under the command of the king Ḥusain. The Rāfiḍīs assembled in a force of a hundred and fifty thousand horsemen and the encounter took place in the plain of Būshanj.[149] Both parties alike held their ground, but finally the battle turned against the Rāfiḍīs, and their sultan, Mas'ūd, fled. Their caliph, Ḥasan, stood firm with twenty thousand men until he was killed along with most of them, and about four thousand of them were taken prisoner. One of those who was present at this battle told me that the fighting began shortly after sunrise and the flight [of the Sarbadārs] was just after midday. The king Ḥusain dismounted after | [the hour of] midday prayer, and when he had performed the prayer food was brought. He and his principal associates then continued to eat while the remainder of the troops were beheading the prisoners. He returned to his capital after this signal victory, when God had supported with His aid the [adherents of the] Sunna at his hands and quenched the fire of discord. This battle took place after my departure from India in the year [seven hundred and] forty-eight.[150]

69

There grew up in Harāt a certain pious man, of eminent virtue and ascetic life, whose name was Niẓām al-Dīn Mawlānā.[151] The citizens of Harāt held him in high esteem and used to follow his instructions, while he would admonish them and discourse to them [on the punishment of the wicked in Hell]. They made a compact with him to 'redress the evil',[152] and were joined in this undertaking by the khaṭīb of the city, known as Malik Warnā, who was the paternal cousin of the king Ḥusain and married to his father's widow. (He was one of the most handsome of men in form and conduct, and the king was afraid of him for his own sake and [got rid of him as] we shall relate). Whenever they learned of some action

[149] The battle was fought at Zāwa (see p. 583 below) in July 1342.

[150] A singular example of I.B.'s haphazard dating; see the two preceding notes.

[151] So in the printed text, but MS. 2289 omits 'Mawlānā'. For the following narrative see the note of the French translators (pp. 456–7) from the historian Khwāndemīr, who confirms I.B.'s account in its general lines, but with considerable variation in details.

[152] A traditional Qur'ānic phrase for the punishment or suppression of acts contrary to the Sacred Law.

contrary to the law, even were it on the part of the king himself, they redressed it. |

70 *Anecdote.* It was told me that they were apprised one day that there was committed an unlawful act in the palace of the king Ḥusain, whereupon they assembled for the purpose of redressing it. The king barricaded himself against them inside his palace, but they gathered at the gate to the number of six thousand men, and in fear of them he allowed the jurist [Niẓām al-Dīn] and the principal citizens to be admitted. He had in fact been drinking wine, so they executed upon him the legal penalty[153] inside his palace, and withdrew.

Narrative on [154] *the cause of the killing of the aforementioned jurist Niẓām al-Dīn.* The Turks who inhabit the environs of the city of Harāt and who live in the open country, along with their king Ṭughaitumūr (whom we have already mentioned),[155] to the number of about 50,000, used to be a cause of terror to the king Ḥusain, and he would send gifts to them every year and endeavour to gain their good will. This was before his defeat of the Rāfiḍīs; after routing the latter, 71 he imposed his control on the Turks [also]. It was | a custom of these Turks to visit the city of Harāt from time to time, and they often drank wine in it, or a man of them would come to it in a state of intoxication; then Niẓām al-Dīn would inflict the legal penalty upon those of them that he found drunk. Now these Turks are pugnacious and violent, and they continually make descents on the towns in India, and carry off [their inhabitants] as captives or kill [them]. Sometimes they would take captive some of the Muslim women who live in the land of India among the infidels, and when they brought them back to Khurāsān Niẓām al-Dīn would release the Muslim women from the hands of the Turks. The mark of Muslim women in India is that they do not pierce their ears, whereas the infidel women have their ears pierced. It happened once that one of the amīrs of the Turks called Ṭumūraltī captured a woman and conceived a violent passion for her.[156] She stated that she was a Muslim, whereupon the jurist forced

[153] The *ḥadd* or canonical penalty for wine-drinking is, under the Ḥanafī code, eighty lashes in the case of a free man.

[154] MS. 2289 reads *wahiya.*

[155] See p. 576 above.

[156] MS. 2289 vocalizes *kalifa.*

him to release her. This action enraged the Turk; he rode out with some thousands of his men, raided the horses of Harāt in | their pasturage in the plain of Badghīs, carried them off 72 and left nothing for the men of Harāt to ride on or to milk. They took them up into a mountain in those parts where no one could prevail against them, and neither the sultan nor his soldiers could find horses with which to pursue them. The sultan then sent an envoy to them, to request them to restore the cattle and horses that they had seized and to remind them of the pact between them and himself. They replied that they would not restore their booty until he should allow them to lay hands on the jurist Niẓām al-Dīn, but the sultan refused to consent to this. The shaikh Abū Aḥmad al-Jishtī, the grandson of the shaikh Mawdūd al-Jishtī,[157] enjoyed a great reputation in Khurāsān and his word was held in high esteem by its people. This man rode [to the sultan] with a mounted company of his disciples and mamlūks and said 'I shall personally conduct the faqīh Niẓām al-Dīn to the Turks, so that they may be placated by this, and then | I shall bring 73 him back again.' Since those present were in favour of his proposal, the faqīh Niẓām al-Dīn, seeing their unanimous agreement upon it, rode out with the shaikh Abū Aḥmad and arrived at [the camp of] the Turks. The amīr Tumūraltī rose up at his approach, and, saying to him 'It was you who took my woman from me,' struck him with his mace and smashed his brain, so that he fell dead. The shaikh Abū Aḥmad, vexed and disconcerted, returned from the place to his town, and the Turks restored the horses and cattle that they had seized.

Some time later this same Turk who had killed the faqīh came to the city of Harāt. He was met by a body of the faqīh's associates who came up to him as though to salute him, but with swords under their robes, and they killed him, while his companions fled for their lives. After this event the king Ḥusain sent his uncle's son Malik Warnā, who had been the partner of the faqīh Niẓām al-Dīn in [the campaign for] the

[157] I.e. al-Chishtī (from the village of Chisht in Sijistān), one of the founders of the famous Eastern order of the Chishtīya (see *E.I.*, s.v.), d. 1132/3. In the contemporary *Ta'rīkh Nāma-i Harāt* (Calcutta, 1944, p. 647) Abū Aḥmad is mentioned (with the title *Shaikh al-Islām*) in company with Niẓām al-Dīn.

74 reform | of unlawful conduct, as envoy to the king of Sijistān.[158] On his arrival there, the king Ḥusain sent an order to him to remain in Sijistān and not to return to him. He set out to go to India, in consequence, and I met him, as I was leaving the country, at the city of Sīwasitān in Sind.[159] He was an excellent man, who had a natural liking for positions of authority, and for hunting, falcons, horses, slaves, attendants, and royal garments made of rich stuffs. Now a man of this order will find himself in no happy situation in the land of India. In his case, the king of India made him governor of a small town, and he was assassinated there on account of a slave-girl by one of the men of Harāt who were living in India. It was said that the king of India had secretly employed the man to assassinate him at the instigation of the king Ḥusain, and it was for this reason that the king Ḥusain acknowledged the king of India as his suzerain after the death of the aforementioned Malik Warnā. The king of India exchanged gifts with him and gave him the city of Bakār in Sind, whose tax-yield is fifty thousand silvar dinars a year.[160] |

75 Let us return now to our narrative: From Harāt we travelled to the city of al-Jām, a place of middling size, pretty, with orchards and trees, abundance of springs, and flowing streams. Most of its trees are mulberries, and silk is to be had there in quantities.[161] The town takes its name from the self-denying and ascetic saint Shihāb al-Dīn Aḥmad al-Jām, whose history we shall relate shortly. His grandson was the shaikh Aḥmad, known as Zāda, who was executed by

[158] Sijistān (Sīstān) was ruled under the Mongols and their successors by a line of descendants from the Ṣaffārid house, which had survived through all the vicissitudes of the preceding centuries. The ruling princes at this time were Quṭb al-Dīn Muḥammad (1331–45; succeeded by his son Tāj al-Dīn, d. 1350) and his brother 'Izz al-Dīn (1333–82).

[159] A statement referring to his visit to the Sultan Muḥammad ibn Tughluq during the latter's stay in Sīwasitān, when I.B. asked to be allowed to go to the Ḥijāz (see p. 766 below).

[160] Presumably Bhakkār, on the left bank of the Indus, about 120 miles north of Multān. These negotiations with the king of Herāt are apparently passed over in silence by the Indian historians.

[161] In modern times called Turbat-i Shaikh Jām, formerly Būzjān or Pūchkān, in Quhistan on the borders of Bādghīs, and on the direct road from Herāt to Nīshāpūr and Ṭūs. Mustawfī (p. 171) gives the distances as 30 farsakhs from Herāt to Pūchkān, and 38 from Pūchkān to Nīshāpūr. Shaikh Aḥmad of Jām lived 1049–1142.

the king of India, and the city is now in the hands of his sons. It is exempted from paying taxes to the sultan, and [the members of the shaikh's house] live there in well-being and opulence. It was told me by a person in whom I have confidence that the sultan Abū Sa'īd, the king of al-'Irāq, came to Khurāsān on one occasion and encamped in this city, in which is the hospice of the shaikh. Whereupon the shaikh [Aḥmad] entertained him with an immense [display of] hospitality; he gave one sheep to every tent in the sultan's *maḥalla*, one sheep to every four men, and to every riding-beast in the *maḥalla*, whether | horse, mule, or ass, one night's forage, so that not a single animal was left in the *maḥalla* without receiving [its share of] his hospitality. 76

History of the Shaikh Shihāb al-Dīn, after whom the city of al-Jām is named: It is related that [in his youth] he was given to pleasure and addicted to drinking. He had about sixty drinking-companions, and it was their custom to meet for one day in the house of each one of them, so that each man's turn came round every two months. They continued in this fashion for a time. At length one day when the turn of the shaikh Shihāb al-Dīn arrived, on the eve of his turn he made a resolution to repent and determined to set himself aright with his Lord. He said to himself, 'If I say to my associates that I repented before their meeting in my house, they will impute my statement to inability to entertain them,' so he made the same preparations as had formerly been made by | any one of his fellows in the way of food and drink, and put the wine into wineskins. His companions arrived, and on preparing to drink opened a skin, but when one of them tasted it he found it to be sweet.[162] They then opened another, found it the same, then a third, and found it likewise, and proceeded to expostulate with the shaikh on this score. Thereupon he confessed to them the true state of his affair, made a clean breast of the circumstances,[163] and informed them of his repentance, adding 'By God, this wine is no different from what you have been in the habit of 77

[162] Arabic *ḥulwan*, apparently in the sense of 'non-intoxicating'.

[163] I use this idiomatic phrase to reproduce the Arabic idiom, 'He told them truthfully the age of his young camel.' For the variant, but certainly incorrect, readings see the French editors' note on p. 457.

drinking in the past.' Whereupon they all repented, turning to God Most High, built that hospice, and devoted themselves to the service of God Most High. Many miraculous graces and divinations[164] have been made manifest at the hand of this shaikh.

We travelled on from al-Jām to the city of Ṭūs, which is one of the largest and most illustrious cities of Khurāsān, the home-town of the celebrated Imām Abū Ḥāmid al-Ghazālī (God be pleased with him), and the place of his tomb.[165] Thence we went on to the city of Mashhad al-Riḍā, al-Riḍā being 'Alī b. Mūsā al-Kāẓim b. Ja'far al-Ṣādiq b. Muḥammad al-Bāqir b. 'Alī Zain | al-'Ābidīn b. Ḥusain al-Shāhid, son of 'Alī b. Abī Ṭālib (God be pleased with them).[166] This too is a large and important city, with abundance of fruits, streams, and grinding-mills. Living there was al-Ṭāhir Muḥammad Shāh (*al-Ṭāhir* has among them the same significance as *al-Naqīb* among the people of Egypt, Syria, and al-'Irāq).[167] The people of India and Sind and Turkistān say 'Al-Sayyid al-Ajall'.[168] Also at this sanctuary was the qāḍī, the sharīf Jalāl al-Dīn (I met him in India), and sharīf 'Alī[169] and his two sons, Amīr Hindū and Dawlat Shāh—these accompanied me from Tirmidh to India.[170] They were [all] men of eminent virtue.

78

[164] For this sense of *mukāshafāt* cf. vol. II, p. 471, 2 lines from foot.

[165] Ṭūs, a few miles to the north of Meshed, was destroyed by the Mongols in 1220, but apparently recovered, since it had a Mongol governor and a Nestorian bishop (see *E.I.*, s.v.). Al-Ghazālī (d. 1111) was one of the greatest of the mediaeval doctors in Islam, and is the subject of a vast literature. The site of his tomb is not now known.

[166] The eighth Imām of the 'Twelver' Shī'ites (see vol. II, p. 325, n. 175), who died (or, according to the Shī'ites, was poisoned) at the village of Sanābādh, outside Ṭūs, in 818, after being proclaimed heir-presumptive by the 'Abbāsid caliph al-Ma'mūn, son of al-Rashīd. His shrine became 'one of the most venerated of holy places', in the words of I.B.'s contemporary Mustawfī, who adds that 'at the present day it has become a little town' (tr. 149). See also *E.I.*, s.v. Meshhed.

[167] I.e. Marshal of the Sharīfs; see vol. I, p. 258, n. 50. *Ṭāhir* means literally 'pure, free from vice'.

[168] 'The Most Eminent Sayyid', i.e. the most excellent among the Sayyids.

[169] Apparently the same as the sharīf Amīr 'Alī, mentioned later in this volume. But he does not mention the sharīf Jalāl al-Dīn elsewhere. MS. 2289 vocalizes the last name as Dūlat Shah, and reads 'He (i.e. Sharīf 'Alī) was a man of eminent virtue'.

[170] The Sharīf 'Alī and his two sons joined I.B. at Tirmidh and accompanied him to India.

The noble sanctuary is surmounted by a great dome inside a hospice, with a college and a mosque adjoining it. All these buildings are of elegant construction, | their walls being colourfully decorated[171] with Qāshānī [tiles]. Over the tomb is a wooden staging coated with plaques of silver, with a silver candelabra suspended above it. The threshold of the door of the dome-chamber is of silver, and over the door itself is a curtain of gold-embroidered silk. The chamber is carpeted with different sorts of rugs. Facing this tomb is the tomb of Hārūn al-Rashīd, the Commander of the Faithful (God be pleased with him), and over it is a staging on which they place candlesticks (which the people of the Maghrib call by the name of *ḥasaka* and *manāra*).[172] When a Rāfiḍī enters to visit [the tomb of al-Riḍā], he kicks the tomb of al-Rashīd with his foot and pronounces a blessing on al-Riḍā.[173]

79

We went on next to the city of Sarakhs, after which is named the pious shaikh Luqmān al-Sarakhsī (God be pleased with him).[174] Thence we travelled to the city of Zāwa, which is the city of the pious shaikh Quṭb al-Din Ḥaidar, who has given his name to the Ḥaidarī group of poor brethren.[175] These are [the faqīrs] who put iron rings in their hands, necks, and ears, and they go so far as to put them also on their penes | so that they cannot perform the act of copulation.

80

We continued our journey from there and came to the city of Naisābūr, which is one of the four metropolitan cities of Khurāsān.[176] It is [sometimes] called 'Little Damascus',

[171] I read *maṣbūgh* with MS. 2289. For *qāshānī* see vol. I, p. 256, n. 42.

[172] The text has *shama'dānāt,* a term presumably unknown in Morocco, hence I.B.'s explanation by a word of local use (*ḥasaka* in literary Arabic meaning 'thistle') and a common Arabic term for any kind of stand for a light.

[173] Hārūn al-Rashīd died at Ṭūs while leading an expedition to Khurāsān in 809. According to the geographer al-Qazwīnī (cited by Le Strange, *Lands,* 390), the caliph al-Ma'mūn (see n. 166 above) made both graves exactly alike so that they could not be distinguished.

[174] Luqmān is mentioned (without dates) by Jāmī, *Nafaḥat al-Uns,* 296–7.

[175] A devotee in the thirteenth century, associated with the Qalandarī darwīshes (see vol. I, p. 37, n. 108). According to al-Maqrīzī, 'Treatise on Hemp' (trans. S. de Sacy, *Chrestomathie arabe,* Paris 1806, II, 120–34), he is credited (obviously without foundation) with having introduced the use of *ḥashīsh* into Persia.

[176] The old city of Nīshāpūr, which survived the Mongol invasion, was destroyed by an earthquake in 1280 and a new city built in its vicinity (Mustawfī, 147; the translation has 629 (A.H.) for 679).

because of its quantities of fruits, orchards and streams, and by reason of its beauty. It is traversed by four canals, and its bazaars are excellent and extensive. Its mosque is exquisite; it is situated in the centre of the bazaar and close by it four colleges, with an abundant supply of running water. They are inhabited by a great host of students studying the Qur'ān and jurisprudence, and are among the good colleges of that land. [But] the colleges of Khurāsān, the two 'Irāqs, Damascus, Baghdād and Cairo, although they attain the highest architectural skill and beauty, yet all of them fall short of the college established by our Master, the Commander of the Faithful, al-Mutawakkil 'ala'llāh, the warrior in the cause of God, the man of learning among kings, | and the centrepiece of the necklace of justice-loving Caliphs, Abū 'Inān (God extend his felicity and give victory to his army),[177] namely the college near the *qaṣba*[178] of the capital city of Fez (God Most High protect her). For this college has no rival in size, elevation, or the decorative plasterwork in it—[indeed] the people of the East have no ability to produce such [plasterwork].[179] There are manufactured at Naisābūr silk fabrics of *nakh, kamkhā'*[180] and other kinds, and these are exported from it to India. In this city is the hospice of the shaikh and learned imām, the devout Pole Quṭb al-Dīn al-Naisābūrī, one of the saintly homiletic preachers and scholars, with whom I lodged. He gave me excellent and most generous hospitality, and I was witness to some astonishing proofs[181] and graces accorded to him.

A miraculous grace of his. I had purchased in Naisābūr a Turkish slave-boy, and this shaikh, seeing him with me, said to me 'This boy is no good to you; sell him.' I said to him 'Very well', and sold | the boy on the very next day, when he

[177] For Sultan Abū 'Inān see vol. I, p. 3, n. 8, and for the Bū 'Inānīya college ibid., p. 53, n. 166.

[178] Arabic *al-qaṣaba*, originally and commonly meaning 'fortress', but frequently applied in North Africa to the fortified quarter of a city which contained the palace and its dependencies; see G. Marçais, *L'Architecture musulmane d'Occident*, Paris 1954, 407–8.

[179] On the special techniques applied to stucco work in Granada and the Maghrib see G. Marçais, op. cit., 228–31, 331–2.

[180] For these fabrics see vol. II, p. 445, n. 117, and 446, n. 122.

[181] 'Proofs' (*barāhīn*) in the sense of evidentiary miracles testifying to his quality as a saint.

was bought by a certain merchant. I took leave of the shaikh and went on my way; afterwards when I stopped in the city of Bisṭām, one of my friends wrote to me from Naisābūr to relate that this slave-boy had killed a Turkish boy and been put to death in retaliation for him. This is an evident miraculous grace accorded to this shaikh (God be pleased with him).

From Naisābūr I went on to the city of Bisṭām, which has given its name to the celebrated shaikh and knower [of the mysteries] Abū Yazīd al-Bisṭāmī.[182] In this city is his tomb, beside which, under the same cupola, is [the tomb of] one of the sons of Ja'far al-Ṣādiq (God be pleased with him).[183] In Bisṭām also is the tomb of the pious shaikh and saint Abu'l-Ḥasan al-Kharaqānī.[184] My lodging in this city was in the hospice of the shaikh Abū Yazīd al-Bisṭāmī (God be pleased with him).

I continued my journey from this city by way of Hindukhīr[185] to Qundūs and Baghlān, which are [regions of] villages where there are to be found shaikhs and pious men, and with fruit-gardens and streams.[186] We encamped | at Qundūs by a flowing river,[187] where there was a hospice belonging to one of the shaikhs of the poor brethren, an Egyptian who was called *Shīr Siyāh*, and that means 'The Black Lion'.[188] We were entertained there by the governor of that land, who

83

[182] Commonly called Bāyezīd, one of the most famous of the ecstatic mystics of Islam, d. 874; see *E.I.*², s.v. Abū Yazīd, and L. Massignon, *Lexique technique de la Mystique musulmane*, Paris 1922, 243–56. There is a photograph of the tomb in E. Diez, *Kunst der islamischen Völker*, Berlin, 1917, p. 69.

[183] Not mentioned elsewhere, and perhaps a confusion with the reputed tomb of Muḥammad b. Ja'far al-Ṣādiq in Jurjān (Mustawfī, tr., 156).

[184] Abu'l-Ḥasan 'Alī b. Aḥmad, d. 1035, a later disciple of Bāyezīd; see al-Sam'ānī, *Ansāb*, s.v. al-Kharaqānī.

[185] This is the reading adopted by the French editors from MS. 2289, but the preferable reading is that of two other MSS, Hindukhā, for Hindakhū. Their suggestion that this stands for Andakhūdh (now Andkhoy), 100 miles west of Balkh, is apparently confirmed by the marginal reading *Indkhū* in *Ḥudūd al-'Ālam* (tr. V. Minorsky, London, 1937, p. 107, n. 2).

[186] Qundūz still exists with the same name, on the lower course of the river called after it, before its junction with the Amu Darya. Baghlān (now an industrial centre) was the name of the region on its middle reaches (here called Surkhāb) between Qundūz and Bāmiyān. See J. Humlum, *La Géographie de l'Afghanistan*, Copenhagen 1959, p. 155.

[187] Literally 'by a stream of water'.

[188] Not known.

was a man from al-Mawṣil, living in a large garden thereabouts. We remained on the outskirts of this village for about forty days, in order to pasture the camels and horses. At that place there are excellent pastures and quantities of herbage, and security there is universally established by reason of the severity of the judgements given by the amīr Buruntaih.[189] We have already said that by the laws of the Turks anyone who steals a horse must [restore it and] give along with it nine like it; if he cannot find this [number] his sons are taken in their place, and if he has no sons he is slaughtered like a sheep. The people [there] leave their animals to graze at will, without any herdsman, after each one has branded his animals on their thighs, and so also did we do in this country. 84 It happened that we made a check of | our horses after we had camped there for ten nights, and found three of them missing, but after half a month the Tatars brought them to us at our camp, for fear of what might befall them from the [application of the] laws. We used to picket two horses opposite our tents every night to deal with anything that might happen at night-time. We did lose two horses one night [just before] we set out from there, and twenty-two days later they brought them both back to us while we were on the road.

Another reason for our halt was fear of the snow. For upon this road there is a mountain called Hindūkūsh, which means 'the slayer of the Indians',[190] because the slave-boys and girls who are brought from the land of India die there in large numbers as a result of the extreme cold and the great quantity of snow. [The passage of] it extends for a whole day's march. We stayed until the warm weather had definitely set in and crossed this mountain, [setting out] about the 85 end of the night | and travelling on it all day long until sunset. We kept spreading felt cloths in front of the camels for them to tread on, so that they should not sink in the snow.

[On setting out from Baghlān][191] we journeyed to a place

[189] See p. 561 above, and for the laws on horse-stealing vol. II, p. 474.

[190] This seems to be the earliest, or one of the earliest, occurrences of this name.

[191] See n. 186 above.

called Andar.[192] There existed there in former times a city, whose traces have been obliterated, and we alighted in a large village in which there was a hospice belonging to an excellent man named Muḥammad al-Mahrawī. We lodged with him and he treated us with consideration. When we washed our hands after eating, he would drink the water in which we had washed because of his strong belief [in our merits] and his benevolence. He travelled with us until we scaled the mountain of Hindūkūsh mentioned above. We found on this mountain a spring of warm water, but when we washed our faces with it the skin peeled off and we suffered sorely in consequence.

[After crossing the mountain] we halted at a place called Banj Hīr (*banj* means 'five' and *hīr* means 'mountain', so that the name means 'five mountains').[193] There was there [in former times] a fine and populous city | on a great river of blue water, resembling a sea,[194] which comes down from the mountains of Badakhshān (it is in these mountains that there are found the rubies that are called by people *balakhsh*).[195] This land was devastated by Tankīz, the king of the Tatars, and has not recovered its prosperity since. In this city is the mausoleum of the shaikh Sa'īd al-Makkī, who is greatly venerated among them.[196]

86

We came to the mountains of Pashāy, where there is the hospice of the saintly shaikh Aṭā Awliyā'.[197] *Aṭā* means, in Turkish, 'father', and *awliyā'* is Arabic [meaning 'friends [of God]', i.e. saints], so his name means 'Father of the Saints'.

[192] Andarāb, on the headwaters of the Doshi (Surkhāb) river. It was the place at which the silver from the mines of Panjhīr was formerly minted as dirhams; see V. Minorsky, *Ḥudūd al-'Ālam*, p. 341. The valley of Andarāb leads to the Khāwak Pass (13,000 feet); the hot springs in the upper valley have temperatures of 108° and 124° Fahr. (H. Yule, *Cathay and the Way Thither*, IV, 258, n. 2).

[193] Panjhīr was formerly of great importance for its silver mines, and noted for its unruly population. In modern times the ancient term *hīr* (=mountain) was replaced by *shīr* (=lion).

[194] Not 'blue like the sea', but in volume 'comparable to a sea'. The Panjhīr river is the principal tributary of the Kābul river.

[195] See p. 571 and n. 124 above.

[196] Not known.

[197] Literally 'Father of the Saints', but not identified. Pashai is the name of a tribe (formerly *kāfir*, i.e. pagan) in the Panjhīr valley and the region to the south of it, still called Kāfiristān (see *E.I.*, s.v.); cf. Marco Polo, cap. xxx (Yule, I, 164–5).

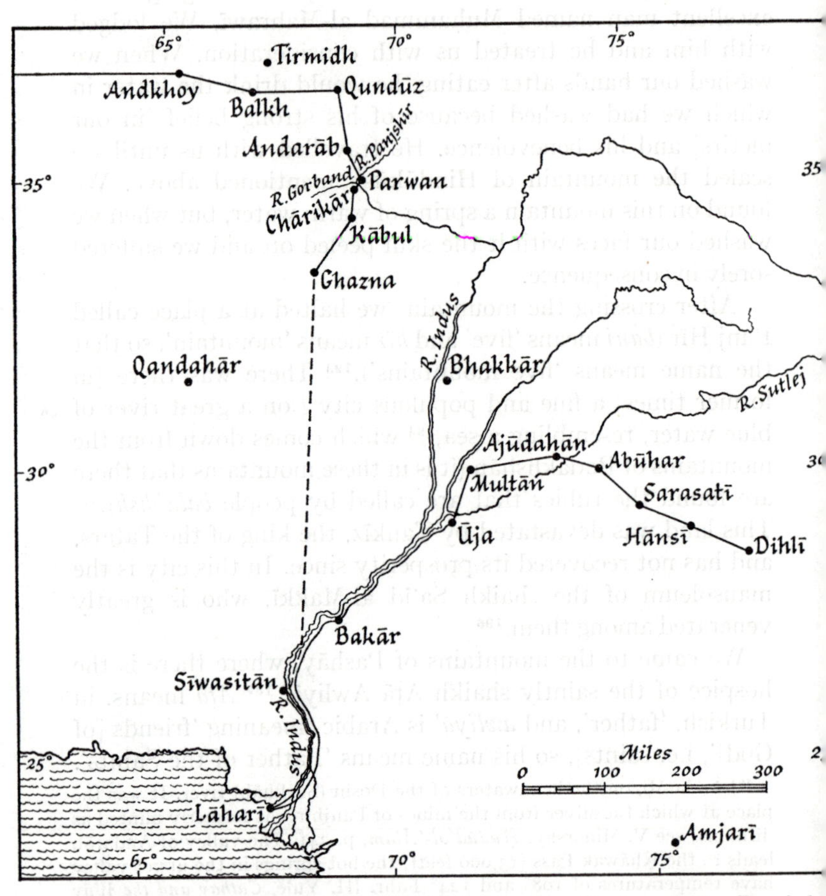

2. Ibn Baṭṭūṭa's itineraries in Afghanistan, Sind and the Punjab

He is called also by the name of *Sīṣad Sālah, sīṣad* in Persian meaning 'three hundred', and *sālah* meaning 'year', since they state that his age is three hundred and fifty years. They have a strong belief in his merits [as a saint], | and come to visit him from the towns and villages, and the sultans and the princesses visit him too. He showed us honour and entertained us as his guests. We encamped by a river near his hospice and went to visit him, and when I saluted him he embraced me. His skin is fresh and smoother than any that I have seen; anyone seeing him would take him to be fifty years old. He informed me that every hundred years there grew on him [new] hair and teeth, and that he had seen Abū Ruhm, whose tomb is at Multān in Sind. I asked him whether he had any Traditions [of the Prophet] to transmit,[198] and he told me a lot of tales. I had some doubts about him, and God knows how much truth there was in what he claimed. 87

We went on next to Parwan,[199] where I met the amīr Buruntaih. He made gifts to me, showed me consideration and wrote to his deputies in the city of Ghazna that they should treat me honourably. I have already | spoken of him, and have mentioned the immensity of stature with which he was endowed.[200] He had in his company a group of shaikhs and poor brethren, hospice folk. We travelled next to the village of al-Charkh, a large place with many fruit-gardens and excellent fruit.[201] We arrived there in the height of summer, and found in it a company of poor brethren and students of religion. We prayed the Friday prayers in it, and its governor, Muḥammad al-Charkhī, offered us hospitality. I met him [again] later in India. 88

We then journeyed to the city of Ghazna, the town [associated with] the sultan and warrior for the Faith Maḥmūd b. Subuktakīn, of famous name.[202] He was one of the greatest

[198] The hearing of Traditions from aged persons was eagerly sought, since they shortened the chain of transmittors from the original source; cf. vol. I, p. 155.

[199] At the junction of the Panjhīr and Ghōrband rivers, 45 miles north of Kābul.

[200] See p. 561 and n. 80 above.

[201] Chārikār, ten miles south of Parwan.

[202] In Persian pronunciation Ghaznī, 75 miles south by west of Kābul; see *E.I.*, s.v. It was the capital of the dynasty of Turkish princes called after it Ghaznevids (962–1186), and suffered severely from the Ghūrids and later invaders.

of rulers, was given the title of Yamīn al-Dawla,[203] and made frequent incursions into the land of India, where he captured cities and fortresses. His tomb is in this city, with a hospice around it. The greater part of the town is in ruins, with nothing but a fraction of it still standing, although it was
89 [formerly] a great city. It has an exceedingly | cold climate, and the inhabitants move out of it in the cold season to the city of al-Qandahār.[204] This is a large and fertile place, but I did not visit it; it is three nights' journey from Ghazna. We encamped outside Ghazna, in a village there on a stream [that flows] below its citadel. We were honourably received by its governor, Mardak Aghā (*mardak* meaning [in Persian] 'little [man]' and *aghā* meaning 'of great family').[205]

We travelled next to Kābul. This was in former times a great city,[206] and on its site there is now a village inhabited by a tribe of Persians called al-Afghān.[207] They hold mountains and defiles and have powerful forces at their disposal, and the majority of them are brigands. Their principal mountain is called Kūh Sulaimān.[208] It is related that the Prophet of God Sulaimān (peace be upon him) climbed this mountain and looked out over the land of India, which was
90 [then] covered with darkness, | but returned without entering it, so the mountain was named after him. It is in this mountain that the king of Afghān resides. At Kābul is the hospice

[203] Maḥmūd (reigned 999–1030) acquired an immense reputation by his raids into India, by which the foundations were laid for the future Islamic sultanate of Dihlī. The title of 'Right Hand of the State' was conferred on him by the 'Abbāsid caliph al-Qādir; see *E.I.*, s.v., and M. Nazim, *The Life and Times of Sultan Mahmud of Ghazna*, Cambridge 1931. The later history of his tomb is related ibid., p. 124, n. 3.

[204] Ghazna, at an altitude of 2,220 metres, has a mean January temperature of −6·7° Cent., Kandahār, 200 miles to the south-west, at an altitude of 1,040 metres, has +5·6° (Humlum, p. 56).

[205] See vol. II, p. 434, n. 80.

[206] This is probably a reminiscence of the expeditions to Kābul in the early centuries of Islam, but al-Idrīsī also speaks of Kābul as a great Hindu city; see *E.I.*, s.v. It is difficult to see how I.B. could have visited Ghazna from Parwan without first passing through Kābul; most probably the paragraph on Kābul precedes that on Ghazna.

[207] At this time the term seems to have been applied only to the tribes in the south-eastern region of modern Afghanistan; see *E.I.*, s.v.

[208] The Sulaimān range, to the east of Quetta, overlooking the plain of the Indus, the highest point of which (11,295 ft.) is called Takht-i Sulaimān ('Solomon's Throne').

of the shaikh Ismā'īl al-Afghānī, the disciple of the shaikh 'Abbās, who was one of the great saints.[209]

From there we rode to Karmāsh, which is a fortress[210] between two mountains, where the Afghān intercept travellers. During our passage of the defile we had an engagement with them. They were on the slope of the mountain, but we shot arrows at them and they fled. Our party was travelling light [without baggage-train] and had with them about four thousand horses. I had some camels,[211] as a result of which I got separated from the caravan, along with a company, some of them being Afghān. We jettisoned some of our provisions, and abandoned the loads of those camels that were jaded on the way, but next day our horsemen returned to the place and picked them up. We rejoined the caravan after the last evening prayer, and spent the night at the station of Shāshnagār, which is the last inhabited place on the confines of the land of the Turks.[212] From there | we entered the great desert, 91 which extends for a space of fifteen nights' march;[213] it cannot be entered except in one season of the year, namely after the rains have fallen in the land of Sind and India, which is in the first days of the month of July. There blows in this desert the deadly *samūm* wind, which causes bodies

[209] Probably the mausoleum of Jābir al-Anṣārī (5th/11th cent.), son of the Herāt philosopher and poet 'Abdallāh al-Anṣārī: see Wolfe, *An Historical Guide to Kabul*, Kabul, 1965, p. 95.

[210] MS. 2289 reads 'a narrow defile', as against the other MSS. From the context it would seem that the original reading was 'a fort in a narrow defile'. Karmāsh is a mountainous tract to the south-east of Gardīz, which is 35 miles east of Ghazna (H. G. Raverty, *Afghanistan and Part of Baluchistan*, London, 1880, p. 91).

[211] MS. 2289 reads 'a fever' (*ḥummā*).

[212] Shāshnagār is commonly identified with the district of Hashtnagar, 16 miles north-east of Peshāwar, but this cannot be reconciled with the probable identification of Karmāsh (n. 209 above), nor with the following narrative.

[213] The Indus river at Attock is only 40 miles from Hashtnagar, so that the journey from there should require less than two days. The statement in the text requires a journey of well over 300 miles. In conjunction with I.B.'s later statement that he crossed the Indus at some point three or four days' journey from Siwāsitān (Sehwan; see pp. 596–7 below), the only plausible identification of his route is one that went southwards from Ghazna through the desert west of the Sulaimān range (note his reference to it, p. 590 above), thence into the plain of Sind, and reached the Indus at some point in the district of Lārkāna, a total distance of about 350 miles from the point indicated here.

to crumble through putrefaction, so that when a man dies his limbs fall apart. We have already mentioned that this wind blows also in the desert between Hurmuz and Shīrāz.[214] A large party, which included Khudhāwand-Zāda, the qāḍī of Tirmidh,[215] had preceded us, and they lost by death many camels and horses. Our company arrived safely (praise be to God Most High) at Banj Āb, which is the water of Sind. *Banj* means 'five' and *āb* means 'water', so the [whole] name means 'The five rivers'.[216] These flow into the main river 92 and irrigate those districts, as we shall mention later, | if God will. Our arrival at this river was on the last day of Dhu'l-Ḥijja, and there rose upon us that night the new moon of al-Muḥarram of the year 734.[217] From this point the intelligence officers wrote a report about us to the land of India, and gave its king a detailed account of our circumstances.

Here ends what we have to say concerning the first journey. Praise be to God, Lord of the Worlds.

[214] See vol. II, p. 404 and n. 130.

[215] On p. 565 above Khudhāwand Zāda is called the ruler of Tirmidh, and clearly distinguished from the qāḍī, but in the later narrative (p. 606 below) he is again called the qāḍī.

[216] *Banj* for Persian *panj*. As already seen (vol. I, p. 50), I.B. does not clearly distinguish the Indus proper from the five-river complex of the Panjāb. His term 'water of Sind' in the preceding sentence probably reflects the Persian usage.

[217] 12 September 1333.

CHAPTER X

Sind and North-Western India

In the Name of God, the Merciful, the Compassionate and the Blessing and Peace of God be upon our lord Muḥammad, and his House, and his Companions. 93

The shaikh Abū 'Abdallāh Muḥammad, son of 'Abdallāh, son of Muḥammad, son of Ibrāhīm, of the tribe of Luwāta, of the city of Tangier, known by the name of Ibn Baṭṭūṭa (God's mercy upon him) related as follows:

On the day of the new moon of the holy month of Muḥarram, the first day of the year 734, we came to the river of Sind called Banj Āb, which means 'the Five Waters'. This is one of the greatest rivers on earth. It rises in flood in the hot season, and the inhabitants of that country sow at the time of its flood, just as the people of Egypt do during the Nile flood. This river is the frontier | of the territories 94 of the exalted Sultan Muḥammad Shāh, king of Hind and Sind.[1]

When we reached this river the officials of the intelligence service who are charged with that duty came to us and wrote a report about us to Quṭb al-Mulk, the governor of the city of Multān.[2] The chief of the amīrs of Sind at this time was one of the Sultan's mamlūks, named Sartīz. He is the inspector-general of the mamlūks, and all the Sultan's troops parade before him for review.[3] His name means 'the Sharp-

[1] For Sultan Muḥammad b. Tughluq, see chap. XII below. The distinction between Hind and Sind (whose name is derived from the Sanskrit name of the Indus, Sindhu) derives, for Muslim writers, from the fact that Sind, having been conquered by the Arabs in 712, constituted a province of the Islamic Empire from that time, whereas India was first invaded by Maḥmūd of Ghazna (see p. 589 above) in the eleventh century.

[2] See p. 605 below.

[3] See p. 563 above. The latter phrase seems to define precisely the significance of his title.

headed', because *sar* means [in Persian] 'head' and *tīz* means 'sharp'. At the time of our arrival he was in the city of Siwasitān in Sind,[4] which is ten days' journey from Multān. From the province of Sind to the Sultan's capital, the city of Dihlī, it is fifty days' journey, but when the intelligence officers write to the Sultan from Sind the letter reaches him in five days by the postal service. |

95 *Description of the* Barīd [*Postal Service*].[5] The postal service in India is of two kinds. The horse-post, which they call *ūlāq*,[6] consists of horses belonging to the Sultan [with relays] every four miles. The service of couriers on foot has within the space of each mile three relays, which they call *dāwa*,[7] the *dāwa* being a third of a mile, and a mile itself is called by them *kurūh*.[8] The manner of its organization is as follows. At every third of a mile there is an inhabited village, outside which there are three pavilions. In these sit men girded up ready to move off, each of whom has a rod two cubits long with copper bells at the top. When a courier leaves the town he takes the letter in the fingers of one hand and the rod with the bells in the other, and runs with all his might. The men in 96 the pavilions, on hearing | the sound of the bells, get ready to meet him and when he reaches them one of them takes the letter in his hand and passes on, running with all his might and shaking his rod until he reaches the next *dāwa*, and so they continue until the letter reaches its destination. This post is quicker than the mounted post, and they often use it to transport fruits from Khurāsān which are regarded as great luxuries in India; the couriers put them on [woven baskets like] plates and carry them with great speed to the Sultan. In the same way they transport the principal criminals; they place each man on a stretcher and run carrying the stretcher on their heads. Likewise they bring the Sultan's drinking water when he resides at Dawlat Ābād, carrying it

[4] See p. 597 below.

[5] On the *barīd*, see vol. I p. 51, n. 159.

[6] A messenger or courier on a relay of post horses (Turkish).

[7] Persian *daw*, 'running'; MS. A reads 'which they call dāw, each dāwa being a third of a mile'. This would correspond more accurately to Arabic usage, *dāw* being the collective and *dāwa* the noun of unity. But the autograph MS. 2291 has *dāwa* in the passage on p. 618 below.

[8] Urdu *kuroh*, a third of a *farsakh* (see vol. I, p. 34 n. 93). Its equivalence with the Arabic mile (or two kilometres) is only approximate.

from the river Kank [Ganges], to which the Hindus go on pilgrimage and which is at a distance of | forty days' journey from there. 97

When the intelligence officials write to the Sultan informing him of those who arrive in his country, the letter is written with the utmost precision and fulness of description.[9] They report to him that a certain man has arrived of such-and-such appearance and dress, and note the number of his party, slaves and servants and beasts, his behaviour both on the move and at rest, and all his doings, omitting no details relating to all of these. When the newcomer reaches the town of Multān, which is the capital of Sind, he stays there until the Sultan's order is received regarding his entry and the degree of hospitality to be extended to him. A man is honoured in that country only according to what may be seen of his actions, conduct, and zeal, since no one there knows anything of his family or parentage. The king of India, the Sultan Abu'l-Mujāhid Muḥammad Shāh, makes a practice of honouring strangers and showing affection to them and singling them out for governorships or high dignities of state. | The majority of his courtiers, palace officials, ministers of state, judges, and relatives by marriage are foreigners, and he has issued a decree that foreigners are to be called in his country by the title of *'Azīz* [Honourable], so that this has become a proper name for them. 98

Every person proceeding to the court of this king must needs have a gift ready to present to him in person, in order to gain his favour. The Sultan requites him for it by a gift many times its value. We shall have much to tell later on about the presents made to him by foreigners. When people became familiar with this habit of his, the merchants in Sind and India began to furnish each person who came to visit the Sultan with thousands of dinars as a loan, and to supply him with whatever he might desire to offer as a gift or for his own use, such as riding animals, camels and goods. They place both their money and their persons at his service, and stand before him like attendants. When he reaches the Sultan, he receives a magnificent gift from him | and pays off his debts and his dues to them in full. So they ran a flourishing trade 99

[9] The MSS readings vary slightly, but all amount to the same thing.

and made vast profits, and it became an established usage amongst them. On reaching Sind I followed this practice and bought horses, camels, white slaves and other goods from the merchants. I had already bought in Ghazna from an 'Irāqī merchant, a man from Takrīt by the name of Muḥammad al-Dūrī, about thirty horses and a camel with a load of arrows, for this is one of the things presented to the Sultan. This merchant went off to Khurāsān and on returning later to India received his money from me. He made an enormous profit through me and became one of the principal merchants. I met him many years later, in the city of Aleppo, when the infidels had robbed me of everything I possessed, but I received no kindness from him. |

100 *Description of the Rhinoceros*. After crossing the river of Sind called Banj Āb, we entered a forest of reeds, following the track which led through the midst of it, when we were confronted by a rhinoceros. In appearance it is a black animal with a huge body and a disproportionately large head. For this reason it has become the subject of a proverb, as the saying goes *Al-karkaddan rās bilā badan* (rhinoceros, head and no torso). It is smaller than an elephant but its head is many times larger than an elephant's. It has a single horn between its eyes, about three cubits in length and about a span in breadth. When it came out against us one of the horsemen got in its way; it struck the horse which he was riding with its horn, pierced his thigh and knocked him down, then went back into the thicket and we could not get at it. I saw a rhinoceros a second time on this road after the hour of afternoon prayer. It was feeding on plants but when we

101 approached it | it ran away. I saw a rhinoceros yet another time when in the company of the king of India we had entered a jungle of reeds. The sultan was mounted on an elephant and we too were mounted on elephants along with him. The foot-soldiers and horsemen went in and beat it up, killed it and conveyed its head to the camp (*maḥalla*).

After two days' march from [the crossing of] the river of Sind we reached the town of Janānī, a large and fine town on the bank of the river Sind.[10] It has beautiful bazaars and has

[10] Janānī no longer exists and is apparently not mentioned elsewhere. From this description it lay somewhat to the north of Sehwan but its

been inhabited from ancient times by a people called the Sāmira,[11] whose ancestors established themselves there on the conquest of Sind in the time of al-Ḥajjāj [A.D. 712], as the chroniclers of the conquest of Sind have noted. The shaikh, the learned imām, the ascetic doer of the law, and devout Rukn al-Dīn, son of the shaikh and virtuous doctor of the law Shams al-Dīn, son of | the shaikh, the devout and ascetic imām Bahā' al-Dīn Zakariyā, the Qurashite (he was one of the three whom the shaikh and virtuous saint Burhān al-Dīn the lame told me in the city of Alexandria that I should meet them in the course of my journey, and I did meet them, God be praised),[12] told me that his earliest ancestor was called Muḥammad ibn Qāsim the Qurashite,[13] and he took part in the conquest of Sind in the army which al-Ḥajjāj ibn Yūsuf dispatched for that purpose during his governorship in al-'Irāq and settled there and founded a numerous family. These people called the Sāmira never eat with anyone nor may anyone observe them while they are eating, nor do they marry anyone outside their clan, nor do they allow anyone to marry into it. They had at this time an amīr called Wunār whose history we shall relate in due course.[14] 102

From Janānī we travelled | to Sīwasitān [Sehwan],[15] a large town, outside which is a sandy desert, treeless except for acacias. Nothing is grown on the river here except melons, and the food of the inhabitants consists of sorghum and peas, which they call *mushunk*[16] and of which they make 103

identification with Halānī (proposed by Sir W. Haig) is very dubious. See also Mahdi Husain, intro. p. lxxvi.

[11] I.B. applies the familiar Arabic term for the Samaritans to the Rajput tribe of the Sūmras, who had maintained their independence in lower Sind from the eleventh century until shortly before this time.

[12] See Vol. I, pp. 23–4. Bahā' al-Din Zakariyā (1183–1267) was the effective founder of the Indian branch of the Suhrawardī order (see Vol. II, p. 297). His grandson Rukn al-Dīn Abu'l Fatḥ, son of Ṣadr al-Dīn 'Ārīb, died in Multān in 1335. I.B. curiously omits to say whether he met this shaikh in Janānī, or, as seems more probable, in Multān.

[13] Since Muḥammad b. Qāsim was commander of the Arab army which conquered Sind in 712, the claim is open to question, and indeed contradicted by the Indian biographers who relate that Bahā' al-Dīn's grandfather emigrated to Multān from Khurāsān.

[14] See p. 599 below.

[15] A small town 120 miles north of Karachi, at some distance from the present bed of the Indus river.

[16] Persian *mushang*, glossed as 'a kind of grain', or 'small pea'.

bread. There is a plentiful supply of fish and buffalo milk, and the people there eat skinks. These are little animals resembling the lizard[17] (which the Moroccans call the garden snakelet) except that it has no tail. I have seen them digging the sand and fetching it out of it; they slit open its stomach, throw out the contents and stuff it with curcuma [turmeric]. This (which they call *zard shūbah*,[18] meaning yellow stick) takes the place of saffron with them. When I saw this small animal and them eating it, I took a loathing at it and would 104 not eat it. We entered Sīwasitān | during the hottest period of the summer. The heat was intense, and my companions used to sit naked except that each had a cloth round his waist and another soaked with water on his shoulders; this would dry in a very short time and he had to keep constantly wetting it again.

In this town I met its preacher, whose name was al-Shaibānī. He showed me the letter of the Commander of the Faithful, the Caliph 'Omar ibn 'Abd al-'Azīz (God be pleased with him) to his remote ancestor, appointing him to the office of preacher to this town, which they have inherited generation after generation from that time to the present day. The text of the letter [is as follows]: 'This is the command issued by the servant of God, the Commander of the Faithful, 'Omar ibn 'Abd al-'Azīz to N.' It is dated in the year 99 and there is written on it in the handwriting of the Commander of the Faithful 'Omar ibn 'Abd al-'Azīz 'Praise be 105 to God alone', as | the above-mentioned preacher assured me.[19]

Another person I met there was the aged shaikh Muḥammad al-Baghdādī, who lived in the hospice built at the tomb of the pious shaikh 'Othmān al-Marandī. He was said to be more than 140 years old and to have witnessed the death of al-Musta'ṣim billāh, the last of the 'Abbāsid Caliphs, when he was killed by the infidel Hulāwun, son of Tankīz the Tatar.[20]

[17] *Umm ḥubain*, glossed as lizard, and also as 'male chameleon' (see Lane, s.v. *ḥirbā'*), but the *ḥunaishat al-janna* is the wall lizard.

[18] Persian *zard chūbah*.

[19] 'Omar b. 'Abd al- 'Azīz, caliph of Damascus 717–720 (see Vol. I, p. 93). That at this date a caliph should have issued a diploma of appointment to a local khaṭīb is highly improbable.

[20] I.e. in 1258; see vol. II, p. 334 and p. 553 above. The form Hulāwun, for the more usual Hūlagū, is in fact a more accurate rendering of the Mongol Hüle'ü (cf. Marco Polo's Alau).

In spite of his great age this shaikh was still sound of body and able to walk on his own feet.

Living in this town were the amīr Wunār al-Sāmirī,[21] to whom I have already referred, and the amīr Qaiṣar al-Rūmī, who were both in the Sultan's service and had under their command about 1,800 horsemen. There was living in it also a certain Indian infidel named Ratan, a person skilled in calculation and writing. He entered the service of the king of India along with a certain amīr | and having gained the Sultan's favour, the latter gave him the title of Chief of Sind, made him governor of that country with Sīwasitān and its dependencies as his appanage, and conferred on him the 'honours', namely drums and flags, a privilege accorded to the principal amīrs. When he came to this country Wunār, Qaiṣar, and other persons resented the superior rank given to the infidel over them and resolved to kill him. Some days after his arrival they persuaded him to go out into the districts attached to the town to inspect their affairs, so he went out with them. When night fell they set on foot a tumult in the camp, asserting that it was attacked by a lion, and made for the infidel's tent and killed him. They then returned to the town and seized monies belonging to the Sultan which were collected there, amounting to 12 laks. The lak is 100,000 [silver] dinars, which is equivalent to 10,000 dinars in Indian gold coins, and the Indian dinar is worth two dinars | and a half in the gold coinage of the Maghrib.[22] They then set the above-mentioned Wunār at their head, entitling him Malik Fīrūz. He distributed the

106

107

[21] The following narrative is the only known source for this rebellion. It has apparently some relation to the rise of the Rajput Sammas to power in Sind, under a line of rulers with the dynastic title of Jām, the first of whom was Jām Unār. Whether I.B.'s Wunār was in reality a Samma, or a Sūmra associated with the Sammas, remains problematical. See Mahdi Husain, intro., pp. lxxv–lxxvi, and *Indian Gazetteer*, s.v. Sind.

[22] At this time the principal coinage of the Sultanate of Delhi consisted of two coins called *ṭanka*, of gold and silver respectively, the former of 170, the latter of 175 grains, the latter have a formal value of one tenth of the former, see Yule, *Cathay and the Way thither*, vol. IV, 54–62. I.B. calls the gold coin *tanga* and the silver coin the *dīnār*, and distinguishes it from a smaller silver coin, the *'ardalī* of 140 grains, which he calls *dīnār darāhim*. The actual value and weight of the gold *ṭanka* varied considerably (from 98 to 163 grains) during Sultan Muḥammad's reign: see Mahdi Husain, *Muḥammad b. Tughluq*, London 1938, 233–238.

monies amongst the troops, but subsequently became alarmed for his safety owing to his remoteness from his own tribe and so went out to rejoin them along with those of his relatives who were with him.

The remainder of the troops appointed Qaiṣar al-Rūmī as their chief. News of the revolt was brought to 'Imād al-Mulk Sartīz, the Sultan's mamlūk, who was at that time chief amīr in Sind and residing in Multān, whereupon he assembled his troops and equipped an expedition both by land and on the river Sind. It is a ten days' journey from Sīwasitān to Multān. Qaiṣar came out to meet him, but when the armies clashed he and his associates were ignominiously defeated and barricaded themselves in the town. Sartīz besieged them, setting up siege artillery against them, and when the siege had gone on for forty days and they were hard pressed by it, 108 they asked for and were granted | terms. When they came out to him, however, he broke his word to them, seized their property and ordered their execution. Every day he would strike off the heads of some of them, cut some of them in half, flay others of them alive and fill their skins with straw and hang them on the city wall. The greater part of the wall was covered with these skins fixed on crosses, striking with terror those who saw them. He also collected their heads in the middle of the town where they formed a mound of some size. It was [shortly] after these events that I lodged at a large college in this town. I used to sleep on the roof of the college and when I woke up during the night I would see these skins attached to the crosses; they filled me with horror and I could not bear to stay in the college, so I went elsewhere.

Now the worthy and equitable jurist 'Alā al-Mulk of Khurāsān, entitled Fasīḥ al-Dīn, formerly qāḍī of Harāt, 109 had come to join the service | of the king of India, and had been appointed governor of the town and dependencies of Lāharī in Sind. He had assisted 'Imād al-Mulk Sartīz in this operation with his own troops. I resolved to travel with him to the town of Lāharī. He had fifteen ships with which he had come on the river of Sind, carrying his baggage-train, so I set out with him.

The journey on the river of Sind and the order observed

during it. The jurist 'Alā al-Mulk had amongst his vessels one called by the name of *ahawra*, somewhat like a *ṭarīda* in our country, but broader and shorter.[23] In the centre of it there was a wooden cabin[24] to which one climbed up by steps, and on the top of this there was a place prepared for the governor to sit in. His suite sat in front of him and the mamlūks stood to right and left, while the crew of about | forty men rowed. 110 Accompanying the *ahawra* were four vessels to right and left, two of which carried the governor's 'honours', i.e. standards, kettledrums, trumpets, bugles and reedpipes (that is *ghaiṭas*),[25] and the other two carried singers. First the drums and trumpets would be sounded and then the musicians would sing, and they kept this up alternately from early morning to the hour of the midday meal. When this moment arrived the ships came together and closed up with one another and gangways[26] were placed from one to the other. The musicians then came on board the governor's *ahawra* and sang until he finished eating, when they had their meal and at the end of it returned to their vessel. They then set off again on their journey in the manner described until nightfall. When it became dark, the camp was set up on the bank of the river, the governor disembarked and went to his tents, the repast was spread[27] | and most of the troops joined in the 111 meal. After the last evening prayer, sentries were posted for the night in reliefs. As each relief finished its tour of duty one of them cried in a loud voice 'O lord king,[28] so many hours of the night are past.' Then the next relief would come on duty,

[23] The *ṭarīda* in Mediterranean usage was a vessel for transport of horses and heavy goods (see vol. IV, 109 Ar.) as distinct from the galley (*shūn* or *shawna*). The commonly found identification with the *tartane* is extremely dubious, this latter being a lighter vessel resembling a schooner or xebeck. See Kindermann, '*Schiff' in Arabischen*, s.v. In spite of the similarity of sound, the Hindi *hūri* (fishing boat or canoe) is obviously a different kind of vessel.

[24] The term (*mu'arrash*) implies a platform shaded by a trellis or other covering. It is not clear whether it was reached by a ladder or by a stair.

[25] See vol. II, p. 343, n. 242.

[26] Arabic *iṣqālāt*, obviously from Italian *scala*, used of ladders of all kinds, also for portable gangways.

[27] The *simāṭ*, literally the mat upon which the dishes were arranged, was the ceremonial meal at which a prince, commander, or high official ate in the company of his suite and his troops: cf. p. 669 below.

[28] *Malik* ('King') was a title applied in Indian usage, as will be frequently seen below, to high officers. The original term *malik* is generally retained in this translation.

and when it finished its tour, their spokesman also called out to give notice of how many hours had passed. At dawn the trumpets and drums sounded and the dawn prayer was said, then food was brought, and when the meal was finished they resumed their journey.

If the governor wishes to travel on the river he travels on shipboard in the order which we have described. If he wishes to travel on land [the order of march is as follows]. The drums and trumpets are sounded and his *ḥājibs*[29] take the lead; they are followed next by the foot-soldiers, preceding the governor himself. In front of the *ḥājibs* ride six horsemen, 112 three of whom carry | drums slung round their necks, and three with reedpipes. When they approach a village or an elevation in the ground, these six sound their drums and reedpipes and are followed by the drums and trumpets of the main body. To the right and left of the *ḥājibs* are the singers, who sing alternately, but when the hour of the midday meal comes the whole body encamps.

After I had travelled for five days with ʿAlā al-Mulk, we reached the site of his province. This is the city of Lāharī, a fine town on the sea-coast where the river of Sind discharges itself into the ocean,[30] and two seas meet.[31] It possesses a large harbour, visited by men [i.e. merchants] from al-Yaman, Fārs, and elsewhere. For this reason its contributions to the Treasury and its revenues are considerable; the governor ʿAlā al-Mulk told me that the tax-yield from this town amounted to sixty laks per annum. How much a *lak* is we have already said. The governor receives *nim dah yak*, 113 meaning the half of | the tenth of this,[32] that being the footing on which the Sultan hands over the provinces to his governors, that they take for themselves one twentieth of the yield.

A curiosity which I visited outside this town. I rode out one day with ʿAlā al-Mulk, and we came to a plain called Tārna,

[29] I.e. chamberlains and indoor staff in general.

[30] The ruins of Lāharī, formerly known as Larrybunder, lie on the northern side of the Rāho channel or creek, some 28 miles south-east of Karachi. Owing to the shoaling of its entrance it was supplanted about 1800, first by Shāhbandar (see *Indian Gazetteer* s.v.) and then Karachi.

[31] This has no local geographical significance, but is a Qur'ānic allusion: see vol. II, p. 276, n. 20.

[32] *nīm dah yak*, one half of one tenth; on this Persian phrase see the note of the French editors, p. 459.

seven miles from Lāharī, where I saw an innumerable quantity of stones resembling the shapes of men and animals.[33] Many of them were disfigured and their forms effaced, but there remained among them the figure of a head or a foot or something of the sort. Some of the stones also had the shape of grains of wheat, chickpeas, beans and lentils and there were remains of a city wall and house walls. We saw too the ruins of a house with a chamber of hewn stones, | in the midst of which there was a platform of hewn stones resembling a single block, surmounted by a human figure, except that its head was elongated and its mouth on one side of its face and its hands behind its back like a pinioned captive. The place had pools of stinking water and an inscription on one of the walls in Indian characters. 'Alā al-Mulk told me that the historians assert that in this place there was a great city whose inhabitants were so given to depravity that they were turned to stone, and that it is their king who is on the platform in the house we have described, which is still called 'the king's palace'. They add that the inscription on one of the walls there in Indian characters gives the date of the destruction of the people of that city, which occurred about a thousand years ago. 114

When I had spent five days in this city with 'Alā al-Mulk, he gave me a generous travelling provision and I left for the city | of Bakār,[34] a fine city intersected by a channel from the river of Sind. In the middle of this canal there is a fine hospice at which food is supplied to all travellers, built by Kishlū Khān during his governorship of Sind, as will be told later on.[35] I met in this town the jurist and imām Ṣadr al-Dīn al-Ḥanafī, also its qāḍī, who was called by the name of Abū Ḥanīfa, and the devout and ascetic shaikh Shams al-Dīn Muḥammad of Shīrāz, one of those granted length of years;[36] I was told that he was more than 120 years old. 115

[33] The only plausible suggestion for the identity of these ruins is that (made by Haig in *JRAS* 1887) they are those known as Morā-mārī, eight miles N.E. of Lāharī.

[34] Bukkur (Bhakhar), a fortified island in the Indus, lying between the town of Sukkur and Rohri, 110 miles north of Sehwan.

[35] See p. 650 below.

[36] Arabic *al-mu'ammarīn*, men of exceptionally advanced age, who were highly regarded in religious circles, cf. p. 589, n. 198 above.

Thereafter I set out from Bakār and came to the city of Ūja [Uch], a large and well-built town which lies on the bank of the river of Sind and has fine bazaars and good buildings.[37] The governor there at the time was the excellent king, the Sharīf Jalāl al-Dīn al-Kījī, a gallant and generous man, and it was in this town that he died, as the result of a heavy fall from his horse. |

116 *A generous act of this king.* A friendship grew up between me and this king, the Sharīf Jalāl al-Dīn, and developed into firm ties of comradeship and affection, and [later on] we met at the capital Dihlī. When the Sultan left for Dawlat Ābād (as we shall relate) and bade me remain in the capital, Jalāl al-Dīn said to me 'You will require a large sum for expenses and the Sultan will be away for a long time, so take my village and use its revenues until I return'. I did so and gained from it about five thousand dinars—may God give him richest recompense. In the town of Ūja I met the devout and ascetic shaikh the Sharīf Quṭb al-Dīn Ḥaidar al-'Alawī,[38] who invested me with the patched robe. He was one of the great saints, and the garment in which he robed me remained in my possession down to the time when the infidel Hindus despoiled me at sea.

From Ūja I travelled to the city of Multān, the capital of 117 the land | of Sind and residence of its ruling amīr. On the road to Multān and ten miles distant from it is the river called Khusrū Ābād, a large river that cannot be crossed except by boat.[39] At this point the goods of all who pass are subjected to a rigorous examination and their baggage searched. Their practice at the time of our arrival was to take a quarter of everything brought in by the merchants, and to

[37] Now reduced to a group of three villages in the state of Bahāwalpur (see *Indian Gazetteer*, s.v.), Uch was at this time a prominent centre of Muslim activity, developed under the leadership of the Suhrawardī shaikh, Sayyid Jalāl al-Dīn Bukhārī (1199–1291).

[38] I.e. descendant of 'Alī, but not necessarily of the Prophet's daughter Fāṭima (see vol. I, p. 46, n. 140). The investiture with the patched robe (*khirqa*, see vol. I, p. 80, n. 47) indicates that this Sharīf was a leading member of a ṣūfī order, but there is nothing to show whether he was related to Sayyid Jalāl al-Dīn, or belonged to another order.

[39] Generally taken to be the Ravi, which at this time flowed by Multān (*Indian Gazetteer*, XVIII, 24), but the reason for so strange a name for a river is not known.

exact a duty of seven dinars for every horse. Two years after our arrival in India the Sultan abolished these duties and ordered that nothing should be taken from people except the alms tax (*zakāt*) and the tenth. This was at the time when he recognized the 'Abbāsid Caliph Abu'l-'Abbās.[40]

When we set about the crossing of this river and the baggage was examined, the idea of having my baggage searched was very disagreeable to me, for though there was nothing much in it, it seemed a great deal in the eyes of the people, and I did not like | having it looked into. By the grace 118 of God Most High there arrived on the scene one of the principal officers on behalf of Quṭb al-Mulk, the governor of Multān, who gave orders that I should not be subjected to examination or search. And so it happened, and I gave thanks to God for the mercies which He had vouchsafed me. We spent that night on the bank of the river and next morning were visited by the postmaster, a man named Dihqān, originally from Samarqand, who is the person who writes to the Sultan to inform him of affairs in that city and district and of all that happens in it and all who come to it. I was introduced to him and went in his company to visit the governor of Multān.

The Governor of Multān and the ordering of affairs at his court. The governor of Multān is Quṭb al-Mulk, one of the greatest and most excellent of the amīrs. When I entered his presence, he rose to greet me, shook my hand, and bade me sit beside him. I presented him with a white slave, a horse, and some | raisins and almonds. These are among the greatest 119 gifts that can be made to them, since they do not grow in their land but are imported from Khurāsān. This governor [in his public audience] sat on a large carpeted dais, having the qāḍī, whose name was Sālār, and the preacher whose name I forget, beside him. To right and left of him were [ranged] the commanders of the troops, and armed men stood at his back, while the troops were passed in review

[40] See p. 674 below, where this edict is dated 741 A.H. (1340–41), although the 'Abbāsid caliph Abu'l 'Abbās was appointed only during the last days of that year (mid-June 1341) (Ibn Taghrībirdī, *Nujūm*, x.4): see the narrative relative to this in vol. I, 225–6. The dating of this event 'two years' after I.B.'s arrival is impossible, and although *sanatain* might be a textual error for *sinīna* ('several years') it is more likely a slip of memory.

before him. They had a number of bows there, and when anyone comes desiring to be enrolled in the army as an archer he is given one of the bows to draw. They differ in stiffness and his pay is graduated according to the strength he shows in drawing them. For anyone desiring to be enrolled as a trooper there is a target set up; he puts his horse into a run and tries to hit it with his lance. There is a ring there too, suspended to a low wall; the candidate puts his horse into a run until he comes level with the ring, and if he lifts it off 120 with his lance | he is accounted among them a good horseman. For those wishing to be enrolled as mounted archers, there is a ball placed on the ground; each man gallops towards it and shoots at it, and his pay is proportioned to his accuracy in hitting it.

When we visited this governor and saluted him, as we have related, he gave orders for us to be lodged in a house outside the town belonging to the disciples of the devout shaikh Rukn al-Dīn, whom I have already mentioned.[41] It is their practice that [the governors] do not give hospitality to anyone until orders are received from the Sultan to do so.

Account of the foreigners whom I met in this city, making their way to the capital of the King of India. Amongst them was Khudhāwand-Zāda Qiwām al-Dīn, qāḍī of Tirmidh, who had come with his womenfolk and children and was joined at Multān by his brothers, ʿImād al-Dīn, Ḍiyāʾ al-Dīn and 121 Burhān al-Dīn.[42] Others were Mubārak-Shāh, one of | the notables of Samarqand; Arun-Bughā, one of the notables of Bukhārā; Malik-Zāda, son of the sister of Khudhāwand-Zāda; and Badr al-Dīn al-Faṣṣāl. Each one of these had with him his associates, servants, and followers.

Two months after we reached Multān one of the Sultan's chamberlains, Shams al-Dīn of Būshanj, and the 'king' Muḥammad al-Harawī, the *kutwāl*,[43] arrived in the town. These two had been sent by the Sultan to meet and escort Khudhāwand-Zāda, and were accompanied by three eunuchs sent by al-Makhdūmah Jahān, the Sultan's mother, to escort

[41] See p. 597, n. 12 above.

[42] See p. 571 above.

[43] An Urdu term (meaning 'keeper of the citadel (*kūt*)' used for chief of police.

the wife of this same Khudhāwand-Zāda. They brought also robes of honour for them both and for their children, and [had instructions] to arrange for the journey [to Dihlī] of [all] those who had come on one mission or another. They came to me together and asked me why I had come [to India]. I told them that I had come to enter permanently the service of *Khūnd 'Ālam* ['Master of the World'], namely | the 122 Sultan, this being how he is called in his dominions. He had given orders that no one coming from Khurāsān should be allowed to enter India unless he came with the intention of staying there. So when I told them that I had come to stay they summoned the qāḍī and notaries and drew up a contract binding me and those of my company who wished to remain in India, but some of them refused to take this engagement.

We then prepared for the journey to the capital, which is forty days' march from Multān through continuously inhabited country. The chamberlain and the other officer who had been sent with him provided everything that was needed for the entertainment of Qiwām al-Dīn and took about twenty cooks with them from Multān. The chamberlain himself went ahead [with them] every night to prepare his meals, etc. at the next station, and no sooner did Khudhāwand-Zāda arrive than his meal was already prepared. Each one of the newcomers whom we have mentioned used to camp separately | in his tents with his companions, but 123 they often joined in the meal which was prepared for Khudhāwand-Zāda. I myself was present at it only once.

The order observed at this meal was [as follows]. They would serve bread (their bread consists of thin round cakes like those we call *jardaqa*);[44] then they cut up the roasted meat into large pieces of a size such that one sheep makes four or six pieces, and they put one piece before each man. They served also round dough cakes made with ghee, resembling the bread called *mushrik* in our country,[45] which they stuff with the sweet [called] *ṣābūnīya*,[46] and on top of

[44] Arabicized from Persian *girda*, 'round', glossed in mediaeval texts as 'thick bread-cakes' (see al-Jāḥiẓ, *al-Bukhalā*, ed. I. Ḥājīrī, Cairo, 1948, p. 267), but in the usage of Fez meant a *faṭīra*, a kind of pancake. Presumably I.B. means a *chapati*.

[45] Ar. *mushrak*: See Lane, 1001 Nights, III, 640 (*shuraik*).

[46] A concoction made in Egypt of starch, almonds, honey and sesame oil,

each dough cake they put a sweet cake which they call *khishtī* (which means 'brick-shaped'), made of flour, sugar and ghee. Then they serve in large porcelain bowls meat cooked with ghee, onions, and green ginger. After that they serve something which they call *samūsak*,[47] made of meat hashed and cooked with almonds, walnuts, pistachios, 124 onions, and spices, put inside a piece of thin bread | fried in ghee. They put five pieces of these before each person, or perhaps four. Next they serve rice cooked in ghee with chickens on top of it, follow this with *bouchées du juge*,[48] which they call *hāshimī*, and then set down the *qāhirīya*.[49] The chamberlain stands beside the table-mat before the food is served and he does homage in the direction of wherever the Sultan may be and all those who are present do homage at the same time. This homage with them consists in bending the head rather like the 'bowing' of the prayers. When they have done that, they sit down to eat and vessels of gold, silver, and glass are brought filled with sugared water, that is to say syrup[50] diluted with water. They call that *shurba* [sherbet] and drink it before [beginning to] eat. The chamberlain then says *bismillāh* which is the signal for them to start eating. When they finish eating they are given jugs of barley-water,[51] and after drinking this they are given betel and areca nut, which we have described already.[52] When they have taken betel and areca nut the chamberlain says *bis-* 125 *millāh*, | whereupon they rise and do homage as they did before, and separate.

On our journey from the city of Multān they continued to observe this order in the manner which we have set down until we reached the land of al-Hind. The first town we

---

the name of which was transferred to the Persian *fālūdhaj*, made of starch and honey.

[47] From Pers. *sanbūsa*, 'triangular'.

[48] This French term is the most elegant translation for *luqaimāt al-qāḍī*, which would seem to imply some kind of small sweet cakes: cf. p. 757 below.

[49] Another sweetmeat, of what kind is unknown.

[50] It is clear from the parallel passage, vol. I, p. 154 (Ar. 247), that *jullāb* is used for syrup of some kind, but not necessarily that implied by the Persian etymology ('rose-water').

[51] *fuqqā'*, an effervescent drink made from barley.

[52] See vol. II, p. 387.

entered was the city of Abūhar,[53] which is the first of these lands of Hind, a small but pretty place with a large population, and with flowing streams and trees. There are not to be found in India any trees of our country except the lote-tree,[54] but there it is of great girth and its fruit is about as large as a gall nut, and very sweet. They have many trees none of which are to be found either in our country or elsewhere.

Description of the trees of India and their fruits. One of them is the *'anbah* [mango];[55] it is a tree which resembles orange trees | but is larger in size and more leafy. The shade which it 126 gives is the densest of any, but it is oppressive and if one sleeps beneath it he becomes enervated. Its fruit is of the size of a large pear. When the fruit is green and not yet fully ripe the people gather those of them that fall, put salt on them and pickle them as limes and lemons are pickled in our country. The Indians pickle also green ginger and clusters of pepper, which they eat with meat dishes, taking after each mouthful a little of these pickled [fruits]. When the mango ripens in the season of autumn [rains] its fruit becomes yellow and then they eat it like apples, some people cutting it with a knife while others simply suck it. The fruit is sweet, with a little acidity mingled with its sweetness, and has a large stone which they plant, like orange pips and other fruit stones, and the trees sprout from them.

Then there are the *shakī* and the *barkī*.[56] | These are trees of 127 great age with leaves like those of the walnut, and their fruits come out from the trunk of the tree itself. Those of them that are next to the ground are the *barkī* and those higher up are the *shakī*. The former are sweeter and better-flavoured; the latter resemble large gourds and have a skin like oxhide. When it yellows in the season of autumn they gather it and

[53] In the Ferozepur (Firuzpur) district of the Panjab; I.B. has placed it by error before Ajodhan (see n. 71 below).

[54] Called by I.B. the *nabq*, strictly the fruit of the loti-tree (*Ziziphus lotus*), which is of anything from shrub size to a small tree. The Indian tree is the jujube-tree (*Z. jujuba*), 30 to 50 feet high.

[55] From Hindi *āmb*. The English *mango* is derived from the Tamil name *mānkāy*.

[56] The jack-tree (*Artocarpus integrifolia*). The *barkī* is like a melon, weighing three or four pounds; it pierces the bark of the tree next to the ground. The *shakī* is like a large gourd and weighs 25 or 30 pounds. A single *shakī* provides a meal for four or five persons.

split it in half; inside each fruit there are from one to two hundred pods resembling cucumbers, between each of which there is a thin yellow skin. Each pod has a kernel resembling a large bean and when these kernels are roasted or boiled they taste like beans [and take the place of them] since beans are not to be found in that country. They store up these kernels in red earth and they keep until the next year. This *shakī* and *barkī* is the best fruit in India.

128 Another is the *tandū*, the fruit | of the ebony tree, of about the size and colour of an apricot and very sweet.[57] Then there is the *chumūn*,[58] whose trees are of great age, and whose fruit resembles an olive; it is black in colour and has a single stone like the olive. Also the sweet orange, which is very plentiful in their country, but the bitter orange is seldom found; there is a third kind between sweet and bitter, about the size of a lime, which has an excellent flavour and I used to enjoy eating it. Another species is the *mohwa*,[59] long-lived trees, with leaves like those of the walnut except that there is red and yellow in them. Its fruit resembles a small pear and is very sweet. At the top of each fruit there is a smaller fruit of the size of a grape, but hollow; its taste is like that of grapes,
129 but eating too many of them gives a splitting headache. | A surprising thing is that when these fruits are dried in the sun they taste just like figs, and I used to eat them in place of figs, which are not to be found in India. They call this [small] fruit *angūr*, which in their language means grapes.[60] Grapes themselves are very rare in India and are to be had only in certain districts, in the capital Dihlī and in the territory of. . . .[61] The *mohwa* bears fruit twice a year and from its kernels they make oil, which they use for lamps. Another of their fruits is one which they call *kasīra*[62] and which they dig out of the ground; it is very sweet and resembles a chestnut. India has of the fruits of our country the pomegranate,

[57] The *tandū* (*Diospyros melanoxylon*) is the fruit of the ebony tree.

[58] For the *jamūn* (so spelled in spite of I.B.'s careful spelling with *ch*) i.e. the jambol or black plum, see vol. II, p. 379, n. 57.

[59] The *mohwa* (*Bassia latifolia*) is used also to make spirits (called toddy or pariah).

[60] In Persian.

[61] All MSS have a blank at this point, clearly for some other place name.

[62] The *kasīra* (*kaserū*; *Scirpus kysoor*) is dug out of the ground.

which bears fruit twice a year. I have seen some in the islands of Dhība al-Mahal which bore fruit continuously. The Indians call it *anār*; | I think this must be the origin of the name jullanār because *jul* in Persian means flower and *anār* means pomegranate.[63] 130

Account of the cereals which the people of India sow and use for food. The Indians sow twice a year. When the rain falls in their country in the hot season they sow the autumn crop, and harvest it sixty days later. Among these autumn grains in their country are *kudhrū*, a kind of millet which is the commonest of the grains in their country; *qāl* which resembles [the type of millet called] *anlī*; and *shāmākh* which is smaller in the grain than *qāl*, and often grows without being sown.[64] It is the food of the devotees and ascetics, and of the poor and needy. They go out to gather what has sprung up of this plant without cultivation; each of them holds a large basket | in his left hand and has in his right a whip with which he beats the grain so that it falls into the basket. In this way they collect enough of it to supply them with food for the whole year. The seed of this *shāmākh* is very small; after gathering, it is put out in the sun, then pounded in wooden mortars; the husk flies off leaving its pith, a white substance, from which they make gruel. They cook this with buffalo's milk and it is pleasanter [prepared in this way] than baked as bread; I used often to eat it in India and enjoyed it. Other grains are *māsh* which is a kind of pea, and *munj* which is a species of *māsh*, differing from it in having elongated grains and in its clear green colour. They cook *munj* with rice and eat it with ghee; this dish they call *kishrī* and they breakfast on it every day. It takes the place with them of *ḥarīra* in the lands of the Maghrib.[65] Then there is *lūbiyā*, a kind of bean, and *mūt*, | which resembles *kudhrū* but has smaller grains.[66] It is used as fodder for draught animals in that country and 131 132

[63] The Arabic *jullanār*, 'pomegranate flower', is in fact derived from Persian *gul-anār* (*gul*, however, properly meaning 'rose').

[64] The *kudhrū* (*Paspalum scrobiculatum*) is the common millet.

[65] The *māsh* is the common order of the pulses (*Phaseolus radiatus*). The *munj* is apparently a similar kind (*P. mungo*). *Kishrī* is the well-known kedgeree. These are both species of the vetch called *dāl*.

[66] The *lūbiyā* (*Vigna cattiang*) is a Persian name for the small bean. The *mūt* (*Cyperus rotundus*) is apparently a sort of *kudhrū*.

fattens them; the barley in their country has no strength in it, and fodder for the animals is furnished by this *mūt* or else by chickpeas, which they pound and soak with water before feeding it to them. In place of green fodder, too, they feed them with *māsh* leaves, but first each animal is given ghee to drink for ten days, three to four pounds a day, and is not ridden during this time, and after that they feed it with *māsh* leaves, as we have said, for a month or so.

The cereals which we have mentioned are autumn crops. When they harvest these sixty days after sowing them, they sow the spring cereals, which are wheat, barley, chickpeas, and lentils. They are sown in the same ground where the 133 autumn crops are sown | for their land is generous and of good heart. As for rice, they sow it three times a year, and it is one of the principal cereals in their country. They sow also sesame and sugarcane along with the autumn grains that we have mentioned.

To return to what we were saying, we continued our journey from the city of Abūhar across open country extending for a day's journey. On its borders are formidable mountains, inhabited by Hindu infidels who frequently hold up parties of travellers. Of the inhabitants of India the majority are infidels; some of them are subjects [ryots] under Muslim rule,[67] and live in villages governed by a Muslim headman appointed by the tax-collector or subordinate officer in whose fief[68] the village lies. Others of them are rebels and warriors, who maintain themselves in the fastnesses of the mountains and plunder travellers. |

[67] Literally 'under the *dhimma* of the Muslims' i.e. protection on payment of tribute taxes; see vol. II, p. 425, n. 50. The term translated 'headman' (*ḥākim*) vaguely indicates a person who exercises some judicial or civil authority. The *'āmil* in this context is clearly not to be taken in any peculiarly Indian technical sense but in the common Arabic meaning of 'tax-collector' (or 'tax-farmer') and *khadīm* (strangely rendered 'eunuch' in the French translation) which implies only 'a subordinate' (translated 'servitor' in vol. I, p. 223), can here, in view of the assignment of fiefs to such persons, only mean 'officer of lower rank'.

[68] I have retained the traditional translation of *iqṭā'* by 'fief', in spite of the well-justified protests of mediaeval historians, since the Muslim *iqṭā'* carried diverse social and economic status and is not identical with the West-European *feodum*. See W. H. Moreland, *The Agrarian System of Moslem India* (Cambridge, 1929) pp. 8–11, where the differences between 'representatives', 'assignees', 'grantees', and '[tax] farmers' are explained.

Account of an engagement which we had on this road, being the first engagement which I witnessed in India. When we made ready to set out from Abūhar, the main party left the town in the early morning, but I stayed there with a small party of my companions until midday. We then set out too, numbering in all twenty-two horsemen, partly Arabs and partly non-Arabs [i.e. Persians and Turks], and were attacked in the open country there by eighty infidels on foot with two horsemen. My companions were men of courage and vigour[69] and we fought stoutly with them, killing one of their horsemen and about twelve of the footsoldiers, and capturing the horse of the former. I was hit by an arrow and my horse by another, but God in His grace preserved me from them, for there is no force in their arrows. One of our party had his horse wounded, but we gave him in exchange the horse we had captured from the infidel, and killed the wounded horse, which was eaten by | the Turks of our party. We carried the heads of the slain to the castle of Abū Bak'har,[70] which we reached about midnight, and suspended them from the wall. 134 135

After two days' journey from this place we reached the town of Ajūdahān,[71] a small town belonging to the pious shaikh Farīd al-Dīn al-Badhāwunī, the very person whom the pious shaikh and saint Burhān al-Dīn the lame had told me, at Alexandria, that I should meet.[72] And meet him I did, God be praised. He was the spiritual preceptor of the king of India, who made him a gift of this town. But he is afflicted by secret imaginings (God preserve us from them); thus he never shakes anyone by the hand, nor comes near him, and if his robe should brush against the garment of any other person he washes it. I went into his hospice and when I met him I

[69] Read, with MSS 2289 and 2291 (4–907), *ghanā'*.

[70] The name no longer exists, but it is mentioned in a text cited by Mahdi Husain as a small place with a hospice twenty miles from Ajodhan.

[71] Ajodhan was the principal ferry across the Sutlej river, and was renamed Pākpaṭṭan ('holy ferry') by Akbar, in honour of the saint (Bābā) Farīd al-Dīn, mentioned below, whose shrine is widely venerated.

[72] See vol. I, p. 23. I.B., in calling him Farīd al-Dīn, has confused his name with that of his grandfather, the founder of the line of Chishti shaikhs at Ajodhan, who died in 1271 and was succeeded by his son Badr al-Dīn Sulaimān (d. 1281), and the latter by his son 'Alam al-Dīn Mawj-Daryā (d. 734/1334). It was 'Alam al-Dīn also who was the shaikh (spiritual preceptor) of Sultan Muḥammad.

gave him the greetings of Shaikh Burhān al-Dīn. He was 136 astonished and said 'I am not worthy of | that.' I met also his two virtuous sons, Mu'izz al-Dīn, the elder, who when his father died succeeded to his shaikhly function, and 'Alam al-Dīn,[73] and visited the tomb of his grandfather, the sainted Pole, Farīd al-Dīn called al-Badhāwunī,[74] after the town of Badhāwun in the land of as-Sambal.[75] When I was about to leave this town, 'Alam al-Dīn said to me, 'You must not go without seeing my father.' I saw him accordingly; he was on top of a terrace in his hospice, and was wearing white robes and a large turban with a tassel, which was inclined to one side. He gave me his blessing and sent me a present of sugar and sugar candy.

Account of the Indians who burn themselves to death. As I returned from visiting this shaikh, I saw people hurrying out from our camp, and some of our party along with them. I asked them what was happening and they told me that one 137 of the Hindu infidels had died, | that a fire had been kindled to burn him, and his wife would burn herself along with him. After the burning my companions came back and told me that she had embraced the dead man until she herself was burned with him. Later on I used often to see in that country an infidel Hindu woman, richly dressed, riding on horseback, followed by both Muslims and infidels and preceded by drums and trumpets; she was accompanied by Brahmans, who are the chiefs of the Hindus. In the Sultan's dominions they ask his permission to burn her, which he accords them and then they burn her.

Sometime later I happened to be in a town inhabited by a majority of infidels, called Amjarī.[76] Its governor was a

[73] Mu'izz al-Dīn was subsequently appointed by Sultan Muḥammad governor of Gujerat, and was killed in a rebellion there in 1348. 'Alam al-Dīn was appointed *Shaikh al-Islām* (i.e. chief muftī) in Delhi.

[74] This was one of the most famous of the Chishtī saints in India, known by the nickname of Shakarganj ('sugar store') conferred on him by his teacher Quṭb al-Dīn Bakhtiyār [see p. 625 below], whom he succeeded as the head of the Chishtī order in India. In assigning him to Badaun, I.B. has confused him with his successor in the Chishtī headship, Niẓām al-Dīn Awliyā' (pp. 653–4 below).

[75] The district of Sambhal in Uttar Pradesh.

[76] Amjhera, in Gwalior state, 12 miles west of Dhar. For the Sāmira see p. 597, n. 11 above.

Muslim, one of the Sāmira of Sind. In its neighbourhood were some unsubdued infidels, and when one day they made an attack on the road the Muslim amīr went out to engage them, | together with his subjects both Muslim and infidel. 138 There was severe fighting between them, in the course of which seven of the infidel subjects were killed, three of whom had wives, and the three widows agreed to burn themselves. The burning of the wife after her husband's death is regarded by them as a commendable act, but is not compulsory;[77] but when a widow burns herself her family acquire a certain prestige by it and gain a reputation for fidelity. A widow who does not burn herself dresses in coarse garments and lives with her own people in misery, despised for her lack of fidelity, but she is not forced to burn herself.

When these three women to whom we have referred made a compact to burn themselves, they spent three days preceding the event in concerts of music and singing and festivals of eating and drinking, as though they were bidding farewell to the world, and the women from all around came [to take part]. On | the morning of the fourth day each one of them 139 had a horse brought to her and mounted it, richly dressed and perfumed. In her right hand she held a coconut, with which she played, and in her left a mirror, in which she could see her face. They were surrounded by Brahmans and accompanied by their own relatives, and were preceded by drums, trumpets and bugles. Everyone of the infidels would say to one of them 'Take greetings from me to my father, or brother, or mother, or friend' and she would say 'yes' and smile at them. I rode out with my companions to see what exactly these women did in this [ceremony of] burning. After travelling about three miles with them we came to a dark place with much water and trees with heavy shade, amongst which there were four pavilions, each containing a stone idol. Between the pavilions there was a basin of water over which a dense shade was cast by trees so thickly set that the sun could not penetrate them. | The place looked like a spot in 140 hell—God preserve us from it! On reaching these pavilions they descended to the pool, plunged into it and divested

[77] I.B. seeks to put the practice into the legal categories familiar to Muslims so that they should not get the wrong impression.

themselves of their clothes and ornaments, which they distributed as alms. Each one was then given an unsewn garment of coarse cotton and tied part of it round her waist and part over her head and shoulders. Meanwhile, the fires had been lit near this basin in a lowlying spot, and *raughan kunjut*,[78] that is oil of sesame, poured over them, so that the flames were increased. There were about fifteen men there with faggots of thin wood, and with them about ten others with heavy balks in their hands, while the drummers and trumpeters were standing by waiting for the woman's coming. The fire was screened off by a blanket held by some 141 men | in their hands, so that she should not be frightened by the sight of it. I saw one of them, on coming to the blanket, pull it violently out of the men's hands, saying to them with a laugh, *mārā mītarsānī az aṭash man mīdānam ū aṭash ast rahā kunī mārā*; these words mean 'Is it with the fire that you frighten me? I know that it is a blazing fire.'[79] Thereupon she joined her hands above her head in salutation to the fire and cast herself into it. At the same moment the drums, trumpets and bugles were sounded, and men threw on her the firewood they were carrying and the others put those heavy balks on top of her to prevent her moving, cries were raised and there was a loud clamour. When I saw this I had all but fallen off my horse, if my companions had not quickly brought water to me and laved my face, after which I withdrew.

The Indians have a similar practice of drowning them-142 selves, and many of them do so in the river Gang, | the river to which they go on pilgrimage, and into which the ashes of these burned persons are cast. They say that it is a river of Paradise.[80] When one of them comes to drown himself he says to those present with him, 'Do not think that I drown myself for any worldly reason or through penury; my purpose is solely to seek approach to Kusāy,' Kusāy being the name of God in their language.[81] He then drowns himself, and when

[78] Persian *kungud*, 'sesame' or rape-seed.

[79] It seems unlikely that a Hindu woman would speak in Persian. Presumably the words were those of the person who translated them to I.B. The Arabic translation omits the last phrase, 'let me be'.

[80] This is a more probable interpretation of the Arabic (*min al-jannati*) than the alternative 'comes from Paradise'.

[81] *Kusāy* represents Krishna, as the French translation suggests.

he is dead they take him out and burn him and cast his ashes into this river.

Let us return to our original topic. We set out from the town of Ajūdahan, and after four days' march reached the city of Sarasatī,[82] a large town with quantities of rice of an excellent sort which is exported to the capital, Dihlī. The town produces a very large revenue; I was told how much it was by the *ḥājib* Shams al-Dīn al-Būshanjī, | but have for- 143 gotten the figure. Thence we travelled to the city of Ḥānsī,[83] an exceedingly fine, well built and populous city, surrounded by a great wall, whose builder they say was one of the great infidel sultans called Tūra, of whom they have many tales and stories to relate. It is from this city [came] Kamāl al-Dīn Ṣadr al-Jahān, the Grand Qāḍī of India, and his brother Qutlū Khān, the preceptor of the Sultan,[84] also their two brothers Niẓām al-Dīn and Shams al-Dīn, who renounced the world for the service of God and sojourned at Mecca to the time of his death.

We set out thereafter from Ḥānsī and arrived two days later at Mas'ūd Ābād, which is ten miles from Dihlī,[85] and stayed there three days. Ḥānsī and Mas'ūd Ābād belong to the exalted king Hūshanj, the son of the king Kamāl Gurg (the word | *gurg* means 'wolf'), of whom we shall have more to say 144 later.[86]

The Sultan of India, to whose capital we had come, was absent from it at the time in the district of the city of Qanawj,[87] which is ten days' march from Dihlī. But the Sultan's mother, who is called al-Makhdūma Jahān[88] (*Jahān* is the name for *al-dunyā* [i.e. the world]) was in the capital as well as his vizier, the *Khwāja Jahān*, a person named Aḥmad

[82] Ṣarsatī was the old town, abandoned in 1726, and replaced by Sirsa in 1837.

[83] Hānsī was involved in the rebellion of Sayyid Ibrāhīm, which was put down in 1336.

[84] See below pp. 628, 718, and for Niẓām al Dīn p. 731. The apparently superfluous *huwa* in the text comes from the autograph MS. 2291, and suggests that some words have been omitted before 'Kamāl al-Dīn'.

[85] Its ruins lie one mile east of Najafgarh, and six miles west by north of Palem station.

[86] P. 718 below.

[87] See also vol. IV, pp. 25 ff. (Ar.). The absence of the Sultan was the consequence of the expedition into the Dūāb, to the south and west of Delhi.

[88] See p. 736 below.

ibn Aiyās, a *rūmī* by origin.[89] The vizier sent his officers to receive us, designating for the reception of each of us a person of his own rank. Among those whom he appointed to receive me were the Shaikh al-Bisṭāmī, the *sharīf* al-Māzanderānī, who was the chamberlain of the strangers, and the doctor 'Alā' al-Dīn al-Multānī, known by the name of Qunnara. He wrote to inform the Sultan of our arrival, sending the letter 145 by | the *dāwa*, that is by courier post, in the manner we have already described,[90] and his letter reached the Sultan and he received the Sultan's reply during the three days that we spent at Mas'ūd Ābād. Thereafter the qāḍīs, jurists and shaikhs, and some of the amīrs came out to meet us. The Indians call the amīrs 'kings'; where the people of Egypt and elsewhere say 'amīr' these people say 'malik'. There came out to meet us also the shaikh Ẓahīr al-Dīn al-Zanjānī, who is a personage of high dignity at the Sultan's court.[91]

We then set out from Mas'ūd Ābād and halted near a village called Pālam,[92] belonging to the sayyid and sharīf Nāṣir al-Dīn Muṭahhar al-Awharī,[93] one of the Sultan's familiars, and of those who enjoy his entire favour. On the next day we arrived at the royal residence of Dihlī, the 146 metropolis of the land of al-Hind, | a vast and magnificent city, uniting beauty with strength. It is surrounded by a wall whose equal is not known in any country in the world,[94] and is the largest city in India, nay rather the largest of all the cities of Islam in the East.

[89] See pp. 654–6 below.
[90] See p. 594, n. 7 above.
[91] Not mentioned elsewhere.
[92] See n. 85 above.
[93] Already mentioned by I.B. (see vol. I, p. 259) as a former Marshal of the Ashrāf at al-Najaf in Iraq.
[94] See vol. II, p. 348.

CHAPTER XI

The City of Dihlī and Its Sultans

Description of the City. The city of Dihlī is of vast extent and population, and made up now of four neighbouring and contiguous towns. One of them is the city called by this name, Dihlī; it is the old city built by the infidels and captured in the year 584 (A.D. 1188).[1] The second is called Sīrī,[2] known also as 'Abode of the Caliphate'; this was the city given by the Sultan to Ghiyāth al-Dīn, the grandson of the 'Abbāsid Caliph al-Mustanṣir when he came to his court.[3] In it was the residence of the Sultan 'Alā al-Dīn and his son Quṭb al-Dīn, of whom we shall speak later. The third is called Tughluq Ābād,[4] after | its founder, the Sultan Tughluq, the 147 father of the Sultan of India to whose court we came. The reason why he built it was that one day as he stood before the Sultan Quṭb al-Dīn he said to him 'O master of the world, it were fitting that a city should be built here.' The Sultan replied to him ironically 'When you are Sultan, build it.' It came to pass by the decree of God that he became Sultan, so he built it and called it by his own name. The fourth is called Jahān Panāh,[5] and is set apart for the residence of the Sultan, Muḥammad Shāh, the reigning king of India, to whose court we had come. He was the founder of it, and it was his intention

[1] The mediaeval city of Dihlī was founded by a Rajput chief in the eleventh century and captured by Quṭb al-Dīn Aibak (see p. 628 below) in 588/1192. It lies ten miles to the south of the Mughal city of Dihlī (properly called Shāhjahānābād). For the successive cities see the maps and plans in the article 'Dihlī' in the *Encyc. of Islam*, new edition, and Sir Gordon Hearn, *The Seven Cities of Delhi*, second edition, Calcutta, 1928.

[2] Two to three miles to the north-east of old Delhi.

[3] See vol. I, pp. 225–6, and below, pp. 679–85.

[4] Four to five miles east by south of old Delhi. For Sultan Tughluq see pp. 648–56 below. See Plate 3.

[5] Literally 'Refuge of the world', i.e, 'of universal fame'. It occupied an area of some four miles in breadth between old Delhi and Sīrī.

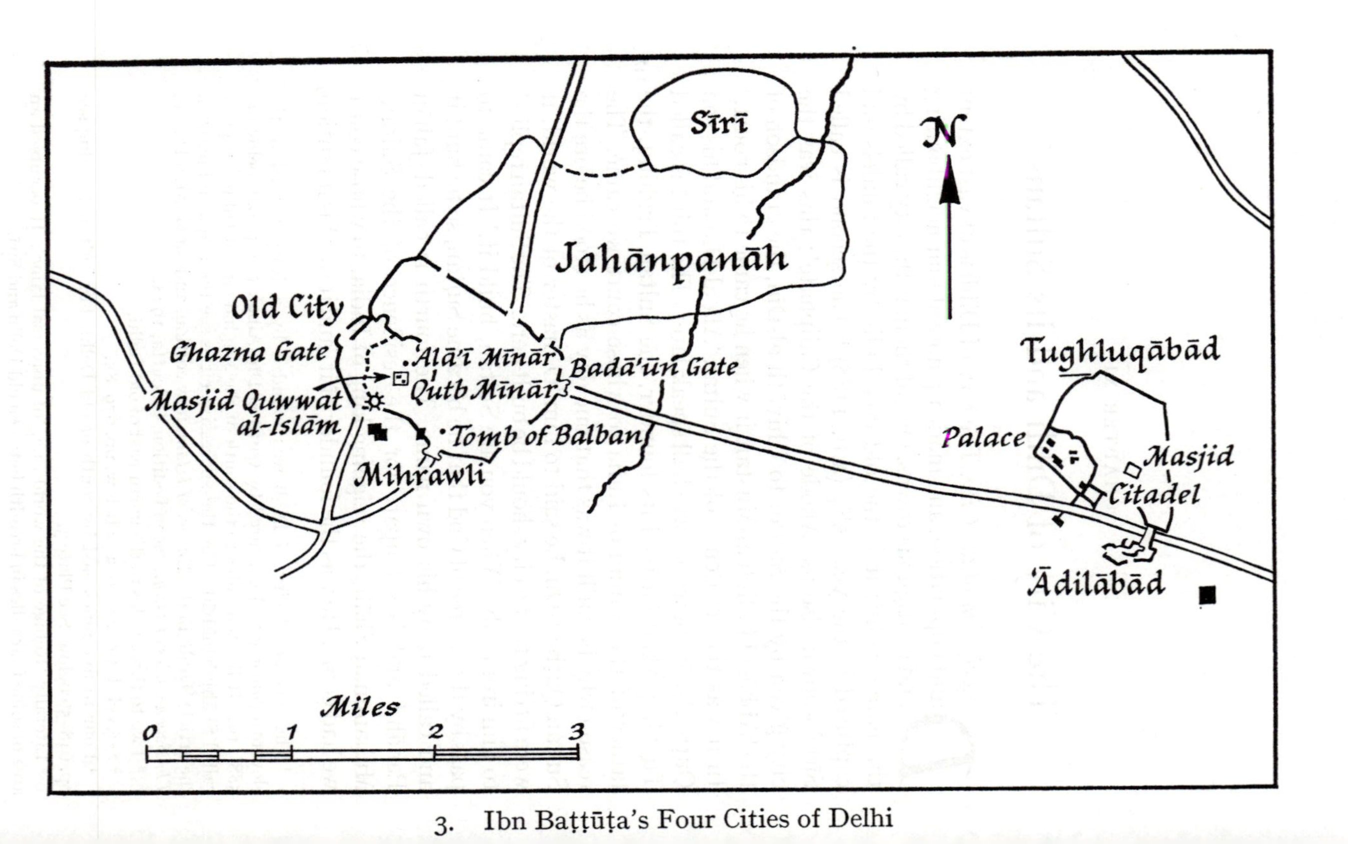

3. Ibn Baṭṭūṭa's Four Cities of Delhi

to unite these four towns within a single wall, but after building part of it he gave up the rest because of the great expense entailed in its construction.

Description of the wall and gates of Dihlī. The wall which surrounds the city of Dihlī | is unparalleled. The breadth of 148 the wall itself is eleven cubits, and inside it there are rooms where night-watchmen and keepers of the gates are lodged. The wall contains also stores for provisions, which they call 'granaries',[6] as well as stores for war equipment and for mangonels and stone-throwing machines.[7] Grain keeps in it for a very long time without going bad or becoming damaged. I have seen rice brought out of one of these stores, and although it had gone black in colour it was still good to the taste. I have also seen *kudhrū* (millet)[8] taken out of them. All these stores had been laid up by the Sultan Balaban[9] ninety years before. There is room inside the wall for horsemen and infantry to march from one end of the town to the other, and it has window openings pierced on the town side, through which the light enters. The lower courses of this wall are constructed with stone and the upper courses with baked brick, and its towers are numerous and set at short intervals. |

The city has twenty-eight gates. Their name for gate is 149 *darwāza*. Amongst these gates is the darwāza of Badhāwun, which is the largest gate; the darwāza of *al-Mindawī*,[10] beside which is the grain market; the darwāza of Jul,[11] where the gardens are; the darwāza of Shāh, which is the name of a man; the darwāza of Pālam, the name of a village which we have already mentioned; the darwāza of Najīb, the name of a man; the darwāza of Kamāl, the same; the darwāza of Ghazna, called after the city of Ghazna, in the province of Khurāsān, and outside which is the place set apart for festival

[6] *Anbārāt*, a Perso-Arabic formation from Pers. *anbār* 'fuel'.

[7] *raʿādāt*, apparently a popular form of *ʿarrādāt*, which were much lighter than the heavy mangonels resembling rather the ballista. For these see Cl. Cahen, 'Un Traité d'Armurerie composé pour Saladin', in *Bull. d'Études Orientales*, XII (Beyrouth, 1948), pp. 141–3, 157–9.

[8] See p. 611, n. 64 above.

[9] See p. 633 below. This is the spelling of the autograph.

[10] So vocalized in the autograph; but the French translators in a note on p. 461 seem to prefer *mandwī*. The word itself means 'grain market'.

[11] Persian *gul*, 'rose, flower'.

prayers[12] as well as some cemeteries; and the darwāza of al-Bajāliṣa.[13] Outside this gate are the cemeteries of Dihlī. This is a beautiful place of burial; they build domed pavilions in it and every grave must have a [place for prayer with a] miḥrāb beside it, even if there is no dome over it.[14] They plant
150 in it flowering trees | such as the tuberose,[15] the *raibūl*,[16] the *nisrīn*[17] and others. In that country there are always flowers in bloom at every season of the year.

Description of the Mosque of Dihlī.[18] The Cathedral Mosque occupies a vast area; its walls, roof, and paving are all constructed of white stones, admirably squared and firmly cemented with lead. There is no wood in it at all. It has thirteen domes of stone, its *minbar* also is of stone, and it has four courts. In the centre of the mosque is the awe-inspiring column of which [it is said] nobody knows of what metal it is constructed. One of their learned men told me that it is called *Haft Jūsh*, which means 'seven metals', and that it is composed of these seven.[19] A part of this column, of a finger's length, has been polished, and this polished part gives out a
151 brilliant gleam. Iron makes no impression | on it. It is thirty cubits high, and we rolled a turban round it, and the portion which encircled it measured eight cubits. At the eastern gate of the mosque there are two enormous idols of brass prostrate on the ground and held by stones, and everyone entering or leaving the mosque treads on them. The site was formerly occupied by a *budkhāna*,[20] that is idol temple, and was converted into a mosque on the conquest of the city. In the

[12] *Muṣallā*; see vol. I, p. 13, n. 20.

[13] A station in the vicinity of Qanawj, visited later by I.B.: see vol. IV, p. 27 (Ar.).

[14] The text is ambiguous, but appears to mean that some of the miḥrābs are under domes and some open to the sky.

[15] Persian *gul-i shabbo* ('night scented rose'): cf. p. 739 below.

[16] The identity of this plant is dubious; Mahdi Husain translates 'jessamine', i.e. white jasmine.

[17] Here apparently the musk-rose, with white and yellow flowers.

[18] Called *Quwwat al-Islām* ('the strength of Islam') in the original Rajput city, and, as I.B. correctly states below, built on the site of a Hindu temple.

[19] The iron pillar, still standing, was taken from a fourth-century temple of Vishnu. It is 24 feet in height. *Haft gūshe* would mean, not 'seven metals' but 'heptagonal'; *haft gush*, 'of seven temperaments', seems more likely in view of its resistance to rust. See Plate 2.

[20] Persian *but-khānah*, 'idol-house'.

PLATES

1. The Quṭb Minār with the iron pillar

3 Courtyard of the Quwwat al-Islām Mosque

3. The walls of Tughluqābād

4 The Hall of the Thousand Columns

5. Mausoleum of the Sultan Ghiyāth al-Dīn Tughluq Shāh, in which his son Sultan Muḥammad is said to have been buried

northern court of the mosque is the minaret, which has no parallel in the lands of Islam.[21] It is built of red stone, unlike the stone [used for] the rest of the mosque, for that is white, and the stones of the minaret are dressed. The minaret itself is of great height; the ball on top of it is of glistening white marble and its 'apples'[22] are of pure gold. The passage is so wide that elephants can go up by it. | A person in whom I 152 have confidence told me that when it was built he saw an elephant climbing with stones to the top. It was built by the Sultan Mu'izz al-Dīn, son of Nāṣir al-Dīn, son of Sultan Ghiyāth al-Dīn Balaban.[23] The Sultan Quṭb al-Dīn wished to build in the western court an even larger minaret, but was cut off by death when [only] a third of it had been completed.[24] The Sultan Muḥammad intended to bring it to completion, but afterwards gave up the idea as being unlucky. This [unfinished] minaret is one of the wonders of the world for size, and the width of its passage is such that three elephants could mount it abreast. The third of it built equals in height the whole of the other minaret we have mentioned in the northern court. I climbed to the top of it on one occasion; I saw most of the houses of the city, and the walls for all their elevation and loftiness looked to me quite low. The people at the foot of the minaret appeared to me like little children, although to one looking at it from below | it does not seem 153 so high because of its great bulk and breadth.

[21] The famous Quṭb Minār, now 234 feet (69·7 metres) in height, actually in the southern court. See Plate 1.

[22] Evidently 'ball shaped ornaments', and presumably those smaller ones on the stem of the spire above the minaret. The original top storey of the Quṭb Minār has, however, been lost in the course of its frequent dilapidation and rebuilding (see the following note).

[23] I.B., or his informant, has confused the Mu'izz al-Dīn (Kaiqubād), who reigned at Delhi 1287–90 (see pp. 635–8 below), with the suzerain of the conqueror of Delhi, Quṭb al-Dīn, (see p. 628 below), the Ghūrid sultan Mu'izz al-Dīn Muḥammad b. Sām who is eulogized in inscriptions on the Minār. The minaret was actually begun by Quṭb al-Dīn, on the model of the Ghūrid minaret at Jām (see *Le Minaret de Djam*, edd. Maricq and Wiet, Paris, 1959) and completed by Shams al-Dīn Lalmish (Iletmish) about 1229. It suffered repeated damage from lightning and decay, and was restored to its present condition only in 1828–1829.

[24] The incomplete base storey of this monument (the base diameter of which is twice that of the Quṭb Minār) still stands in the northern court of the mosque. It was the work of sultan 'Alā' al-Dīn (1295–1315), the father of Quṭb al-Dīn Mubārak Shāh (see pp. 638–43 below).

The sultan Quṭb al-Dīn had intended also to build a cathedral mosque in Sīrī, the so-called 'Abode of the Caliphate',[25] but he completed only the wall in the direction of Mecca and the miḥrāb. It is built with white, black, red and green stones; if it were finished there would be nothing like it in the world. Sultan Muḥammad proposed to complete it and commissioned the master masons to estimate its cost. They asserted that he would spend thirty-five laks in completing it, so the Sultan gave up the idea as being too costly. One of his intimate associates, however, told me that he gave it up not because of its excessive cost but because he regarded the project as unlucky, since Sultan Quṭb al-Dīn had been killed before finishing it. |

154 *Description of the two great tanks outside Dihlī.* Outside Dihlī is the large reservoir named after the Sultan Shams al-Dīn Lalmish,[26] from which the inhabitants of the city draw their drinking water. It lies close to the *muṣallā*.[27] Its contents are collected from rain water, and it is about two miles in length by half that breadth. Its western side, in the direction of the *muṣallā*, is constructed with stones, and disposed like a series of terraces one above the other, and beneath each terrace are steps leading down to the water. Beside each terrace there is a stone pavilion containing seats for those who have come out to visit the place and to enjoy its attractions. In the centre of the tank there is a great pavilion built of dressed stones, two stories high. When the reservoir is filled with water it can be reached only in boats, but when 155 the water is low the people go into it. | Inside it is a mosque, and at most times it is occupied by poor brethren devoted to the service of God and placing their trust in Him (i.e. dependent upon charity). When the water dries up at the sides of this reservoir, they sow sugar canes, gherkins, cucumbers, and green and yellow melons there; the latter are very sweet but of small size. Between Dihlī and the 'Abode of the Caliphate' is the 'private tank', which is larger than that of

[25] See p. 619 above.

[26] See pp. 629–30 below.

[27] I.e. outside the Ghazna gate (see p. 621 above), i.e. on the western side. This reservoir is identified with the Shemsi tank to the west of Mihrawli (Fanshawe, quoted Mžik, p. 64 n.) and was constructed by Sultan Iltutmish (Iletmish).

the Sultan Shams al-Dīn.[28] Along its sides there are forty pavilions, and round about it live the musicians. Their place is called Ṭarab Ābād ('City of Music') and they have there a most extensive bazaar, a cathedral mosque, and many other mosques besides. I was told that the singing girls living there, of whom there are a great many, take part in a body in the *tarāwīḥ* prayers in these mosques during the month of Ramaḍān,[29] and the imāms lead them in these prayers. The male musicians do the same. I myself saw the male musicians on the occasion of | the wedding of the amīr Saif al-Dīn 156 Ghadā son of Muhannā,[30] when each one of them had a prayer mat under his knees, and on hearing the *adhān* (call to prayer) rose, made his ablutions and performed the prayer.

Account of some of its places of visitation. One of these is the tomb of the pious shaikh Quṭb al-Dīn Bakhtiyār al-Ka'kī.[31] The blessed power of this tomb is manifest and it enjoys great veneration. The reason why this shaikh was called al-Ka'kī is that he used to give all those debtors who came to him to complain of need or poverty, or who had daughters and had not the wherewithal to send them with proper outfits to their husbands, a *ka'ka* of gold or silver, and so he became known for that reason as al-Ka'kī;[32] God have mercy on him! Among them also are the tomb of the eminent legist Nūr al-Dīn al-Kurlānī, and that of the legist 'Alā al-Dīn al-Kirmānī,[33] | named after the province of Kirmān. The blessed 157 power of this tomb is manifest and it streams with light. The place which it occupies serves to indicate the *qibla* of the

[28] *Ḥawḍ al-Khāṣṣ*, about two miles north of the mosque and the same distance west of Sīrī.

[29] See vol. I, p. 239, n. 195. [30] See pp. 685–92 below.

[31] A native of Ūsh, in Farghāna, he became a disciple of Mu'in al-Dīn Chishtī, the founder of the Chishtī order in India, and established the order in Delhi, where he enjoyed immense influence both with the Sultan and the population and died in 1235/36. His tomb in Mihrawli is still a popular place of pilgrimage (see Fanshawe, p. 281).

[32] *Ka'k* is a flat cake or biscuit, but one wonders where I.B. obtained his explanation of this name. The more usual interpretation, and one more attuned to Ṣūfī tradition, attributes it to the saint's supernatural or miraculous supply of these cakes.

[33] Al-Kurlānī has not been identified. Several members of the Kirmānī family of Ḥusainid sharīfs were religious notables at Delhi; 'Alā' al-Dīn was probably Sayyid Muḥammad b. Maḥmūd (d. 1311), a close friend of the saint Niẓām al-Dīn Awliyā (see pp. 653–4 below).

muṣallā for the festival prayers, and thereabouts are the tombs of a large number of pious men, God give us profit of them.

Account of some of its scholars and pious men. Amongst them is the pious and learned shaikh Maḥmūd al-Kubbā; he is one of the great saints and the people assert he is able to draw on the resources of creation, because to all outward seeming he has no property of his own, yet he supplies food to all comers and makes gifts of gold and silver coins and garments. Many miraculous graces have been operated through him and he has acquired a great reputation for them.[34] I saw him many times and profited from his blessed power. Another is the pious and learned shaikh 'Alā al-Dīn [called] 158 al-Nīlī as though he were named after | the Egyptian Nile, but God knows.[35] He was a disciple of the learned and pious shaikh Niẓām al-Dīn al-Badhāwunī. He preaches to the people every Friday and multitudes of them repent before him and shave their heads and fall into ecstasies of lamentation, and some of them faint.

Anecdote. I was present one day when he was preaching, and the Qur'ān-reader recited in his presence 'O ye men, fear your Lord. Verily the quaking of [the earth at] the Hour is a thing of terror. On the day when ye see it every nursing woman shall be unmindful of what she has suckled, and every carrying female shall bring forth her burden, and thou shalt see men reeling as drunkards, yet are they not drunkards, but the chastisement of God is terrible.'[36] [When the reader finished,] the doctor 'Alā al-Dīn repeated these words, and a 159 certain poor brother | somewhere in the mosque uttered a loud cry. The shaikh repeated the verse and the faqīr cried out again and fell dead. I was one of those who prayed over him and joined in his funeral cortège.

Another of the pious men of Dihlī is the learned and saintly shaikh Ṣadr al-Dīn al-Kuhrānī.[37] He used to fast continually

[34] No important shaikh of this name is mentioned in Indian sources, and it has been suggested that he is no other than the celebrated Chishtī saint Naṣīr al-Dīn Maḥmūd, known as *Chirāgh-i-Dihlī* (the lamp of Delhi'), the spiritual successor of Niẓām al-Dīn (see pp. 653–4 below), d. 1356.

[35] 'Alā' al-Dīn Nīlī was a native of Oudh, became one of the khalīfas of Niẓām al-Dīn, and died at Delhi in 1361.

[36] Sūra xxii, vv. 1–2.

[37] Nothing is known of this shaikh.

and stand all his nights [in prayer]. He renounced the world entirely and rejected all its goods, and wore nothing but a woollen cloak. The Sultan and the officers of state used to visit him but he often refused to see them, and when the Sultan asked permission to give him a grant of some villages, from the revenues of which he could supply food to poor brethren and visitors, he would have nothing to do with it. Visiting him another day the Sultan brought him a present of ten thousand dīnārs, but he refused to accept it. It was said that he broke his fast only after three nights and that when someone remonstrated with him about this he replied 'I do not break fast until I am under such compulsion that carrion becomes lawful for me.'[38]

Another of them is the learned and saintly imām, | the abstinent and humble-minded devotee, Kamāl al-Dīn 'Abdallāh al-Ghārī, the outstanding and unique personality of his age.[39] He is called al-Ghārī ['the cave-man'] from a cave which he used to inhabit outside Dihlī, near the hospice of Shaikh Niẓām al-Dīn al-Badhāwunī. I visited him in this cave three times. 160

A miraculous grace of his. I had a slave boy who ran away from me, and whom I found in the possession of a certain Turk. I had in mind to reclaim the slave from him, but the shaikh said to me 'This boy is no good to you. Don't take him'. The Turk wished to come to an arrangement, so I settled with him that he paid me a hundred dīnārs and I left him the boy. Six months later the boy killed his master and was taken before the Sultan, who ordered him to be handed over to his master's sons, and they put him to death. When I experienced this miracle on the part of the shaikh I attached myself entirely to him, withdrawing from the world and giving all that I possessed | to the poor and needy. I stayed with him for some time,[40] and I used to see him fast for ten and twenty days on end and remain standing [in prayer] most of the night. I continued with him until the Sultan sent for me and I became entangled in the world once again—may 161

[38] 'Carrion' (*maita*), i.e. the flesh of any animal that has not been ritually slaughtered, is unlawful food (see vol. II, p. 392, n. 91), but a familiar legal maxim declares that 'necessity makes the forbidden lawful'.

[39] See p. 766 below.

[40] See p. 766 below.

God give me a good ending! Later on, if God will, I shall tell the whole story, and how it was that I returned to the world.

Account of the capture of Dihlī and of the kings who reigned there successively. I was told by the jurist and imām, the most learned Grand Qāḍī in Hind and Sind, Kamāl al-Dīn Muḥammad ibn al-Burhān of the town of Ghazna, entitled Sadr al-Jahān,[41] that the city of Dihlī was captured from the hands of the infidels in the year 584. I have myself seen this date inscribed on the miḥrāb of the great mosque there.[42] He told

162 me also that it | had been captured by the amīr Quṭb al-Dīn Aibak, who was called by the title of Sipāh[43] Sālār, the meaning of which is 'commander of the armies', who was one of the mamlūks of the exalted Sultan Shihāb al-Dīn Muḥammad ibn Sām the Ghūrid, king of Ghazna and Khurāsān,[44] the same who conquered the kingdom of Ibrāhīm, son of the warrior Sultan Maḥmūd ibn Subuktakīn, who began the conquest of India.

This Sultan Shihāb al-Dīn had despatched the amīr Quṭb al-Dīn with a powerful army and God gave him conquest of the city of Lāhawr.[45] After he settled there his power increased greatly, and he was calumniated to the Sultan, whose intimate friends insinuated to him that Aibak was aiming at constituting himself sole sovereign of India and had indeed already withdrawn his allegiance and revolted. When this report came to the ears of Quṭb al-Dīn [Aibak] he immediately took the initiative, entered Ghazna by night, and presented himself before the Sultan, unknown to those who

[41] Kamāl al-dīn ibn al-Burhān was the chief qāḍī of the mamlūks, and was I.B.'s informant for his history.

[42] The earliest inscription in the mosque is dated 587/1191 (see Edward Thomas, *Chronicles of the Pathan Kings of Delhi*, London, 1871, pp. 21–22). I.B., scanning the lofty inscription from far below, mistook the first letter of 7 (*s.b.*') for the first two letters of 4 (*arb.*').

[43] As noted in the French edition, the autograph reads *s.yāh* for *s.bāh*.

[44] Shihāb al-Dīn was the earlier title of the Ghūrid Mu'izz al-Dīn (see p. 623, n. 23 above). For the Sultans of Ghūr and Shihāb al-Dīn's conquest of Ghazna in 1173 see Barthold, *Turkestan*, p. 337 and *E.I.* 2, s.v. The Grand Qāḍī's history is somewhat confused. Ghazna had been abandoned by the Ghaznevid sultans some time before. For Maḥmūd of Ghazna, see p. 590, n. 203 above; his grandson Ibrāhīm died in 1099.

[45] In 582/1186. Lahore was the Ghaznevid capital in India, and it was by this victory that the Ghūrids replaced the Ghaznevids as the rulers of Muslim India.

had denounced him. | Next day the Sultan took his seat 163 on his throne, having first placed Aibak underneath the throne so that he was not visible. The royal companions and officers who had calumniated Aibak entered and when they had taken their places the Sultan questioned them on the subject of Aibak. They affirmed to him that Aibak had rebelled and refused his allegiance, adding 'We have absolutely certain information that he has proclaimed himself king'; whereupon the Sultan beat the throne with his foot, clapped his hands and called 'Aibak'. He replied 'Here am I', and came out before them. They were filled with confusion and hastened in terror to kiss the ground. The Sultan said to them 'I forgive you this lapse but beware of any further loose talk about Aibak,' and ordered him to return to India.[46] So he returned to it and conquered the city of Dihlī and other cities, and Islām has been established there down to the present day. Quṭb al-Dīn remained there to the time of his death. |

The Sultan Shams al-Dīn Lalmish.[47] He was the first who 164 exercised independent rule in the city of Dihlī. Before his rise to royal power he was a mamlūk of the amīr Quṭb al-Dīn Aibak, the commander of his army and a deputy for him. On Quṭb al-Dīn's death he seized the sovereign power and ordered the people to take the oath of allegiance to him. The jurists came to him headed by the Grand Qāḍī at that time, Wajīh al-Din al-Kāsānī, and when they entered his audience chamber they took their places before him and the qāḍī sat down beside him according to the regular custom. The Sultan understood from them what it was that they wished

[46] This story has not been traced elsewhere. It appears to be a popular embroidery upon Aibak's visit to Ghazna in the year after his occupation of Delhi, where he was detained for some time by illness but eventually reappointed to the government of India. See M. A. Ahmad, *The Early Turkish Empire of Delhi* (Lahore, 1949), pp. 130–1.

[47] This name is commonly rendered Iltutmish by the Indian historians and is so vocalized in *R.C.É.A.*, vol. XI, I, nos. 4100–1–2–5, etc. and Hikmet Bayur in *Belleten* of the Turkish History Society, vol. XIV (Ankara, 1950), 567–88. The inscriptions on coins, however, and on the Quṭb Minār clearly read Īlitmish (Īletmish) (see Thomas, *Pathan Kings*, pp. 78–9, although he renders the name as Altamsh), as do several other early Persian and Indian texts (see Ahmad, *op. cit.* in n. 46, pp. 155–6). I.B.'s *Lalmish* is surely a popular simplification. He reigned 1210–35, after defeating an obscure successor of Aibak, named Ārām.

to discuss with him, and raising a corner of the carpet upon which he was sitting produced for them a deed formally attesting his enfranchisement.[48] The judge and the legists after reading it unanimously took the oath of allegiance to him; he became sole sovereign and reigned for twenty years. He was just, pious and of excellent character, and among the commendable actions which are remembered of him was his 165 zeal | in redressing wrongs and seeing that justice was done to the oppressed. He gave orders that every person who had been wronged should wear a coloured robe.[49] Now the people of India all dress in white, so when he held public audience or rode out and saw someone wearing a coloured robe he looked into his petition and rendered him his due from his oppressor. Then he carried this practice to extremes[50] saying 'There are some people against whom injustices are committed at night, and I wish to do justice to them without delay,' so he set up at the gate of his palace two marble statues of lions. These were placed on towers there and hung round their necks were two chains of iron attached to which was a large bell. The victim of oppression would come by night and set the bell ringing; the Sultan would hear it, look into his case there and then, and see that justice was done by him. On his death the Sultan Shams al-Dīn left three male children, namely Rukn 166 al-Dīn, who exercised the rule after him, Mu'izz | al-Dīn and Nāṣir al-Dīn, and along with them a daughter Raḍīya, who was the full sister of Mu'izz al-Dīn. He was succeeded as ruler by Rukn al-Dīn, as we have said.

The Sultan Rukn al-Dīn son of the Sultan Shams al-Dīn. When the oath of allegiance had been taken to Rukn al-Dīn after his father's death he began his reign by using violence against his brother Mu'izz al-Dīn and put him to death.[51] Raḍīya, who was the full sister of Mu'izz al-Dīn, showed her

[48] Since a slave could not legally hold any public office of authority, proof of manumission was regularly demanded by the religious lawyers from a former slave before recognizing him by an oath of allegiance.

[49] Mahdi Husain (p. 33, n. 3) quotes texts which imply that this was not an uncommon usage in Iran and India, and that the coloured robe was as a rule made of paper.

[50] The autograph plainly reads *'aghyā*, notwithstanding Dozy's remarks s.v. *'ayy*.

[51] An error of detail—the murdered prince was Quṭb al-Dīn; Mu'izz al-Dīn succeeded his sister Raḍīya as sultan.

disapproval of this act to him and he planned to kill her too. On a certain Friday when Rukn al-Dīn rode out to attend the prayer, Raḍīya mounted to the terrace of the old castle adjoining the great mosque, which is called *Dawlat Khāna*,[52] dressed in the robes worn by persons against whom a wrong has been committed, presented herself to the people, and addressed them from the terrace, saying to them 'My brother killed his brother and now he is trying to kill me as well.' Then she recalled to them the days of her father and his good actions | and his beneficence to them, whereupon they, stirred up to excitement, rushed upon the Sultan Rukn al-Dīn, who was there in the mosque,[53] seized him, and brought him out before her. She said to them 'The slayer shall be slain' so they put him to death in retaliation for the murder of his brother. As their [third] brother Nāṣir al-Dīn was still a child the people agreed to establish Raḍīya as ruler. 167

The Sulṭāna Raḍīya.[54] When Rukn al-Dīn was put to death the troops determined by general consent to confer the sovereignty on his sister Raḍīya and proclaimed her as queen. She held sovereign rule for four years and used to ride abroad just like the men, carrying bow and quiver and[55] (*qurbān*), and without veiling her face. After that she was suspected of relations with a slave of hers, one of the Abyssinians,[56] so the people agreed to depose her and marry her to a husband. She was deposed in consequence and married to one of her relations, and her brother Nāṣir al-Dīn became king. |

Sultan Nāṣir al-Dīn son of Sultan Shams al-Dīn.[57] When Raḍīya was deposed her youngest brother Nāṣir al-Dīn became ruler and exercised the royal power for some time. Subsequently Raḍīya and her husband revolted against him, 168

[52] Persian: 'house of the rulership', the White Palace of Iltutmish (Ahmad, p. 191, n. 2).

[53] A romantic addition to the story. Rukn al-Dīn was on campaign, and was captured by Raḍīya's troops after her elevation to the sultanate.

[54] The Perso-Indian pronunciation is Razīya (r. 1236–40). I.B.'s form *Sulṭāna* is peculiar, and contrary to classical Arabic usage. On her coinage Raḍīya is correctly entitled *Sulṭān* (Thomas, 107–8).

[55] ? Kirpāl (suggestion of Dr. A. Goriawale).

[56] Indian sources assert that she allowed the Abyssinian Master of the Stables (*Amīr ākhūr*) to lift her on to her horse (Ahmad, 193).

[57] I.B.'s informant omits the reigns of Mu'izz al-Dīn (who defeated Raḍīya's attempt to regain the throne) and 'Alā' al-Dīn Mas'ūd-shāh. Nāṣir al-Dīn Maḥmūd reigned 1246–66.

led out a force of their own mamlūks and a body of disorderly elements who followed them, and prepared to fight against him. Nāṣir al-Dīn went out accompanied by his mamlūk and representative Ghiyāth al-Dīn Balaban, who ruled the kingdom after him, and they engaged in battle. Raḍīya's troops were put to flight and she herself fled until, overtaken by hunger and overwhelmed by weariness, she approached a cultivator whom she saw tilling the soil and asked him for something to eat. He gave her a crust of bread which she ate and then fell fast asleep. She was dressed as a man, but when she slept the labourer looked at her sleeping and saw beneath her outer garments a tunic[58] embroidered with jewels. Realizing from this that she was a woman, he killed her, 169 stripped her, drove off her horse, and buried her | in his field, then taking some of her garments he went to the market to sell them. The dealers had some suspicions about him and brought him before the *shiḥna*, that is to say the chief of police,[59] who had him beaten until he confessed to killing her and showed them where she was buried. Her body was disinterred, washed, wrapped in grave clothes and buried again at the same place, and a dome was built over it. Her grave, which is on the bank of the great river called al-Jūn at a distance of one farsakh from the city, is still visited by pilgrims in order to obtain blessing.[60]

After her death Nāṣir al-Dīn enjoyed undisputed sovereignty and continued to rule for twenty years. He was a pious king; he used to write copies of the Holy Book with his own hand, sell them and buy his food with the proceeds. The qāḍī Kamāl al-Dīn showed me a Qur'ān copied by him in an elegant and well-executed writing. Subsequently his deputy[61] 170 | Ghiyāth al-Dīn Balaban killed him and became king after

[58] *qabā'*. See Dozy, *Vêtements*, 352.

[59] *Shiḥna* generally means the military governor of a city, who was usually in command of the police also. For *ḥākim* cf. Vol. I, p. 114, n. 168.

[60] The tomb and its site are described by Mahdi Husain, p. 35, n. 4.

[61] This is the lexical equivalent of *nā'ib* (*nāyib* in the autograph) and the official designation (*nā'ib al-mulk*) of the office held by Balban. But he was in fact the Regent of the empire, with powers and insignia equal to those of the Sultan (Ahmad, p. 230, n. 2). His title at this time was *Ulugh-khān*, and his chief occupation was to put down the numerous revolts by subordinate officers against Nāṣir al-Dīn. There is no contemporary confirmation that the latter was killed by Balban.

him. This Balaban had a remarkable history which we shall relate.

The Sultan Ghiyāth al-Dīn Balaban. His name is spelt with two *b*'s separated by an *l*, each followed by the vowel *a*, and an *n* at the end. When Balaban killed his master Sultan Nāṣir al-Dīn, he ruled as sovereign after him for twenty years, having previously been deputy to him for twenty years more. He was one of the best of sultans, just, clement, and upright. Among his generous acts was the building of a house, which he called 'The House of Safety'. If any debtor entered it his debt was paid; if any person fled to it for refuge he was secure; if anyone entered it after killing someone, satisfaction was given on his behalf to the relatives of the person killed; and if anyone who had committed an injury or punishable offence entered it his prosecutors were given satisfaction likewise. It was in this house that he was buried when he died and I have visited his tomb.[62] |

His strange history. It is related that a certain poor brother at Bukhārā, seeing there this Balaban, who was of short stature, unprepossessing and ugly, said to him *yā Turkak*, which is a phrase used to express contempt. Balaban replied 'At your service, *yā khūnd*',[63] which so pleased the faqīr that he said to him, pointing to some pomegranates which were being sold in the bazaar, 'Buy me some of those pomegranates.' Balaban replied 'Certainly', and taking out a few coppers which were all that he had, bought some of those pomegranates for him. As he took them, the faqīr said to him 'We give you the kingdom of India.' Balaban kissed his own hand saying 'I accept it with pleasure,' and the thing remained fixed in his mind. It happened that Sultan Shams al-Dīn Lalmish sent a merchant to buy mamlūks for him at Samarqand, Bukhārā, and Tirmidh, and he bought a hundred mamlūks, one of whom was Balaban. The Sultan, when the merchant brought the mamlūks before him, was satisfied with | all of them except Balaban, because of his insignificant

171

172

[62] The tomb of Balban (reigned 1266–87) still exists, near the mosque of Jamālī (Ahmad, 287, n. 3). Adjoining it is the tomb of his son, the 'Martyr Khān' (see p. 635 below).

[63] *Turkak*, i.e. 'miserable little Turk'. *Khūnd*, shortened form of Pers. *Khudāwand*, 'lord, sovereign' (cf. vol. II, p. 291, n. 68). So also a few lines below, *Khūnd 'ālam*, 'master of the world'.

appearance, as we have described, and said 'I do not accept this man.' Balaban said to him 'Oh master of the world, for whom have you bought these mamlūks?' The Sultan laughed at him and said 'I have bought them for myself,' then Balaban said to him 'Buy me for the sake of God High and Mighty.' The Sultan consented, accepted him and enrolled him among his mamlūks; nevertheless little account was taken of him and he was assigned to the [corps of] water-carriers.

Now the astrologers versed in the science of the stars used to tell the Sultan Shams al-Dīn that one of his mamlūks would seize the kingdom from the hand of his son and take possession of it. Although they continued to predict this to him, he paid no attention to their predictions because of his uprightness and probity of character, until they said the same thing to the principal khātūn, the mother of his sons, and she spoke to him about it. This made an impression on him; he sent for the astrologers and said 'Would you recognize the mamlūk who will seize my son's kingdom if you saw him?' 173 They replied | 'Certainly, we have in our possession a sign by which we would recognize him.' Thereupon the Sultan gave orders for a parade of his mamlūks and held a special session for that purpose, when they were passed in review before him rank by rank, while the astrologers watched them and said 'We have not seen him yet.' Then mid-day passed and the water-carriers said among themselves 'We are hungry, so let us pool some of our money and send one of our number to the market to buy food for us.' Having collected the money, they sent Balaban with it, seeing there was no one amongst them of less account than he, but he was unable to find what they wanted in the market and went off to another market and so was delayed. Meanwhile it came to the turn of the water-carriers for review, and since he had not yet come back they took his waterskin and his equipment, strapped the latter on the shoulder of a boy, and presented him as if he were Balaban. When his name was called the boy passed before them, and the parade ended without the astrologers having 174 seen the figure which they were expected to find.[64] | Balaban returned after the end of the review in accordance with God's

[64] The autograph reads *ṭulibū bihā*, carefully pointed.

will to execute His decree.[65] Later on his distinction became apparent and he was promoted to the command of the water-carriers, then entered into the ranks of the fighting troops, and in due course became one of the amīrs. Furthermore Sultan Nāṣir al-Dīn married his daughter before his succession to the kingship, and when he became king he made Balaban deputy for him for a period of twenty years.[66] Then Balaban killed him and occupied his kingdom for twenty years more, as has been related.

The Sultan Balaban had two sons, one of whom was 'The Martyr Khān', his heir; he was governor for his father in the territory of Sind, residing in the city of Multān, and was killed in warfare with the Tatars, leaving two sons Kay Qubādh and Kay Khusrū.[67] The Sultan Balaban's second son was named Nāṣir al-Dīn and was his father's governor in the territories of Laknawtī and Bengal.[68] When the 'Martyr Khān' was killed fighting for the faith the Sultan Balaban transferred | the succession to Kay Khusrū, diverting it from 175 his own son Nāṣir al-Dīn. Now Nāṣir al-Dīn also had a son, called Mu'izz al-Dīn, living at Dihlī with his grandfather, and it was he who succeeded to the kingdom after his grandfather's death in strange circumstances which we shall relate, although his father was still alive at the time, as we have said.

The Sultan Mu'izz al-Dīn son of Nāṣir al-Dīn son of the Sultan Ghiyāth al-Dīn Balaban. When the Sultan Ghiyāth al-Dīn died during the night, after assigning the succession to Kay Khusrū, the son of his son the Martyr, as we have related, and his [other] son Nāṣir al-Dīn being absent in the province of Laknawtī, the 'king' of the amīrs, who was the

[65] This is, of course, the whole point of the story. Balban was, in fact, purchased in Baghdad and was a favoured slave from the first, as a member of the Sultan's household corps.

[66] See n. 61 above.

[67] He was killed during a raid on Sind by a Mongol noble named Timar Khān in 1285. The following narrative is historically accurate, except that Kay Qubādh was not the son of the 'Martyr Khān' Muḥammad, but precisely the Mu'izz al-Dīn mentioned below as the son of Nāṣir al-Dīn Bughrā Khān. The names Qubādh (with *dh*) and Khusrū are clearly so written and vocalized in the autograph.

[68] Laknawti or Lak'hnawti, now the ruined site of Gaur, in the Rajshahi division of East Bengal (Pakistan) was the capital of the Muslim governors and princes of Bengal. I.B.'s spelling of Bengal is *Banjāla*.

deputy of the Sultan Ghiyāth al-Dīn,[69] was an enemy of Kay Khusrū and he plotted a stratagem against him which succeeded. He wrote an act of allegiance in which he forged the handwriting of the great amīrs witnessing to their oath of allegiance to Mu'izz al-Dīn, the grandson of the Sultan 176 Balaban, as their sovereign. He then presented himself | to Kay Khusrū in the character of a loyal counsellor and said to him 'The amīrs have taken the oath of allegiance to your cousin and I fear that they may have designs against you.' Kay Khusrū said to him 'What is to be done?' He replied 'Save yourself by flight to Sind, and to his question how he should leave the town, seeing the gates were closed, said 'The keys are in my hand, I myself shall open them for you.' Kay Khusrū thanked him for this and the 'king' kissed his hand and said to him 'Mount at once.' So the prince rode out with his personal attendants and his mamlūks, and he opened the gate for him, saw him through it, and closed it behind him.

He then asked permission to enter the presence of Mu'izz al-Dīn and took the oath of allegiance to him. Mu'izz al-Dīn said 'How can the kingdom be mine when my cousin has been nominated heir?' The 'king' told him of the trick which he had played on the latter and how he had put him out of the city, whereupon Mu'izz al-Dīn thanked him for his action, 177 went with him to | the palace and sent for the amīrs and principal officers, who swore allegiance to him during the [same] night. Next morning the rest of the population swore allegiance to him also and he was firmly established in the kingdom. Now his father was still alive in the land of Bengal and Laknawtī, and when the news reached him he said 'I am heir to the kingdom; how can my son succeed to the kingdom and enjoy full sovereignty in it while I am still alive?' He therefore set out with his armies on an expedition to the capital, Dihlī, and his son also set out with his armies with the object of driving him away from it. The armies came face to face at the town of Karā,[70] which is on the banks of the river Gang, the same to which the Indians go on pilgrimage.

[69] Malik al-'Umarā' Fakhr al-Dīn Kutwāl, who was high in the favour of Balban. As already mentioned (p. 601, n. 28) the term 'king' (*malik*) was applied to all the chief officers of state in India.

[70] In the province of Allahabad.

Nāṣir al-Dīn camped on the bank on which Karā lies and his son the Sultan Mu'izz al-Dīn encamped on the opposite bank, with the river between them. They had every intention of fighting, but God, exalted be He, desiring to spare the blood of the Muslims, cast into the heart of Nāṣir al-Dīn a tender affection for his son and he said 'If my son is King, | it is an honour to me and I am the one who has most reason to desire it so.' He cast also into the heart of the Sultan Mu'izz al-Dīn a sense of filial submission to his father. Each of them then embarked in a boat, unaccompanied by his troops, and they met in the middle of the river. The Sultan kissed his father's foot and made apologies to him, while his father said to him 'I give you my kingdom and confer the government upon you' and swore allegiance to him. He then wished to return to his province, but his son insisted that he should pay a visit to his territories, and went with him to Dihlī, where he entered the palace and his father bade him sit upon the throne and himself stood before him. This meeting between them on the river was called 'The conjunction of the two auspicious stars',[71] because of the sparing of blood which resulted from it and the offering of the kingdom to one another and the mutual abstinence from conflict, and the poets wrote many panegyrics on this subject. 178

Nāṣir al-Dīn then returned | to his provinces and died there some years later, leaving in them descendants, amongst whom was Ghiyāth al-Dīn Bahādūr, who was taken prisoner by the Sultan Tughluq, and released by his son Muḥammad after Tughluq's death.[72] After this Mu'izz al-Dīn enjoyed undisturbed rule for four years, which were like one long festival.[73] I have seen some of those who remembered those times describing their abundance, their cheap prices and the liberality and generosity of Mu'izz al-Dīn. It was he who built the minaret in the north court of the mosque of Dihlī, and there is nothing like it in the world.[74] One of the inhabitants 179

[71] Probably an allusion to the poetical description of these events by the poet Amīr Khusraw under the title (misquoted by I.B.) of *Qirān al-Sa'dain*.

[72] See pp. 653, 709–10 below.

[73] By this phrase (literally 'like [a series of] festivals') I.B. means something different from the dissipation of the sultan and courtiers described by the Indian historian Baranī (Ahmad, 296–8, 316).

[74] See p. 623, n. 23 above.

of India told me that Mu'izz al-Dīn was much addicted to women and wine and was struck down by a disease which the doctors were unable to cure. One side of him dried up,[75] and then his deputy Jalāl al-Dīn Fīrūz Shāh al-Khaljī revolted against him. |

180 *The Sultan Jalāl al-Dīn.*[76] When the Sultan Mu'izz al-Dīn was seized by the drying up of one of his sides, as we have related, his deputy Jalāl al-Dīn revolted against him, marched out of the city, and took up a position on a hill thereabouts beside a domed tomb called Qubbat al-Jaishānī. Mu'izz al-Dīn sent out the amīrs to engage him, but everyone of them whom he sent took the oath of allegiance to Jalāl al-Dīn and joined his party. The latter then entered the city and besieged the Sultan in the palace for three days. I have been told by an eye-witness that the Sultan Mu'izz al-Dīn suffered the pangs of hunger[77] during those days but found nothing to eat, and a certain sharīf who was one of his neighbours sent him sufficient to remove his affliction. The palace was taken by storm, he was killed, and Jalāl al-Dīn reigned after him.

Jalāl al-Dīn was clement and upright, and it was his clemency that led him to his death, as we shall relate. He 181 exercised undisputed | rule for some years and built the palace which is called by his name,[78] the same one which Sultan Muḥammad gave to his brother-in-law, the amīr Ghadā ibn Muhannā, when he married him to his sister, as we shall relate in due course. The Sultan Jalāl al-Dīn had a son named Rukn al-Dīn and a brother's son 'Alā al-Dīn, whom he married to his daughter and appointed to the governorship of the city of Karā and Mānikbūr and their districts.[79] These are among the most fertile regions in India; they produce

[75] Apparently a paralytic stroke.

[76] First of the line of Khaljī Sultans, reigned 1290–96. The Khalaj were a Turkish tribe long resident in the region of Ghazna, who furnished troops for the expeditions of its Sultans into India. The following narrative is a popular summary of the events which led to their rise to power.

[77] The autograph has 'was afflicted by bitter anxiety [*jaza'* for *jū'*] to the degree that he found nothing to eat'.

[78] Later (p. 685 below) identified by I.B. with the Red Palace (*kushk-i la'l*) in Old Delhi: however, the palace built by Balban, and Jalāl al-Dīn's building, called the Green Palace, was apparently an extension of the palace begun by Mu'izz al-Din at Kailukhrī (Kilok'hri) on the bank of the Jumna, near the later tomb of Humāyūn.

[79] See note 70 above.

large quantities of wheat, rice, and sugar, and have manufactures of fine fabrics which are exported to Dihlī, which is at a distance of eighteen days' journey from them. 'Alā al-Dīn's wife made life disagreeable for him and he so frequently complained of her to his uncle the sultan Jalāl al-Dīn that eventually their relations became strained because of her.

'Alā al-Dīn was a vigorous and brave man, accustomed to conquest and success, and had a fixed ambition to become king, only he had no | wealth except what he could gain for 182 himself by the sword in the way of booty from the infidels. It happened that he went on one occasion on a raid into the territory of Duwaiqīr (it is called also the land of Kataka, and we shall speak of it later),[80] which is the capital of the territories of Mālwa and of Marhata[81] and its sultan was the most powerful of the sultans of the infidels. In the course of this expedition a horse on which 'Alā al-Dīn was riding struck its hoof against a stone and, as he heard a ringing sound from the stone, he gave orders for the ground to be dug up and found under it a vast treasure, which he distributed amongst his followers. When he reached Duwaiqīr its sultan submitted to him, gave him possession of the city without fighting and sent him valuable presents. He then returned to the city of Karā, but sent none of the booty to his uncle. Certain persons[82] incited his uncle against him in consequence and he was sent instructions to come to Dihlī but refused to do so. Thereupon the Sultan Jalāl al-Dīn said 'I shall go to him myself and bring him, for | I look on him as my son'. So he set out with his 183 troops and marched with all speed until he encamped on the bank of the city of Karā, at the same place where the Sultan Mu'izz al-Dīn encamped when he went out to engage his

[80] The later Dawlat Ābād; see vol. I, p. 262, n. 61, and pp. 644, 732 below. *Kataka* (Sanskrit) means a royal camp, adopted in Anglo-Indian as *Cuttack*. A full account of this attack on the Yadava kingdom of Devagiri in 1296, and the submission of its king Ram Chandra is contained in *History of the Khaljis* by K. S. Lal (Allahabad, 1950) pp. 46–57.

[81] The Yadava kings had repeatedly invaded Mālwā (to the north) and occupied the southern Maratha country. I.B. is correct in calling Ram Chandra the most powerful of the Hindu kings at the time.

[82] *Al-nās* is too vague a term to define more precisely than by 'the men concerned in the event' (cf. on the following page), and presumably therefore implies his military officers and palace officials.

father Nāṣir al-Dīn. He embarked on the river in order to meet his nephew, and the latter also embarked on a second vessel, determined on murdering him, and said to his followers 'When I embrace him, kill him.' So when they met in the middle of the river his nephew embraced him and his nephew's attendants killed him as prearranged, and 'Alā al-Dīn took possession of his kingdom and his troops.

The Sultan 'Alā al-Dīn Muḥammad Shāh Khaljī. After he had killed his uncle he seized the sovereign power, and most of his uncle's troops went over to his side. Some of them returned to Dihlī and assembled round Rukn al-Dīn,[83] but 184 when the latter marched out to bar his way, they deserted | in a body to the Sultan 'Alā al-Dīn, and Rukn al-Dīn fled to Sind. 'Alā al-Dīn then entered the royal palace and enjoyed undisturbed rule for twenty years. He was one of the best of sultans, and the people of India are full of his praises. He used to investigate the conditions of his subjects in person and to enquire into the prices which they had to pay, and he used to send for the *muḥtasib*,[84] whom they call the *ra'īs*, every day for that purpose. It is related that he asked him one day why meat was so dear and he told him that it was due to the repeated exactions of toll upon the cattle at the road stages. He gave orders that that practice must cease, sent for the merchants, and gave them money, saying to them 'Buy with this cattle and sheep and sell them; the money received for their sale will go to the treasury and you shall have a commission on their sale.' They did so, and he made the same arrangements with regard to the woven fabrics which were imported from Dawlat Ābād. When the price of grain became very high he opened the stores[85] and sold their grain until the 185 price went down again. | It is said that on one occasion the price rose, and when he ordered that grain was to be sold at a price which he fixed the people refused to sell it at that price. He then gave orders that no one should sell any grain other

[83] The throne-title of Qādir Khān, the younger son of Jalāl al-Dīn. The elder son, Arhalī Khān, was governor of Sind. 'Alā' al-Dīn immediately sent an expedition to Multān, and the two princes were captured and killed.

[84] I.e. the Inspector of Markets; see vol. I, p. 219, n. 130. *Ra'īs* was at that time commonly applied in the East to the officer in charge of police: see Cl. Cahen, in *Arabica*, tom. VI (Paris, 1959), p. 54 and n. 2.

[85] Presumably the grain-stores in the wall, mentioned on p. 621 above.

than store grain, and sold it to the public for six months. Those who had monopolized the stocks became afraid that their grain would be damaged by weevils and petitioned for permission to sell; he then gave them permission, but on condition that they sold it at a price less than that at which they had formerly refused to sell it.

He used never to go on horseback to a Friday prayer nor to a Festival nor on any other occasion. The reason for this was that he had a nephew named Sulaimān Shāh whom he loved and held in high regard. One day when he rode out to hunt taking his nephew with him, the young man determined secretly to act with him as he had acted with his uncle Jalāl al-Dīn, namely to assassinate him. Consequently when the Sultan dismounted for lunch, he shot him | with an arrow and 186 knocked him to the ground, and one of his slaves covered him with a shield.[86] His nephew came up to give him the coup de grâce, but when the slaves told him that he was already dead he believed them, mounted, and entered the palace and seized the private apartments. Sultan 'Alā al-Dīn recovered from his faint, and mounted, his troops assembled around him, and his nephew fled, but was overtaken, brought before him and put to death.[87] After that he would never mount a horse.

He had the following sons: Khiḍr Khān, Shādī Khān, Abū Bakr Khān, Mubārak Khān, i.e. Quṭb al-Dīn who afterwards became king, and Shihāb al-Dīn. Quṭb al-Dīn was harshly treated by him and received little share of fortune or consideration. He gave all his brothers the ceremonial honours, that is to say the banners and drums,[88] and gave him nothing. One day 'Alā al-Dīn said to him 'I must give you the same as I have given your brothers,' to which he replied 'God it is who | will give to me,' a reply which appalled his father and 187 roused his fears. Sometime later the Sultan contracted the disease from which he died. Now his wife, the mother of his son Khiḍr Khān, whose name was Māh-i Ḥaqq (*māh* means 'moon' in their language),[89] had a brother called Sanjar, with

[86] One MS. reads 'with a mantle'.

[87] The fuller story of this episode from the Indian historian Baranī is related by K. S. Lal, *Khaljis*, pp. 184–6.

[88] See vol. I, p. 261.

[89] Her name was Māhrū (Māh-i Ḥaqq looks very like a misread note), with the title of *Malika-i Jahān*. Her brother Sanjar is known in Indian history

whom she made a pact to raise her son Khiḍr Khān to the throne. Malik Nā'ib, the chief of the Sultan's amīrs (he was called al-Alfī because the Sultan bought him for a thousand tankas, that is to say 2,500 in dīnārs of the Maghrib),[90] got wind of this and disclosed their agreement to the Sultan. The Sultan accordingly said to his courtiers 'When Sanjar comes before me I shall give him a robe, and when he puts it on seize him by the sleeves, pull him to the ground and cut his throat.' When Sanjar entered his chamber they acted as arranged and killed him. Khiḍr Khān was away at the time at a place called Sandabat, one day's journey from Dihlī,[91] 188 having gone out | to visit the tombs of some martyrs there, in consequence of a vow which he had taken to walk that distance on foot and to pray for his father's recovery. On hearing that his father had killed his uncle he was deeply grieved and rent the neck of his garment, which it is customary amongst the people of India to do when anyone who is dear to them dies. His father, learning what he had done, was displeased by it and when he appeared before him he angrily reprimanded him, ordered that his arms and legs should be shackled and gave him into the charge of Malik Nā'ib, whom we have mentioned above, with orders to conduct him to the castle of Gāliyūr (or, as it is sometimes called, Guyālyūr). This is an isolated and inaccessible castle, in the midst of the infidel Hindūs, ten nights' journey from Dihlī, and I have stayed in it myself for a time.[92] Having carried him to this castle Malik Nā'ib delivered him to the *kutwāl*, that is the commandant of the castle,[93] and to the 189 *mufradīn*,[94] who are the troops listed in the army register, | and said to them 'Do not say to yourselves that this is the Sultan's son and so treat him with respect; he is in reality

as Alp Khān. For the term *malik nā'ib* see n. 61 above; his name was Kāfūr and he commanded several successful expeditions for 'Alā' al-Dīn.

[90] The *tanka* (*tanga*) was a coin of 175 grains, struck in both gold and silver. The Moroccan dīnār weighed 4·722 grammes (about 73 grains).

[91] Sonpat (Sonepat), on the Jumna, 28 miles north of Delhi. In the following narrative I.B. has telescoped a series of events.

[92] See p. 645 below.

[93] See p. 606 above.

[94] The term seems to imply a body of troops with special functions, but who and what precisely is by no means cleared up by I.B.'s following explanation.

his worst enemy, so guard him as you would guard an enemy.' Later on, when the Sultan's illness increased in severity, he said to Malik Nā'ib 'Send to fetch my son Khiḍr Khān that I may appoint him to the succession.' Malik Nā'ib promised to do so but kept putting him off, and when the Sultan asked him about Khiḍr Khān would say 'He is just coming', until the Sultan died, God's mercy on him.

His son the Sultan Shihāb al-Dīn. When the Sultan 'Alā al-Dīn died, Malik Nā'ib set his youngest son Shihāb al-Dīn on the throne and the people swore allegiance to him. Malik Nā'ib kept him under control, and blinded [his brothers] Abū Bakr Khān and Shādī Khān and sent them to Gāliyūr. He gave orders also for the blinding | of their brother Khiḍr Khān who was imprisoned there, and they were all kept in prison, likewise Quṭb al-Dīn but he was not blinded. The Sultan 'Alā al-Dīn had amongst his personal attendants two mamlūks, one of whom was called Bashīr and the other Mubashshir. The principal khātūn, the wife of 'Alā al-Dīn (she was the daughter of Mu'izz al-Dīn), sent for them, reminded them of their master's generosity and said 'This eunuch, Nā'ib Malik, has treated my sons in the way you know, and now he wants to kill Quṭb al-Dīn.' They replied 'You shall see what we will do.' Now it was their custom to pass the night in the apartment of Nā'ib Malik and to wear their arms in his presence. That night they came in and presented themselves to him when he was in a cubicle made of wood and covered with blanketcloth, which they call *al-khurmaqāh*;[95] during the rainy season he used to sleep in this on the roof of the palace. It happened by chance that he took the sword from the hand | of one of them, brandished it and gave it back to him, whereupon the mamlūk struck him with it and the other joined in. They cut off his head, took it to the prison of Quṭb al-Dīn, threw it down at his feet, and brought him out. Then Quṭb al-Dīn went to the palace of his brother Shihāb al-Dīn and after remaining in attendance on him for a short time as though he were deputy for him, he decided to depose him and did so.[96]

190

191

[95] *Khurmaqah* or *kharmaqah* is the vocalization in the autograph. The Persian term is *khurramgāh* i.e. 'pleasure chamber'.

[96] All these events occurred in the early months of 1316.

The Sultan Quṭb al-Dīn son of the Sultan 'Alā al-Dīn. Quṭb al-Dīn deposed his brother Shihāb al-Dīn, cut off his finger, and sent him to Gāliyūr where he was kept in custody with his brothers, and Quṭb al-Dīn was firmly established as king. Some time later he left the capital Dihlī to go to Dawlat Ābād, which is forty days' journey from there. The road between these two cities is bordered by willows and other trees, so that the traveller on it might imagine himself to be 192 in a garden. For every mile of this road | there are three *dāwāt*, i.e. post-stations, whose organization we have already described,[97] and at each *dāwa* there is everything that the traveller requires, so that he seems to be making his way through one [continuous] bazaar forty days' journey in length. The road continues in the same manner all the way to the land of Tiling and al-Ma'bar, a six months' journey.[98] At each halting place there is a palace for the Sultan and a hospice for travellers, so that the poor man has no need to carry provisions with him on that road.

When the Sultan Quṭb al-Dīn set out on this expedition, some of the amīrs conspired to revolt against him and to raise to the throne the son of his imprisoned brother Khiḍr Khān. The boy was about ten years old at the time and living with the Sultan. When the Sultan heard of this he took his nephew, seized him by the feet and dashed out his brains on the stones. Then he sent one of the amīrs, called Malik Shāh, 193 to Gāliyūr, where | this boy's father and uncles were, with orders to kill them all. This is the story as the qāḍī Zain al-Dīn Mubārak, who was qāḍī of this castle, told it to me in his own words. 'Malik Shāh reached us one day in the forenoon. I was with Khiḍr Khān in his place of confinement, and when he heard of his arrival he became alarmed and changed colour. The amīr [Malik Shāh] came into his chamber, whereupon the prince said to him "What have you come for?" He replied "On the business of the Master of the World." The prince then asked him whether his life was safe and Malik

[97] See p. 594 above.

[98] Tiling stands for Telingāna, a Hindu kingdom between the Godavari and Krishna rivers, with its capital at Warangal. Ma'bar was the Arabic name for the Coromandel coast, south of Telingāna, visited later by I.B. (*Selections*, 261–5). Six months' journey is an excessive estimate, as the total distance is about twice that from Delhi to Dawlatābād.

Shāh gave him an assurance, and afterwards left him and summoned the *kutwāl,* that is the commandant of the castle, and the *mufradīn,* who are the troops on the register[99] and who numbered three hundred men. He then sent for me and for the attestors and produced the Sultan's order. Having read it they went to [the prison of] Shihāb al-Dīn, the deposed Sultan, and beheaded him. He maintained a firm demeanour and showed no fear. They then beheaded Abū Bakr Khān and Shādī Khān. When they came to execute Khiḍr Khān he was terror-stricken and aghast. His mother was with him | but 194 they shut the door on her and killed him. They then dragged them all into a pit without grave clothes or washing, but they were taken out some years later and buried in the sepulchres of their ancestors.' The mother of Khiḍr Khān lived for a long time and I saw her in Mecca in the year 28.

This castle of Gāliyūr is on the top of a steep hill and looks as though it were carved out of the rock, with no high ground facing it.[100] Inside it there are cisterns of water and about twenty wells, attached to the castle by protecting walls on which are placed mangonels and stone-throwers. One goes up to the castle by a broad track which can be ascended by elephants and horses. At the gate of the castle is the image of an elephant carved in stone and with the image of a mahout upon it; anyone seeing it from a distance would not take it to be anything but an elephant in actual reality. At the foot of the fortress there is a fine town, which is built entirely of white free-stone, | both mosques and private houses, and there 195 is no wood in them except for the doors. The same applies to the king's palace there, and to the kiosks and bungalows. The majority of the common people of the town are infidels and there are stationed there 600 horsemen of the Sultan's army, who are constantly engaged in *jihād* because it has infidels all round it.

When Quṭb al-Dīn had put his brothers to death and secured the sovereign power, so that there was none left to

[99] See n. 94 above.

[100] The old fortress of Gwalior is situated on a ridge rising to a height of 300 feet above the plain and $1\frac{3}{4}$ miles in length, 65 miles south of Agra. It was used as a state prison by the Muslim kings. At the Elephant entrance stood the stone image of an elephant with its mahout on it, called the Hāthiya Paur.

compete with him nor to revolt against him, God the Exalted raised up against him his most favoured officer, the chief of his amīrs and the most highly esteemed amongst them in his eyes, Nāṣir al-Dīn Khusrū Khān.[101] This man attacked him by surprise, killed him and took possession of his kingdom. But his enjoyment of the kingship lasted no long time, for God raised up against him also one who killed him after deposing him. This was the Sultan Tughluq, as shall be expounded in detail hereafter, if God will and as we shall record. |

196 *The Sultan Khusrū Khān Nāṣir al-Dīn.* Khusrū Khān was one of the chief of the amīrs of Quṭb al-Dīn and was brave and good-looking. He had conquered the land of Jandīrī and the land of al-Ma'bar,[102] which are among the most fertile lands of India and lie at a distance of six months' journey from Dihlī. Quṭb al-Dīn used to show great affection for him and to single him out for his favours, and it was this that brought about his own death at his hands. Quṭb al-Dīn had a preceptor named Qāḍī Khān Ṣadr al-Jahān, who was chief of his amīrs and *kalīd-dār*,[103] that is to say keeper of the keys of the castle. It was his custom to spend every night on guard at the Sultan's door along with the troops of the guard, numbering a thousand men who mount the night-watch in turns every fourth night. They form two ranks between the doors of the palace, each man with his weapon in front of him, so

197 that no one may enter | without passing between the two files of them, and when night is ended the troops of the day-watch relieve them. The troops of the guard have their own amīrs and clerks who make rounds to inspect them and note in their registers those of them who are absent or present.

The Sultan's preceptor Qāḍī Khān detested the conduct of

[101] The autograph again vocalizes the name here and below as Khusrū. The Indian historians generally write Khusraw. He was not a Khaljī, but a Hindu convert, as mentioned below; Quṭb al-Dīn gave him the rank of vizier and the title of Khusrū Khān. His origin and caste are matters of controversy: see Ishwari Prasad, *Hist. of the Qaraunah Turks*, vol. I (Allahabad, 1936), 8–10 and Lal, *Khaljis*, 348–51.

[102] Chanderi, a Rajput fortress in the province of Mālwā, in the district of Narwar, was already under Muslim government; I.B. has apparently mentioned it by mistake for Warangal, which was conquered by Khusrū Khān in the course of an expedition to Ma'bar (see n. 98 above) on behalf of Quṭb al-Dīn: see Lal, 338–40.

[103] Persian *kalīd*, 'key', from the Greek *kleis*.

Khusrū Khān and was offended by the habit he observed in him of showing preference and special favour to the infidel Indians, for he was of Indian origin. He lost no opportunity of speaking of this to the Sultan, but the Sultan would not listen to him and would say to him 'Let him do as he pleases,' because of God's decree that he should be killed at his hands. On a certain day Khusrū Khān said to the Sultan 'There is a party of Indians who wish to embrace Islām.' Now it is their custom in that country that when a Hindu wishes to become a Muslim, he is introduced before the Sultan, who clothes him with a fine robe and gives him a necklace and bracelets of gold in proportion to his rank. So the Sultan told him to bring them to him and he replied 'They shrink from | coming 198 to you by day because of their relatives and their fellow-Hindus.' The Sultan said to him 'Bring them to me by night,' so Khusrū Khān collected a body of Indian braves and chiefs, among whom was his own brother Khān-i-Khānān.[104] This was in the hot season, when the Sultan used to sleep on the roof of the palace and had no one with him except a few eunuchs.[105]

When the Indians had passed through the four doors, all bristling with weapons, and reached the fifth door, at which Qāḍī Khān was on guard, he disliked the look of them and apprehended some evil. So he stopped them from entering and said 'I must hear from Khūnd 'Ālam with my own ears his permission for their entry, and only then may they go in.' But when he stopped them from entering they assaulted and killed him. All this made a clamour at the door and the Sultan called out | 'What is there?' Khusrū Khān answered 'These 199 are the Indians who have come to embrace Islām; Qāḍī Khān has stopped them from entering.' As the uproar increased the Sultan became alarmed and rose up with the intention of going into the palace; but the door leading to it was barred and the eunuchs were beside it. As he knocked on the door Khusrū Khān seized him in his arms from behind, but the Sultan was more powerful than he and bore him to the

[104] These were a corps of troops from Gujarat, probably belonging to his own Barvar clan or caste. Khān-i Khānān is a title frequently found in Indian history, literally 'khān of khāns'. There are, of course, varying reports on this assassination in the Indian sources. The date was 720/1320.

[105] or 'pages': cf. vol. II, p. 486 n. 269.

ground. The Indians came in and Khusrū Khān said to them 'Here he is on top of me; kill him,' so they killed him, cut off his head and threw it down from the roof of the palace into the courtyard.

Khusrū Khān sent on the spot for the amīrs and maliks who were as yet unaware of what had happened. Each detachment as they entered found him seated on the throne and took the oath of allegiance to him, and in the morning he made public his succession and despatched the *marāsim*, that is to say the edicts, to all the provinces. He sent also to each amīr a robe of honour and they all obeyed and submitted to 200 him except Tughluq Shāh, | the father of Muḥammad Shāh, who was at that time an amīr in Dibāl-Būr[106] in the province of Sind. On receiving the robe of honour from Khusrū Khān he threw it on the ground and sat on it. The Sultan sent against him his brother Khān-i-Khānān but Tughluq defeated him and, to cut a long story short, finally put the Sultan to death as we shall describe in the history of Tughluq.

When Khusrū Khān became king he showed special favour to the Indians and openly committed reprobate actions, including the prohibition of slaughtering oxen, according to the principle of the infidel Hindus.[107] For they do not permit their slaughter and punish anyone who kills an ox by having him sewn up in its skin and burned. They venerate oxen and drink their urine to obtain blessing and for a cure when they fall sick, and they daub their houses and walls with their dung. This was one of the things which rendered Khusrū 201 Khān | odious to the Muslims and caused them to transfer their allegiance from him to Tughluq, so that the period of his government was not long and the days of his reign were cut short, as we shall proceed to describe.

The Sultan Ghiyāth al-Dīn Tughluq Shāh. His name is spelt thus, with two *u*'s. I was told by the pious and learned imām, the strict and devout shaikh Rukn al-Dīn,[108] son of the pious

[106] Dīpālpur, 80 miles S.S.W. of Lahore.

[107] The Muslim tradition was naturally hostile to Khusrū Khān, and accused him and his Barvars of various heathen and anti-Muslim practices. I.B.'s statement is probably the least violent accusation; whether justified or not, it gives evidence of the early conflict between Muslims and Hindus in the matter of killing cows.

[108] See p. 597 above.

shaikh Shams al-Dīn Abū 'Abdallāh, son of the saint and imām, the learned and devout Bahā al-Dīn Zakarīyā al-Qurashī of Multān, in his hospice at that town, that the sultan Tughluq was one of the Turks known by the name of Qarawna, who inhabit the highlands between Sind and the land of the Turks.[109] He was in poor circumstances and came to Sind in the service of a certain merchant, for whom he was acting as *gulwānī*, | that is to say, in charge of his horses.[110] 202 This was in the time of Sultan 'Alā al-Dīn, and the amīr of Sind was then his brother Ūlū Khān.[111] Tughluq entered his service and became attached to him, and was enrolled by him amongst his paid troops in the *biyāda*,[112] i.e. the infantry. Later on his bravery was remarked and he was enrolled in the cavalry, then became one of the lesser amīrs and Ūlū Khān made him master of his horse. After that he became one of the great amīrs and was called by the title of al-Malik al-Ghāzī. I have seen inscribed on the *maqṣūra* of the congregational mosque at Multān, which was built at his orders, 'I fought with the Tatars twenty-nine times and drove them in defeat, whence I gained the title of al-Malik al-Ghāzī.'

When Quṭb al-Dīn succeeded, he made him governor of the city and district of Dibāl-Būr, and appointed his son, who is the present Sultan of India, as master of his horse. The latter was named Jawna and on becoming king | took the name 203 of Muḥammad Shāh. Subsequently, when Quṭb al-Dīn was killed and Khusrū Khān succeeded, he maintained him as master of the horse. When Tughluq resolved on revolt he had with him three hundred of his own troops[113] upon whom he

[109] From all accounts the Qarawnas (Qaraunas) were a body of unsubdued Turkish nomads, mainly in the fringes of Afghanistan. Whether the name was a tribal one or signified a population of mixed origins is still doubtful; in India it is said to have been applied to the offspring of Tatar or Turkish fathers and Indian mothers: see Ishwari Prasad and Pelliot's note. It may be remarked that I.B.'s statement does not in itself convey any tone of depreciation.

[110] The corresponding Persian word is *galah-bān*, apparently assimilated to Hindi *guālā* (*guālīya*), 'cowherd'.

[111] Almās Beg, entitled Ulugh Khān after his brother's accession, governor of Sind 1296–1301 and of Ranthambhor 1301–2. This report is not to be taken at face value.

[112] Persian *pīyāda*, 'foot soldier'.

[113] Literally 'associates', translated fourteen lines below as 'men'.

could rely in battle, and he wrote to Kishlū Khān, who was at that time in Multān,[114] three days' journey from Dibāl-Būr, asking him to give him support, reminding him of the favour shown to him by Quṭb al-Dīn, and urging him to avenge his murder. Kishlū Khān's son was in Dihlī, so he wrote to Tughluq saying 'Were my son with me I should aid you in your design.' Tughluq then wrote to his son Muḥammad Shāh to tell him of his resolve, and bidding him escape to join him and bring with him the son of Kishlū Khān. His son planned a ruse against Khusrū Khān and it succeeded just as he had hoped. He said to him that the horses had 204 grown too fat and heavy and needed | *yarāq*, that is to say thinning exercise.[115] The Sultan permitted him to take them out on exercise, so he used to ride out every day with his men and keep them going for an hour or two hours or three. He went on to four hours, and finally one day absented himself until the sun had passed the meridian, which is the time when they eat. The Sultan then gave orders to ride in pursuit of him, but no information about him was to be had, and he rejoined his father, having brought with him the son of Kishlū Khān.

Thereupon Tughluq Khān declared open rebellion and assembled the troops, and Kishlū Khān joined him with his followers. The Sultan sent his brother Khān-i-Khānān to engage them but they inflicted on him a crushing defeat; his army passed to their side and Khān-i-Khānān went back to his brother, his officers having been killed and his treasuries and his possessions captured. Tughluq Khān now marched on the capital, Dihlī, and Khusrū Khān came out against him with his troops and encamped outside Dihlī at a place 205 called | Āṣyā Ābād, which means 'windmill'.[116] He ordered the treasuries to be opened and distributed the money in bagfuls without weighing or counting. When he and Tughluq confronted one another the Indians fought with the greatest

[114] Kishlū Khān only later became governor of Sind. At this time he was governor of Uch, and called by his name of Bahrām Aibā. Otherwise, I.B.'s narrative seems to be generally correct.

[115] Turkish *yaraq*.

[116] Persian *āsyā-bād*. This was in the plain of Lahrāwat, two or three miles to the north or north-west of Sīrī (see p. 619, n. 2): Mahdi Husain, *Muḥammad bin Tughluq*, 39.

valour and Tughluq's horsemen were routed, his encampment was plundered and he himself was isolated with his three hundred oldest followers. He said to them 'Where can we escape to? Wherever we are caught we shall be killed.' Khusrū Khān's troopers had [in the meantime] become engaged in looting and had dispersed, so that none but a few remained with him. Tughluq and his followers then made towards the place where he was, for the Sultan is recognized in that country by the parasol[117] which is held over his head. This is what is called in Egypt 'the dome and bird' and is hoisted [over the Sultan] during the festivals [only], whereas in India and China it is never removed from the Sultan whether he is travelling or in residence.

When Tughluq and his followers made for the Sultan there was a fierce fight between them and the Indians, ending in the rout | of the Sultan's troops, and not a man remained by him. He took to flight, then dismounted, put off his outer garments and arms, keeping only a single shirt on, and let his hair loose upon his shoulders in the manner of the Indian faqīrs, and went into a grove of trees in that neighbourhood. The troops assembled around Tughluq and he marched on the city. The *kutwāl*[118] brought him the keys; he entered the palace and after occupying a wing of it said to Kishlū Khān 'You shall be Sultan.' Kishlū Khān replied 'No, but you shall be Sultan,' and after some argument said to him 'Well, if you refuse to become Sultan then your son can take over.' Faced with this unwelcome proposal, he then accepted the Sultanate, took his seat upon the throne, and received the allegiance of the officers of state and the commonalty. 206

Three days later Khusrū Khān, who was still hiding in the grove, came out under pressure of hunger, made a circuit of it, and finding the keeper asked him for some food. Since the keeper had no food with him | Khusrū Khān gave him his ring, saying 'Go, pledge it for food.' When the man took the ring to the bazaar the merchants became suspicious of him and took him before the *shiḥna*,[119] who was the chief of police. The latter brought him before the Sultan Tughluq, whom he 207

[117] The *jitr* (Persian *chatr*), see vol. II, p. 377, n. 54. (I.B. rather strangely renders it by *shaṭr* here.)

[118] See p. 606, n. 43.

[119] See p. 632, n. 59.

informed about the person who had given him the ring. The Sultan sent his son Muḥammad to fetch him, and he seized him and brought him mounted on a *tatū*,[120] that is a common horse. Khusrū Khān on appearing before him said to him 'I am hungry, give me something to eat.' The Sultan ordered him to be served with sherbet, then with food, then with *fuqqā'*, and finally with betel. When he finished eating he rose to his feet and said 'O Tughluq, act towards me according to the code of kings, and do not dishonour me.' Tughluq, granting him his request, gave his orders and he was beheaded in the very place in which he himself had killed Quṭb al-Dīn, and his head and body were thrown down from the roof as he
208 had done with the head of Quṭb | al-Dīn.[121] Thereafter he gave orders to wash him and wrap him in grave-clothes, and he was buried in the tomb prepared for him. Tughluq enjoyed undisturbed rule for four years, and he was just and upright [in his government].

Account of his son's attempt to rebel against him, which did not succeed. When Tughluq was firmly established in the capital, he sent his son Muḥammad to conquer the land of Tiling, which is at a distance of three months' journey from the city of Dihlī.[122] With him he sent a great army including the principal amīrs, such as al-malik Tamūr, al-malik Tikīn, malik Kāfūr the *muhrdār* [i.e. seal-keeper], malik Bairām and others. When he reached the land of Tiling he thought of
209 revolting. He had a boon companion, a certain | jurist and poet, by the name of 'Obaid, and he ordered this man to give out to the troops that the Sultan Tughluq had died, imagining that they would at once take the oath of allegiance to him when they heard of this. But when this report was announced to the troops the amīrs turned against him;[123] each one of them beat his own drum and revolted, so that he was left without any troops at all. They proposed to kill him, but malik Tamūr held them back and protected him from them

[120] Hindi *taṭṭū*, a native-bred pony, greatly inferior to an Arab horse (*Hobson-Jobson*, pp. 902–3).

[121] This action is explained by the fact that Tughluq's rebellion was sparked by the motive of revenge for the massacre of the house of 'Alā' al-Dīn. The date was 720/1320.

[122] I.e. Telingāna: see p. 644, n. 98 above.

[123] Literally 'disavowed him'.

and he was able to escape to his father with ten horsemen whom he called *Yārān muwāfiq*, meaning 'the constant friends'.[124] His father gave him money and troops and on his orders he returned to Tiling; but his father learned what his design had been and put the jurist 'Obaid to death. He gave orders also for the execution of malik Kāfūr the *muhrdār*; a stake with a sharpened end was fixed in the ground for him and was driven into his neck till its point came out of his side as he was impaled on it head downwards, and he was left in | this state. The rest of the amīrs fled to the Sultan Shams 210 al-Dīn, son of the Sultan Nāṣir al-Dīn, son of the Sultan Ghiyāth al-Dīn Balaban, and settled at his court.[125]

Tughluq's expedition to the land of Laknawtī, and the events that followed down to the time of his death. The fugitive amīrs remained in the service of the Sultan Shams al-Dīn. Some time later Shams al-Dīn died, after appointing as his successor his son Shihāb al-Dīn, who sat in his father's seat; but he was overpowered by his youngest brother Ghiyāth al-Dīn Bahādūr Būra (which means in the Indian language 'the black'),[126] who seized the kingdom and killed his brother Quṭlū Khān and his other brothers. From among them, however, Shihāb al-Dīn and Nāṣir al-Dīn fled to Tughluq, who set out with them in person on an expedition against their brother, leaving his son Muḥammad as deputy for him in his kingdom. He made a rapid march to the land of Laknawtī, conquered it, | captured its Sultan Ghiyāth al-Dīn Bahādūr and brought 211 him back to his capital as a prisoner.

There was in the city of Dihlī the saint Niẓām al-Dīn al-Badhāwunī,[127] whom Muḥammad Shāh, the Sultan's son,

[124] From Pers. *yār*, 'friend', and Ar. *muwāfiq*, 'one who agrees with or approves'. The Indian historians are divided on whether Jawna (entitled at this time Ulugh Khān) was the victim or the instigator of the mutiny. But it is worth nothing that (contrary to I.B.'s statement in the preceding section) the revolt against Khusrū Khān had been initiated by Jawna himself, not by his father: see Mahdi Husain, *Muḥammad bin Tughluq*, 32–3.

[125] I.e. in Lakhnawti (Bengal) (see n. 68 above). Fīrūz Shāh, with the throne-title of Shams al-Dīn, was the independent ruler of Bengal from 1302 to 1322, but his son Ghiyāth al-Dīn, the governor of Sonargaon, was already claiming the government of Bengal before his death.

[126] Hindi *bhūrā*.

[127] One of the most notable of the Indian Muslim saints, commonly known as Niẓām al-Dīn Awliyā' (1238–1324), of Bukharan origin, a disciple

used continually to visit, showing great respect to his disciples and always asking for his prayers. Now the shaikh was seized [from time to time] by mystical trances which took control of him and the Sultan's son said to his disciples 'When the shaikh is in this state of ecstasy which takes possession of him, let me know.' They informed him, accordingly, when the shaikh was seized by an ecstasy, and he came into his presence. When the shaikh saw him he said 'We give him the kingdom,' and afterwards died during the Sultan's absence, and his son Muḥammad carried his bier upon his shoulder. All this was told to his father, who showed his disapproval and addressed threatening messages to him, [the more so that] several actions of his had already roused the Sultan's suspicions and he strongly resented his son's excessive purchases of mamlūk troops, his extravagance in his gifts, and his efforts to captivate the hearts of the people. 212 So he became more and more enraged against him, | and when he heard that the astrologers had declared that he would never again enter the city of Dihlī after that expedition[128] he used threatening language towards them.

When he approached the capital on returning from this expedition he ordered his son to build him a palace, which they call a *kushk*,[129] by a river-bed in those parts which is called Afghān-būr.[130] Muḥammad Shāh built it in three days, constructing it mostly of wood, raised upon wooden pillars to some height above the ground. He had it skilfully built on a plan which was supervised by al-Malik Zāda, known later by

of Farīd al-Dīn al-Badhāwunī (see pp. 613–14 above) and promoter of the Chishtī order in Dihlī. He was exceedingly popular and influential but not on good terms with Tughluq. His tomb in Delhi is still a popular place of visitation.

128 This prediction is usually ascribed to Shaikh Niẓām al-Dīn who, on being told that the Sultan had ordered him to leave Delhi before his own return, is reported to have said 'Dihlī is yet far off' (*Dihlī hanōz dūr ast*). As mentioned above, however the saint died during the Sultan's absence in Bengal, and more than a year before his return.

129 Persian, shortened form of *kūshak*. It is the origin of the word 'kiosk'.

130 Afghānpūr was a village to the south-east of Tughluqābād, the new city built by Tughluq, about four miles to the east of the old city, (see vol. II, p. 274, n. 12). Whether I.B. was mistaken or not in associating the name with a river bed (*wādī*) cannot now be determined.

the title of Khwāja Jahān, his name being Aḥmad ibn Aiyās, the chief of the wazīrs of Sultan Muḥammad,[131] who was at that time the controller of buildings. The scheme which they excogitated for this kiosk was that whenever the elephants should tread on one particular side of it, the whole building would fall in ruins. The Sultan alighted at the kiosk and after he had given a meal to his troops[132] | and they had dispersed, 213 his son asked his permission to parade the elephants before him in their ceremonial trappings, and he granted it.

The Shaikh Rukn al-Dīn told me that on that day he was with the Sultan, and the Sultan's favourite son Maḥmūd was in their company. Muḥammad, the Sultan's son, came and said to the Shaikh '*Yā khūnd* ["master"], it is the hour of the '*aṣr* prayer; go down and pray.' The shaikh continued the story to me as follows: 'So I went down, and the elephants were led up from one direction, as they had planned. When they walked on that side the pavilion fell in upon the Sultan and his son Maḥmūd. On hearing the noise (continued the Shaikh) I went back without finishing the prayer and found the pavilion in ruins. His son gave orders to fetch axes and mattocks in order to dig for him, but he made a sign to delay and in consequence they were not brought until after sunset. They then cleared away the ruins and found the Sultan with his back bent over his son to protect him from death; some said | that he was brought out dead, but others assert that he 214 was brought out alive and despatched. He was carried by night to the mausoleum which he had built for himself outside the town called Tughluq Ābād after him, and he was buried there.'[133]

We have already related the reason for his building of this town, which contained the treasuries and palaces of Tughluq.

[131] Aḥmad Aiyāz (or Aḥmad ibn Aiyāz) was the name given to Har Deo, a kinsman (hence the name *malik-zāda*, king's son) of the Hindu rajah of Deogīr, on his conversion to Islam at the hand of Niẓām al-Dīn Awliyā', (Mahdi Husain, p. 54, n. 3).

[132] Presumably the customary repast which the Turkish rulers furnished to their regiments.

[133] His tomb still stands, to the south of the city wall. It will be noted that I.B. cites a particularly well-qualified eye-witness of this incident. Although it cannot be accepted with absolute assurance, the statement that Muḥammad's guilt 'has been authentically disproved' (Mahdi Husain, p. 55, n. 1) is a considerable overestimate. See Plate 5.

In it was the great palace whose tiles[134] he had gilded, so that when the sun rose they shone with a brilliant light and a blinding glow, that made it impossible to keep one's eyes fixed on it. He deposited in this town vast stores of wealth and it is told that he constructed a tank and poured into it molten gold so that it became a single block. All these treasures were spent by his son Muḥammad Shāh when he became Sultan. It was to the mechanical skill, which we have described, of the wazīr Khwāja Jahān in constructing the pavilion which fell down upon Tughluq that he owed his 215 privileged position with his son | Muḥammad Shāh and the special favour shown to him by the latter, for there was no one, whether of the wazīrs or of any others, who came near to enjoying the same position with the Sultan nor stood to him on the same level.

[134] The precise usage of *qirmīd* is uncertain. Although usually meaning 'baked brick', it was also applied to tiles (v. Dozy, s.v.), and it seems more likely in this instance that it was the roof that was gilded.

CHAPTER XII

Sultan Muḥammad Ibn Tughluq

The Sultan Abu'l-Mujāhid Muḥammad Shāh, son of the Sultan Ghiyāth al-Dīn Tughluq Shāh, King of al-Hind and al-Sind, at whose court we presented ourselves. When the Sultan Tughluq died his son Muḥammad took possession of the kingdom without competition or opposition. We have said already that his name was Jawna, but when he became king he called himself Muḥammad and took the *kunya*-name of Abu-l-Mujāhid.[1] All that I have related concerning the Sultans of India, or most of it, is derived from what I was told and picked up from the shaikh Kamāl al-Dīn Ibn al-Burhān of Ghazna, the Grand Qāḍī.[2] | On the other hand, my 216 statements about this king are based for the most part on what I myself witnessed in the days when I was in his land.

Description of him. This king is of all men the most addicted to the making of gifts and the shedding of blood. His gate is never without some poor man enriched or some living man executed, and there are current amongst the people [many] stories of his generosity and courage and of his cruelty and violence towards criminals. For all that, he is of all men the most humble and the readiest to show equity and to acknowledge the right. The ceremonies of religion are strictly complied with at his court, and he is severe in the matter of attendance at prayer and in punishing those who neglect it.

[1] The use of 'royal patronymics' compounded with *Abū* was taken over by the Sultans in India from the Ghaznevids and Ghūrids of Afghanistan. Thus Iltutmish, Balban and Tughluq all adopted the title Abu'l-Muẓaffar (Thomas, 52, 134, 189 ff.); the coins of Muḥammad however do *not* bear the title of Abu'l-Mujāhid, but *al-Mujāhid fī sabīl 'llāh* 'the warrior in the cause of God', along with several other Qur'ānic or religious mottoes (Thomas, 207 ff.). This use of *Abū* corresponds to the use of *Malik* in the Egyptian and Syrian Sultanates (cf. vol. II, p. 369, n. 34).

[2] See pp. 617, 628 above, As Kamāl al-Dīn was himself a native of Ghazna, his statement that Tughluq and his son were of Qarauna origin is trustworthy.

He is one of those kings whose felicity is unimpaired and whose success in his affairs surpasses all ordinary experience, but his dominant quality is generosity. We shall mention some examples of this that are marvellous beyond anything 217 heard tell of anyone | before him, and I call God and His Angels and His Prophets to witness that all that I shall relate of his extraordinary generosity is absolute truth, and God is a sufficient witness. I know that some of the stories I shall tell on this subject will be unacceptable to the minds of many persons, and that they will regard them as quite impossible in the normal order of things; but in a matter which I have seen with my own eyes and of which I know the accuracy and have myself had a large share, I cannot do otherwise than speak the truth. In addition, most of these facts are established by numerous independent authorities[3] in the lands of the East.

Description of his Gates and Audience Hall and of the ceremonial observed therein. The Sultan's palace at Dihlī is called *Dār Sarā* and contains many gates.[4] At the first gate there are posted a number of men in charge of it, and beside it sit buglers, trumpeters and pipe-players.[5] When any amīr 218 or person of note arrives, they sound their instruments | and say during this fanfare 'So-and-so has come, so-and-so has come.' The same takes place also at the second and third gates. Outside the first gate are platforms on which sit the *jallādūn*,[6] who are the executioners, for the custom among them is that when the Sultan orders a man to be executed, the sentence is carried out at the gate of the public audience hall,[7] and the body lies there three nights. Between the first

[3] The language of this passage is loaded with technical terms of the science of transmission of the Prophetic Tradition. The last term, *mutawātir,* in particular is used of a tradition guaranteed by its transmission through several separate and independent chains of trustworthy narrators.

[4] As I.B. has already mentioned (p. 619 above), Sultan Muḥammad built a fourth city, Jahānpanāh, between old Delhi and Sīrī. His 'palace' (*Dār Sarā* in Arabo-Persian) in this city has been excavated (see Mahdi Husain, *Muḥammad bin Tughluq,* 241–2), with the inner audience hall of 'a thousand pillars' (*Hazār Sutūn,* see p. 660 below).

[5] *Ṣurnāyāt*: see vol. II, p. 343, n. 242. It is probable that the term is used here to mean wind instruments generally.

[6] Arabic, etymologically meaning 'floggers'.

[7] *Mashwar*: see vol. II, p. 291, n. 66, here obviously meaning the palace complex as a whole.

and second gates there is a large vestibule with platforms built along both sides, on which sit those troops whose turn of duty it is to guard the gates. At the second gate also there are seated the porters who are in charge of it. Between the second and third gates there is a large platform on which the principal *naqīb*[8] sits; in front of him there is a gold mace, which he holds in his hand, and on his head he wears a tall jewelled cap of gold, surmounted by peacock feathers.[9] The other *naqībs* stand before him, each wearing a low gilded cap[10] on his head and a girdle round his waist and holding in his hand | a whip with a gold or silver handle. This second gate 219 leads to a large and commodious audience hall[11] in which the people sit.

At the third gate there are platforms occupied by the scribes of the door. One of their customs is that none may pass through this gate except those whom the Sultan has expressly designated to enter, and for each person he prescribes a number of his companions and men who may enter along with him. Whenever any person comes to this gate the scribes write down 'So-and-so came at the first hour' or the second or later hours, until the close of the day, and the Sultan studies this report after the last evening prayer. They also take note of everything of any kind that happens at the gate, and certain of the sons of the *maliks*[12] are appointed to transmit what they write to the Sultan. Another of their customs is that anyone[13] who absents himself | from the 220 Sultan's palace for three days or more, with or without

[8] The term has various meanings; in this context it is applied to the marshals and ushers, functionaries whose duty it was to see that the proper order was observed.

[9] The use of peacock feathers was borrowed from Hindu usage, as noted by Mahdi Husain (p. 57, n. 3). N.B. The autograph is replaced at this point by a later copyist in MS. 2291.

[10] The Chief Naqīb wore a *kulāh* (cf. vol. II, p. 301) the others a *shāshiya*, a kind of smoking-cap (French *calotte*) that serves as a base for the turban cloth.

[11] Here again I.B. uses the term *mashwar* for what appears to be the antechamber to the inner audience hall.

[12] 'Sons of kings' normally means members of the royal family (see vol. II, p. 484), but evidently not in this context. Since 'king' was in Indian usage the term applied to principal officers, it probably refers here to their sons, who were apparently employed as palace pages.

[13] I.e. any holder of an official position or rank.

excuse, may not enter this door thereafter except by the Sultan's permission. If he has an excuse of illness or otherwise he presents before him a gift such as is suitable [for one of his rank or office] to offer to the Sultan. So also do those who present themselves at the court on return from their[14] journeys; the doctor of the law presents a copy of the Qur'ān or a book or the like, the faqīr[15] presents a prayer-carpet, rosary, toothpick, etc., and the amīrs and such present horses, camels and weapons. This third door opens into the immense and vast hall called *Hazār Ustūn*, which means [in Persian] 'A thousand pillars'.[16] The pillars are of painted[17] wood and support a wooden roof, most exquisitely carved. The people sit under this, and it is in this hall that the Sultan sits for public audience. |

221 *The order of his public audience.* As a rule his audiences are held after the afternoon prayer, although he often holds them early in the day. He sits on a raised seat[18] standing on a dais carpeted in white, with a large cushion behind him and two others as arm-rests on his right and left. [His left foot is tucked under him] in the same way that one sits when reciting the creed during prayers; this is the way in which all the people of India sit. When he takes his seat, the vizier stands in front of him, the secretaries behind the vizier, then the chamberlains behind them. The chief of the chamberlains is Fīrūz Malik, the son of the Sultan's uncle and his deputy,[19] and he is that one of the chamberlains who stands closest to the Sultan. Next to him comes the private chamberlain, then the deputy private chamberlain, then the steward of the palace and his deputy, then [an officer called] 'the honour of the chamberlains', [another officer called] 'the master of the

[14] The nature of the presents listed in this sentence seems to indicate that this is the meaning of the Arabic phrase.

[15] I.e. ṣūfī shaikh.

[16] *Hazār*, literally 'thousand', implies a large number. See Plate 4.

[17] *Mad'hūn* here certainly means 'painted': see glossary to Idrīsī. s.v. *dahana. Naqasha,* on the other hand, is always used by I.B. to mean carving in some form or other.

[18] I.B. does not use here the recognized term for 'throne' (*sarīr*, as in the following paragraph) but *martaba,* which has the senses of both 'dais' and 'cushion', and suggests therefore some kind of cushioned seat; cf. nn. 32 and 48 below.

[19] Son of Rajab, brother and generalissimo of Sultan Tughluq, subsequently succeeded Sultan Muḥammad and reigned 1357–88 as Fīrūz Shāh.

chamberlains', and a group [of officials] | under their orders; 222 and next, following the chamberlains, the naqībs, of whom there are about a hundred.

As the Sultan sits down the chamberlains and naqībs say in their loudest voice *Bismillāh*. Then the 'great king' Qabūla[20] takes his place behind the Sultan, standing with a fly-whisk in his hand to drive off the flies. A hundred armour-bearers[21] stand on the right of the Sultan and a like number on the left, carrying shields, swords, and bows. To right and left all the way down the hall stand the Grand Qāḍī, next to him the chief preacher, then the rest of the qāḍīs, then the chief jurists, then the chiefs of the Sharīfs [descendants of the Prophet], then the shaikhs,[22] then the Sultan's brothers and relations by marriage, then the principal amīrs, then the chiefs of those called *'azīz* (that is to say the foreigners),[23] then the qā'ids.[24]

Then they bring in sixty horses saddled and bridled with the royal harness, some of them with the trappings | of the 223 Caliphate, namely those with bridles and girths of black silk gilded, and some with the same in white silk gilded, which are reserved for the Sultan's exclusive use. Half of these horses are ranged on the right and half on the left, where the Sultan can see them. Next fifty elephants are brought in; these are adorned with silken and gold cloths, and have their tusks shod with iron for service in killing criminals. On the neck of each elephant is its mahout, who carries a sort of iron battle-axe with which he punishes it and directs it to do what is required of it. Each elephant has on its back a sort of large box capable of holding twenty warriors or more or less, according to its bulk and the size of its body. At the corners of [each] such box there are fixed four banners. These elephants are trained to make obeisance to the Sultan and to incline their heads, | and when they do so the chamberlains 224

[20] The *sarjāmdār*, or keeper of the fly whisk; see vol. I, p. 226, and p. 665 below.

[21] The *Silaḥdārs* (so spelled by I.B. in the Persian manner) were a corps of life guards, enjoying special revenues and privileges.

[22] Presumably the shaikhs of the ṣūfī brotherhoods in the capital.

[23] See p. 595 above.

[24] Literally, 'commanders', but the term is applied to holders not only of military commands but of other high administrative posts as well.

cry in a loud voice *Bismillāh*. They also are arranged half on the right and half on the left, behind the persons [already] standing there. As each person enters who has an appointed place of standing on the right or left, he makes obeisance on reaching the station of the chamberlains, and the chamberlains say *Bismillāh,* regulating the loudness of their utterance by the height of reputation of the person who is making his obeisance, and who then retires to his appointed place on the right or left, beyond which he never passes. If it is one of the infidel Hindus who makes obeisance, the chamberlains and the naqībs say to him 'God guide thee'. The Sultan's slaves stand behind all those in attendance, having in their hands shields and swords, and no one can come in [to the hall] between their ranks, but only by passing before the chamberlains who stand in front of the Sultan. |

225 *Description of the entry of strangers and of those presenting gifts to him.* If there should be at the door anyone who has come to offer the Sultan a gift, the chamberlains enter the Sultan's presence in order of precedence. The *amīr-ḥājib*[25] comes first followed by his deputy, then the private chamberlain followed by his deputy, then the steward of the palace followed by his deputy, the 'master' of the chamberlains and the 'honour' of the chamberlains. They make obeisance in three places, and inform the Sultan of the person at the door. If he commands them to bring him in, they place the gift which he has brought in the hands of men who stand with it in front of those present where the Sultan can see it. He then calls in the donor, who makes obeisance three times before reaching the Sultan and makes another obeisance at the station of the chamberlains. If he is a man of rank he stands on a line with the *amīr-ḥājib,* if not, he stands behind him.
226 The Sultan then addresses him | in person with the greatest courtesy and bids him welcome. If he is a person who is worthy of honour, the Sultan takes him by the hand or embraces him, and asks for some part of his present. It is then placed before him, and if it consists in weapons or fabrics he turns it this way and that with his hand and expresses his

[25] Called above 'the chief of the chamberlains'; the unusual combination of the military and civil titles is presumably due to the royal rank of Malik Fīrūz (see n. 19 above).

approval of it, to set the donor at ease and encourage him by his gracious reception. He gives him a robe of honour and assigns him a sum of money to wash his head, according to their custom in this case,[26] proportioned to the donor's merits.

How the gifts of his provincial officers are made to him. When the provincial officers[27] come [to the court] with gifts and sums of revenue collected from taxes in the provinces, they have vessels made of gold and silver, such as basins, ewers and so forth. They also have ingots of gold and silver made like bricks, which they call *khisht*.[28] | The *farrāshūn*,[29] who are 227 the Sultan's slaves, take up their stand in a row, with the gift in their hands, each one of them holding one piece. Then the elephants are brought forward, if there should be any of them included in the gift, next the horses saddled and bridled, then the mules, then the camels carrying the money. I once saw the vizier Khwāja Jahān present his gift when the Sultan arrived from Dawlat Ābād. He met him with his gift outside the city of Bayāna,[30] and the gift was brought in and presented to him with this ceremonial. Amongst the items comprised in it I saw a tray full of ruby stones, another tray full of emerald stones, and a third tray full of magnificent pearls. Ḥājjī Kāwun, the paternal cousin of the Sultan Abū Sa'īd, king of Irāq, was present with him on this occasion, and the Sultan gave him a part of this gift. We shall relate this later on, if God will.[31] |

How he goes out for the two festivals and matters relevant 228 *thereto.* On the eve of the festival the Sultan sends robes of honour to the maliks, the courtiers, the chief officers of state, the foreigners called *'azīz*, the secretaries, chamberlains, naqībs, qā'ids, slaves, and couriers, to each and all of them. On the morning of the feast day all the elephants are adorned with silk, gold, and precious stones. There are sixteen of these

[26] See p. 738 below.

[27] Arabic *'ummāl*, technically applied to fiscal administrators, but often in the more general sense of administrative officers.

[28] Persian, meaning 'brick'.

[29] 'Those who look after the furnishings', i.e. cleaners, handymen, footmen, etc., but by no means always consisting of slaves. 'The Sultan's slaves' presumably shorthand for 'among the slaves of the Sultan'.

[30] Biana, 120 miles south of Delhi; see vol. IV, pp. 5–6 (Ar.).

[31] See pp. 667–9 below.

elephants which no one rides, but they are reserved to be ridden by the Sultan himself, and over them are carried sixteen parasols of silk embroidered with jewels, each one with a shaft of pure gold. On each elephant is a silk cushion[32] adorned with precious stones. The Sultan himself rides on one of these elephants, and in front of him there is carried aloft the *ghāshiya*, that is his saddle-cover,[33] which is adorned with the most precious jewels. In front of him walk his slaves 229 and his mamlūks, | each one of them wearing on his head a cap of gold and round his waist a girdle of gold, which some of them adorn with jewels. In front of him also walk the naqibs, about three hundred in number, each one of them wearing on his head a golden *aqrūf* [high conical hat][34] and round his waist a golden girdle, and carrying in his hand a whip with a handle of gold. Those who ride are the Grand Qāḍī Ṣadr al-Jahān Kamāl al-Dīn al-Ghaznawī, the Grand Qāḍī Ṣadr al-Jahān Nāṣir al-Dīn al-Khwārizmī, the rest of the qāḍīs, and the principal foreigners among the Khurasanians, 'Iraqis, Syrians, Egyptians, and Moors, each one of them mounted on an elephant. All foreigners are called by them Khurasanians. The muezzins also ride on elephants and they keep on calling out *Allāhu akbar.*

The Sultan comes out of the gate of the palace [with his retinue] in this order. Meanwhile the troops await his coming, 230 each amīr | with his company separately, along with his drums and flags. The Sultan advances, preceded by those whom we have mentioned as walking on foot; these again are preceded by the qāḍīs and the muezzins reciting praises to God, and behind the Sultan are his 'honours', i.e. flags, drums, trumpets, bugles, and pipes. Behind them come all the members of his personal entourage, then these are followed by the Sultan's brother Mubārak Khān[35] with his 'honours' and troops, who

[32] Here again I.B. uses *martaba* (see n. 18 above), but the combination of adjectives seems to imply a bejewelled seat covered with a silk cushion.

[33] The hoisting of the *ghāshiya* before the Sultan on his processions became, under the Seljuks and later dynasties in Asia and Egypt, one of the symbols of sovereignty. I.B.'s explanation of the term indicates that the usage was not yet known in the Maghrib.

[34] See vol. II, p. 485, n. 267.

[35] This half-brother is mentioned below (pp. 687, 694), but appears to have played an obscure role in affairs.

is followed by the Sultan's nephew, Bahrām Khān,[36] with his 'honours' and troops, followed by the Sultan's cousin Malik Fīrūz with his 'honours' and troops, then the vizier next with his 'honours' and troops, then the malik Mujīr ibn Dhu'r-rajā[37] with his 'honours' and troops, then the great malik Qabūla with his 'honours' and troops. This malik stands high in the Sultan's esteem, and enjoys immense prestige and vast wealth. The intendant of his revenue-office,[38] Thiqat | al-Mulk 'Alā' al-Dīn 'Alī al-Miṣrī, known as Ibn al-Sharābishī, told me that his allowance[39] and the allowance of his slaves together with their stipends amounted to thirty-six laks[40] a year. Next after him comes the malik Nukbiya[41] with his 'honours' and troops, then the malik Bughra with his 'honours' and troops, then the malik Mukhliṣ[42] with his 'honours' and troops, then the malik Quṭb al-Mulk[43] with his 'honours' and troops. These persons are the great amīrs who are never separated from the Sultan, and these are the officers who ride in his company on festival days with their 'honours', while the other amīrs ride without 'honours'. All those who ride [in the procession] on that day do so wearing armour, both on themselves and on their horses, the majority of them being the Sultan's mamlūks. When the Sultan reaches the gate of the *muṣallā*[44] he halts by the gate | and orders the judges, the principal amīrs, and the chiefs of the foreigners to enter. Then he himself alights, and the imām leads the prayers and delivers the address. If it should be the

231

232

[36] An adopted son of Tughluq, entitled Tatār Khān, and renamed Bahrām Khān by Sultan Muḥammad, subsequently appointed governor of Sunargaon (see pp. 709–10 below).

[37] In the *Ta'rīkh-i Mubārakshāhī* (cited by Mahdi Husain, *Muhammad bin Tughluq*, 102, n. 1) called Mujīr al-Dīn ibn Abī Rajā, but his exact function at this time is not recorded. For Qabūla see vol. I, p. 226, and n. 20 above.

[38] I take *dīwān* here to mean the register of revenues derived from his domains, etc., in agreement with the usage of Mustawfī. The following term *Thiqat al-Mulk* ('trustworthy servant of the kingdom') is purely a civil title.

[39] *Nafaqa*, i.e. the sum allotted for living expenses.

[40] 3,600,000 dinars, presumably silver dinars, of the standard weight of 175 grains.

[41] Chief dawādār, i.e. head of the secretariat; see p. 713 below.

[42] These two offices are apparently not mentioned elsewhere.

[43] Governor of Multān, see p. 605 above.

[44] See vol. I, p. 13, n. 20.

Feast of the Sacrifice, the Sultan brings a camel and stabs it in the throat with a javelin (which they call *nīza*),[45] first putting on over his clothes a silk wrapper to protect himself from the blood; then he mounts the elephant and returns to his palace.

How he holds audience on feast days and an account of the great throne and the great cassolette. On the day of the feast the palace is garnished[46] and adorned in the most sumptuous manner. Over the whole audience hall there is erected the *bārka*, which is like a vast tent[47] supported by many stout poles and surrounded by pavilions on all sides. Artificial trees are made of silk of different colours, with artificial flowers on them; three rows of them are placed | in the hall, and between each pair of trees there is placed a golden chair with a covered cushion upon it. The great throne is set up at the upper end of the hall; it is of pure gold throughout, and its legs are encrusted with jewels. Its length is twenty-three spans and its breadth about the half of that. It is in separate pieces, which are put together to form the whole throne, and each piece of it is carried by a number of men because of the weight of the gold. Upon it there is placed the cushioned seat,[48] and the parasol encrusted with jewels is hoisted over the Sultan's head. As he mounts the throne the chamberlains and naqībs cry with a loud voice *Bismillāh*, then those present come forward to salute him. The first of them to do so are the qāḍīs, preachers, doctors of the law, sharīfs, shaikhs, and the brothers, relatives and relations-in-law of the Sultan; after them come the [principal] foreigners, then the vizier, then the amīrs of the troops, then the shaikhs of the mamlūks, then the chiefs | of the troops. Each one salutes after the other without any elbowing or unseemly pushing.

233

234

One of their customs on the feast day is that every person who owns [the revenues of] a village, of which he is the beneficiary [by royal grant], brings some gold coins wrapped in a piece of cloth with his name written on it, and casts them into a golden basin there. These contributions amount in all to a vast sum, which the Sultan gives to anyone he pleases.

[45] Persian.

[46] Literally, 'spread with carpets'.

[47] Cf. vol. II, p. 494.

[48] The *martaba*, see p. 660, n. 18 above.

When the people have finished presenting their salutations food is set before them according to their ranks. On that day too there is set up the great cassolette, which is a sort of tower of pure gold composed of separate pieces; when they wish to put it together they join them up, and each section of it is carried by a number of men. Inside it are three chambers which are entered by incense-burners, who set fire to *qamārī* and *qāqulī* aloes-wood,[49] ambergris and benzoin,[50] so that the smoke from them fills the whole hall. There are also | gold and 235 silver barrels carried by pages and filled with rose-water, with which they sprinkle those present broadcast.

This throne and this cassolette are not brought out except on the two festival days only. On the remaining days of the feast the Sultan sits on a golden throne of smaller size. A lofty[51] *bārka* is erected [on the first day, as we have said] which has three doors. The Sultan sits inside it, and at the first door stands 'Imād al-Mulk Sartīz,[52] at the second door the malik Nukbiya, and at the third door Yūsuf Bughra. On his right stand the officers of the mamlūks of the corps of Arms-bearers and on his left likewise, and the general body of people stand in the places assigned to them by their ranks. The commandant of the *bārka*, the malik Ṭaghī,[53] carrying in his hand a golden stick, and his deputy, carrying a silver stick, arrange all those present in order and even up the rows. The vizier stands [in his place], with the secretaries behind him, and the chamberlains and naqībs [likewise] stand [in their places]. Then the musicians and dancers come in—first of all the daughters of the infidel Indian kings | who have been 236 taken as captives of war during that year and whom, after they have sung and danced, the Sultan presents to the amīrs and to the distinguished foreigners, then after them the rest of the daughters of the infidels and these, after they have

[49] I.e. of Qamār (Khmer = Cambodia) and Qāqula (in Malaya), see vol. IV, pp. 240–2 (Ar.) and *Selections*, p. 276.

[50] On *lubān jāwī* or 'Sumatran incense' see vol. IV, p. 240 (Ar.). Benzoin was compounded with ambergris in order to give a stronger and more lasting effect to the latter.

[51] For *ba'īd* in the sense of 'high' cf. vol. IV, p. 367, l. 4 (Ar.).

[52] Governor of Sind; see p. 593 above. The maliks Nukbiya and Bughra are mentioned in the preceding account of the procession.

[53] Mahdi Husain calls him 'superintendent of the durbar' (*Muḥammad bin Tughluq*, 185).

sung and danced, he gives to his brothers and kinsmen and relatives by marriage and to the sons of the maliks. The Sultan's session for this purpose takes place after the hour of afternoon prayer. Then on the next day also, after the hour of afternoon prayer, he holds a session after the same manner, to which are brought singing girls whom, after they have sung and danced, he gives to the amīrs of the mamlūks. On the third day he celebrates the marriages of his relatives and makes gifts to them; on the fourth day he emancipates male slaves, on the fifth he emancipates female slaves, on the sixth he marries male slaves to female slaves and on the seventh he distributes alms, and that lavishly.

His ceremonial on his return from a journey. When the 237 Sultan comes back from | his journeys, the elephants are decorated, and over sixteen of them are raised sixteen parasols, some brocaded and some set with jewels. In front of him is carried the *ghāshiya*, that is the saddle-cover, set with precious stones.[54] Wooden pavilions are built, several stories high, and covered with silk cloths, and in each story there are singing girls wearing the most beautiful dresses and ornaments, with dancing girls amongst them. In the centre of each pavilion there is fashioned a large tank made of skins and filled with rose-syrup dissolved in water, from which all the people, that is to say all comers, natives or strangers, may drink, and everyone who drinks receives [at the same time] betel leaves and areca nuts. The space between the pavilions is carpeted with silk cloths, on which the Sultan's horse treads. The walls of the street along which he passes from the 238 gate | of the city to the gate of the palace are hung with silk cloths. In front of him march footmen from his own slaves, several thousands in number, and behind come the squadrons and mounted troops. On one of his entries into the capital I saw three or four small catapults set up on elephants throwing dinars and dirhams[55] amongst the people, and they would be scrambling to pick them up, from the

[54] See p. 664, n. 33 above.

[55] Not 'gold and silver coins', since I.B. clearly defines the regular Indian dinar as a silver coin worth eight silver (*nuqra*) dirhams (vol. IV, pp. 210 [Ar.]). For the catapults (*ra'ādāt*) see p. 621, n. 7 above.

moment when he entered the city until he reached the palace.[56]

The ceremonial at the private meals. In the Sultan's household there are two kinds of meals, the private meal and the public meal. The private meal is that of the Sultan himself, the one of which he partakes. It is his custom to eat in his saloon[57] in company with those who are present, and the persons who attend for this purpose are the amīrs of the household, the amīr-ḥājib who is the son of the Sultan's uncle,[58] 'Imād al-Mulk | Sartīz, and the amīr-majlis.[59] If the Sultan wishes to honour or favour any of the distinguished foreigners or great amīrs he invites that person, who then eats along with them. Sometimes also he wishes to honour one of those present, and taking one of the plates in his hand he puts a piece of bread on it and gives it to him. The recipient takes it and, placing it on his left palm, does homage with his right hand to the ground. Sometimes he sends a portion of that food to a person who is absent from the saloon, and the recipient does homage in the same way as one who is present, and eats it with those who are in his company.[60] I was present many times at this private meal and I noticed that the number of those who attended it was about twenty persons. 239

The ceremonial at the public meals. As for the public meals, the food is brought from the kitchen preceded by the naqībs crying out *bismillāh*; the head of the naqībs walks in front of them | carrying a golden mace, and with him is his deputy carrying a silver mace. When they enter through the fourth 240

[56] It was this passage, describing a well-authenticated Indian usage, which aroused the gravest suspicions of his Moroccan fellow-countrymen, when he related his travels on his return to Fez: see Ibn Khaldūn, *Muqaddima*, Book 3, § 18, tr. F. Rosenthal, vol. I, p. 370: 'they said privately to one another that he was a liar.'

[57] I.B. clearly distinguishes in this and in the following paragraph the *majlis*, in which the meals were served, from the *mashwar* or public audience-hall.

[58] I.e. Fīrūz Malik; see n. 19 above. For Sartīz see n. 52 above.

[59] Literally 'officer in command of the saloon'. Mahdi Husain renders as 'master of ceremonies', but the context suggests an officer of the highest rank, probably the *chāshnīgīr* (in Arabic *jāshankīr*) or supervisor of the royal table (cf. vol. I, p. 160, n. 16).

[60] It is not clear from the Arabic text whether this means those who happen to be present at the time, or those who have come subsequently for this special occasion.

door and those who are present in the audience hall hear their voices they all rise to their feet, and no one remains sitting but the Sultan alone. When the food is placed on the ground the naqībs range themselves in a line and their amīr[61] stands in front of them and makes an oration in which he praises the Sultan with much eulogy, then he does homage and all the naqībs do homage in concert with him, together with all those who are in the audience chamber, both great and small. It is their custom that everyone who hears the voice of the chief of the naqībs on this occasion stands still, if he is walking, and stays in his place should he be standing. No person moves or quits his standing-ground until the end of this oration. After that his deputy also pronounces a similar oration and does homage, and the naqībs and all those present do homage a 241 second time, and thereafter | they all sit down. The clerks of the gate make a written report of the arrival of the food, although the Sultan already knows of its arrival, and this report is given to a boy selected for that duty from among the sons of the maliks, who takes it to the Sultan. On reading it the Sultan appoints whomsoever he chooses of the principal amīrs to assign their places to those present and to preside at the distribution of food to them.

The food which is served to them consists of thin rounds of bread, roast meat, round cakes in portions[62] and filled with sweet confections, rice, chickens, and *samūsak*; we have already described this and explained how it is made.[63] It is their custom that the principal place at the banquet should be taken by the qāḍīs, the preachers, doctors of law, sharīfs and shaikhs; after them come the Sultan's relatives, then the principal amīrs and then the rest of the people. No one sits down except in a place assigned to him, so that there is no pushing and elbowing between them at all. When they sit down, the *shurbadārs*, that is to say cup-bearers, come bearing 242 vessels of gold, silver, | brass and glass, filled with candy-water. The guests drink this before beginning to eat, and when they

[61] This use of a military title for the Chief Usher (called above and below simply *Naqīb al-nuqabā'*) is surprising.

[62] The phrase *dhātu'l-jawānib* (literally 'many-sided') appears to be a particular term; it seems rather improbable that it should simply mean 'split'.

[63] P. 608 above.

have drunk the chamberlains say *bismillāh*. They then start eating and there is set before each person a portion of every dish of which the meal is composed;[64] he eats of it by himself and no person eats with another out of the same dish. When they finish eating barley-water[65] is brought to them in tin mugs, and when they have taken this the chamberlains say *bismillāh*. Then trays are brought in with betel and areca-nut and each person is given a spoonful of powdered areca with fifteen leaves of betel tied in a bunch with red silk thread. When those present take the betel the chamberlains say *bismillāh* and thereupon they all stand up. The amīr who is appointed to preside at the banquet does homage and they all do homage with him and then withdraw. They have meals twice a day,[66] once before noon, and again after the afternoon prayer. |

Some stories of his generosity and open-handedness. On this 243 subject I shall relate only instances at which I was present and which I witnessed with my own eyes. God Most High knows the truth of what I say and He is sufficient as a witness. Besides, what I am about to tell is notorious and confirmed by the evidence of many persons, and the countries which are in the vicinity of India, such as al-Yaman, Khurāsān and Fārs, are full of stories of him, which their inhabitants know to be true. Especially well known is his generosity to foreigners, for he prefers them to the people of India, singles them out for favour, showers his benefits upon them and clothes them in an ample garment of bounty, appoints them to high offices of state, and confers upon them magnificent gifts. One indication of his generous treatment of them is that he has called them by the designation of *'azīz*[67] and has prohibited their being called strangers, for, he said, when a person is called 'stranger' he feels dispirited and downcast. | I shall now mention out of all that could be enumerated a 244 few of his prodigal gifts and largesse, if God will.

[64] Literally, 'included in the *simāṭ*'; *simāṭ*, properly the mat upon which the food vessels are placed, became from early Islamic times the term applied to the ceremonial meal given by the sovereign to his officers and troops.

[65] *fuqqā'*; see p. 608, n. 51 above.

[66] The text does not expressly say that the *simāṭ* is held twice a day, although this meaning may be inferred from the context; but the sentence seems more like a general statement tacked on to the end of this paragraph.

[67] See p. 595 above.

His gift to the merchant Shihāb al-Dīn of Kāzarūn and the story of the latter. This Shihāb al-Dīn was a friend of al-Kāzarūnī, the 'king' of the merchants[68] [in India], surnamed Pīrwīz. The Sultan had given the city of Kanbāya in grant[69] to the 'king' of the merchants and had promised to appoint him to the office of vizier. Thereupon he sent to his friend Shihāb al-Dīn to join him, and the latter arrived, having prepared a gift for the Sultan consisting of a royal enclosure[70] of segmented woollen cloth decorated with gold leaf, a reception marquee of the same kind, a private tent with an annex, and a resting tent—all of this in ornamented woollen cloth—and a large number of mules. Shihāb al-Dīn, on arriving with this gift to join his friend, the 'king' of the merchants, found 245 him | preparing to set out for the capital with the revenues collected from his territories and a gift for the Sultan. The vizier Khwāja Jahān was informed of the Sultan's promise to him to appoint him vizier and was filled with jealousy and dismay at it. Now the territories of Kanbāya and al-Juzarāt [Gujerat] had been previously under the government of the vizier, and their population had a certain attachment and loyalty to him and devotion to his service. Most of them are infidels and some of them are rebels who inhabit inaccessible retreats in the mountains. The vizier therefore sent secret instructions to them to fall upon the 'king' of the merchants when he came out on his way to the capital.

When therefore, he left [Kanbāya] with the treasures and monies, in company with Shihāb al-Dīn and his gift, they encamped one day before noon, as was their usual practice, and the [escorting] troops dispersed and most of them went to sleep. At that moment they were attacked by a considerable force of infidels, who killed the 'king' of the merchants and carried off as booty his money and treasures and Shihāb 246 al-Dīn's present. | Shihāb al-Dīn himself escaped with his life, and the Sultan, on learning of this through his information officers, gave orders that he should be given thirty thousand

[68] *Malik al-tujjār*, i.e. head or spokesman of the merchants (particularly those engaged in overseas trade) in their relations with the government. For Kāzarūn and its significance in seaborne trade see vol. II, pp. 319–20.

[69] For such grants see p. 681, n. 103 below.

[70] The *sarācha* was an ornamented enclosure for the Sultan on his journeys: see pp. 752–3 below.

dinars from the revenues of the province of Nahrawāla,[71] and return to his own country. When this was offered to him, however, he refused to accept it, saying that he had come for the express purpose of seeing the Sultan and kissing the ground before him. They wrote to the Sultan to this effect and he, gratified with what Shihāb al-Dīn had said, commanded him to proceed to the capital as an honoured visitor.

It chanced that the day of his introduction before the Sultan was the same day that we too were introduced before him. He bestowed robes of honour upon us all and gave orders for our residence, and made Shihāb al-Dīn in addition a handsome gift of money. Some days later the Sultan ordered that I should be given six thousand tangahs,[72] as I shall relate[73] in due course, and on that same day enquired the reason of Shihāb al-Dīn's absence. Bahā al-Dīn ibn al-Falakī replied 'O Master of the World, *namīdānam*' | which 247 means 'I do not know.' Then he said to him '*Shunīdam zahmet dārat,*' meaning 'I have heard that he is ill.' The Sultan said to him '*Biraw hamīn zamān, dar khizāneh yak laki tangah zar bagirī wapīsh ū babarī tā dili ū khush shavad,*' which means 'Go at once to the treasury, take from it a hundred thousand tangahs of gold and bear them to him to set his mind at ease.' He executed the command and conveyed the gift to him, and the Sultan gave orders that he should buy with this money what Indian goods he pleased, and that no one else should buy anything at all until Shihāb al-Dīn should be supplied with all his requirements. In addition he ordered three ships to be made ready for his journey furnished with all their equipment and full pay and provisions for the crew. So Shihāb al-Dīn departed and disembarked in the island of Hurmuz, where he built a great house. I saw this house later on, and I saw also Shihāb al-Dīn, having lost all that he had, at Shīrāz soliciting a gift from its Sultan, Abū Isḥāq. | That is the way with riches 248 amassed in these Indian lands; it is only rarely[74] that anyone

[71] The early mediaeval city and kingdom of Anhilvāra, now named Pātan, in the former state of Baroda (23° 57′ N., 72° 10′ E.).

[72] See p. 757 below.

[73] Text: *sanadhkuruhu*, and cf. in the following sentence the rendering of *namīdānam* by *mā nadrī*.

[74] Reading *qallamā* for *falammā* (as the French translation requires also).

gets out of the country with them, and when he does leave it and reaches some other country, God sends upon him some calamity which annihilates all that he possesses, just as it happened to this Shihāb al-Dīn; for everything that he had was taken from him in the civil war between the king of Hurmuz and his nephews,[75] and he left the country stripped of all his wealth.

The story of his gift to the Grand Shaikh Rukn al-Dīn. The Sultan had sent a present to the Caliph in Egypt, Abu'l-'Abbās, with a request that he should send him the decree of appointment to govern the lands of Hind and Sind—this because of a belief which he held about the authority of the Caliphate.[76] The Caliph Abu'l-'Abbās sent him what he had asked for by the hand of the principal Shaikh in the land of Egypt, Rukn al-Dīn.[77] When this envoy reached him he 249 lavished honours upon him | and made him a handsome gift of money, and he used to rise to meet him whenever the envoy entered his presence, and to show him great respect. At length he gave him leave to return and heaped riches upon him. Amongst his gifts to him on this occasion were a quantity of horseshoes with their nails, all made entirely of pure gold, and he said to him 'When you disembark after your journey, shoe your horses with these.' So Rukn al-Dīn set out for Kanbāya to take ship from there to the land of al-Yaman, but then happened the affair of the revolt of the qāḍī Jalāl al-Dīn and his seizure of the property of Ibn al-Kawlamī.[78] The possessions of the Grand Shaikh were seized also and he himself fled to the Sultan along with Ibn al-Kawlamī. When the Sultan saw him he said to him jestingly [in Persian] *Āmadī kazar barī bā digirī ṣanam kharī zar nabarī wasar nihī*, which means 'You came to carry away gold to consume with fair creatures, but you will carry away no gold and leave your 250 head here.' He said this to him in | a tone of amusement and then added 'Take good heart; I am on the point of setting out

[75] See vol. II, pp. 402–3.

[76] See vol. I, pp. 225–8. Abu'l-'Abbās, entitled al-Ḥākim bi'amri'llāh II, held the titular Caliphate in Cairo from 1341 to 1352. Like his contemporary, Ibn Khaldūn, and other Maghribine writers, I.B. regarded this caliphate as an empty pretence.

[77] See vol. I, p. 228, n. 155.

[78] See pp. 730–4 below.

to deal with the rebels and I shall give you many times more than they have taken from you.' I heard after I had left India that the Sultan kept his promise to him and recompensed him for all that he had lost and that he brought it all safely to Egypt.

Account of the gift which he made to the preacher from Tirmidh, Nāṣir al-Dīn. This doctor of the law and homiletic preacher had come to the Sultan's court, and after staying for a year as a pensioner on his bounty, he wished to return to his own country. The Sultan gave him permission to do so, although he had not yet heard him in discourse or homily. When however, the Sultan [prepared to] set out on an expedition to the land of al-Ma'bar[79] he desired to hear him before his departure, and gave orders that there should be prepared for him a pulpit of white sandalwood, called *maqāṣirī*,[80] and its nails and plaques were made of gold and at the top of it there was inserted | an immense ruby. Nāṣir al-Dīn was invested with an 'Abbāsid robe, black,[81] embroidered with gold and encrusted with precious stones, and his turban was to match. The pulpit was set up for him inside the [Sultan's] *sarācha*, which we call *āfrāg*.[82] The Sultan took his seat on his throne with the principal officers on his right and left, and the judges, doctors of law and amīrs took their places; then he delivered an eloquent address followed by a homily and exhortation. There was nothing remarkable in what he did, but his good fortune befriended him, and when he came down from the pulpit the Sultan rose up and came to him, embraced him, mounted him on an elephant and ordered all those present, of whom I was one, to walk before him to a *sarācha* which had been pitched for him in face of the Sultan's *sarācha*. This enclosure was made entirely of coloured silk and its marquee and private tent were both made of silk also. He sat there [for a reception] in which we joined, each sitting in his place. At one side of the *sarācha*

251

[79] See p. 715 below.

[80] See Dozy's note, II, 358–9. The term (pb. to be read *maqāṣarī*) would seem in all probability derived from the island of Maqāṣar (Macassar), now Celebes: cf. *Chau Ju-Kua: Or the Chinese and Arab Trade*, trans. F. Hirth and W. W. Rockhill (St. Petersburg, 1912), pp. 208–9.

[81] The black robe was the official garment of the 'Abbāsid regime.

[82] See pp. 752–3 below.

there were some golden vessels which the Sultan had given 252 him, namely a large vase for holding lamps,[83] | which was big enough to accommodate a man sitting inside it, two cooking pots, plates, I cannot say how many, a number of jugs, a waterskin, a *tamīsanda*,[84] a table with four legs and a book stand, all of these in pure gold. 'Imād al-Dīn al-Simnānī[85] held up two of the tent pegs of the *sarācha*, one of them brass, the other tinned, as if to give the impression that they were of gold and silver, but they were not so and only as we have stated. [Besides this] the Sultan had given him on his arrival a hundred thousand silver dinars and two hundred slaves, some of whom he freed and some he took with him.

Account of his gift to 'Abd al-'Azīz of Ardawīl.[86] This 'Abd al-'Azīz was a jurist and traditionist who had studied in Damascus under Taqī al-Dīn Ibn Taimīya, Burhān al-Dīn ibn al-Barqaḥ, Jamāl al-Dīn al-Mizzī, Shams al-Dīn al-253 Dhahabī | and others. Subsequently he came to the court of the Sultan, who received him generously and made rich gifts to him. It happened one day that he expounded before him a number of traditions relating to the merit of al-'Abbās and his son (God be pleased with them) and some of the memorable deeds of the Caliphs descended from them. The Sultan was highly delighted with this because of his attachment to the house of al-'Abbās and having kissed this scholar's feet gave orders to fetch a golden tray on which there were two thousand tangahs and poured them over him with his own hand, saying 'These are for you, and the tray as well.' We have related this story before in an earlier passage.

Account of his gift to Shams al-Dīn al-Andukānī. The doctor Shams al-Dīn al-Andukānī, who was a philosopher and a gifted poet, wrote a laudatory ode to the Sultan in Persian. The ode contained twenty-seven verses, and the Sultan gave him a thousand silver dinars for each verse. This is a greater 254 reward than those related of former kings, | who used to give

[83] For this meaning of *tannūr* ('oven') see Dozy, s.v.

[84] Or *tīmasanda*.

[85] Entitled in a later passage (p. 687 below) 'the king of kings'.

[86] I.B. has already related this story in somewhat different terms: see vol. II, pp. 312–13. For the Damascene scholars see vol. I, pp. 135, 148; Shams al-Dīn Muḥammad b. Aḥmad al-Dhahabī (d. 1347), was a celebrated historian.

a thousand dirhams for each verse, which is only a tenth of the Sultan's gift.

Account of his gift to 'Aḍud al-Dīn al-Shawankārī. 'Aḍud al-Dīn was a jurist and imām, a worthy man of great eminence, highly reputed and widely known in his own country. The Sultan, on hearing the stories related of him and of his commendable qualities, sent ten thousand dinars to him in his own town of Shawankāra,[87] without ever seeing him or being visited by him.

Account of his gift to the qāḍī Majd al-Dīn. Then too when the Sultan heard the story of the learned and pious qāḍī Majd al-Dīn of Shīrāz, who was distinguished by the famous miracle, whose history we have written in the first volume[88] and of whom more will be said | later on, he sent ten thousand silver dinars to him at Shīrāz along with Shaikh-Zāda al-Dimashqī. 255

Account of his gift to Burhān al-Dīn of Ṣāgharj.[89] Burhān al-Dīn of Ṣāgharj was a preacher and imām so liberal in spending what he possessed that he used often to contract debts in order to give to others. The Sultan heard of him and sent him forty thousand dinars, with a request that he should come to his capital. He accepted the money and paid his debts with it, but went off to the land of al-Khaṭā, and refused to come to the Sultan, saying 'I shall not go to [the court of] a Sultan in whose presence scholars have to stand.' |

256 *Account of his gift to Ḥājjī Kāwun and history of the latter.* Ḥājjī Kāwun was the son of the paternal uncle of the Sultan Abū Sa'īd, king of 'Irāq, and his brother Mūsā was a king in one of the regions of 'Irāq.[90] Ḥājjī Kāwun came to visit the Sultan and was received with princely hospitality, and loaded

[87] Or Shabānkāra, the south-eastern division of Fārs, so named from the Shabānkāra tribe of Kurds (or Dailamites), who settled there in the twelfth century. The chief cities were Darābjird and Īg, the latter being at this time the capital (G. le Strange, *Lands*, 288–9; *Mustawfī*, trans., 137–8).

[88] See vol. II, pp. 300 sqq.

[89] Ṣāgharj or Ṣāghirj, a township about 15 miles north-west of Samarqand. Burhān al-Dīn is mentioned as a celebrated mystic, resident at the court of 'the king of Khaṭāy' (J. K. Teufel, *Eine Lebensbeschreibung des Scheichs 'Alī-i Hamadānī*, Leiden 1962, p. 72, note x, and cf. p. 17). For al-Khaṭā see above p. 551.

[90] Mūsā Khān b. 'Alī Baidū was briefly recognized as the successor of Abū Sa'īd by a confederacy of chiefs in northern Iraq, but was defeated and killed by Shaikh Ḥasan in July, 1337 (see vol. II, p. 341, and n. 231). His brother Ḥājjī Kāwun seems to be otherwise unknown.

with gifts. One day when the vizier Khwāja Jahān presented his gift [as we have related already],[91] including three trays, one filled with rubies, the second with emeralds, and the third with pearls, Ḥājjī Kāwun was present, and I myself saw the Sultan give him a large portion of this gift. Subsequently he made him another immense gift, and Ḥājjī Kāwun set out for 'Irāq, where he found that his brother had died and that Sulaimān Khān reigned in his stead.[92] He claimed his brother's inheritance, declared himself king and received the homage of the troops, then set out for the land of Fārs and encamped at the city of Shawankāra, the city in 257 which the imām 'Aḍud | al-Dīn, whom we have just mentioned, was living. When he encamped outside there was some delay before the shaikhs went out to present themselves to him, and when they did so he said to them 'What hindered you from coming out at once to do homage to me?' They apologised to him but he refused to accept their excuses and said to his armour-bearers *qilij tikhār*,[93] which means 'draw your swords', whereupon they drew their swords and beheaded them, a considerable number in all. When the amīrs who were in the vicinity of this city heard what he had done they were indignant and wrote to Shams al-Dīn al-Simnānī,[94] who was one of the high-ranking amīrs and jurists, to inform him of what had happened to the men of Shawankāra and to ask his assistance in fighting against Ḥājjī Kāwun. He set out on a campaign with his troops, and the inhabitants of the region assembled to demand vengeance for those shaikhs whom Ḥājjī Kāwun had killed. They attacked his army during the night and routed it; Ḥājjī Kāwun himself was in 258 the citadel | of the town[95] and they surrounded it and, finding

[91] P. 663 above. In view of the following sentence, this occasion can be dated to the early months of 1337.

[92] Sulaimān b. Yūsuf Shāh, a descendant of Abaqa, married to Sāṭī Beg (see vol. II, p. 337, n. 217), maintained himself against Shaikh Ḥasan in Adharbāijān from 1339 to 1343/4, and thereafter in Eastern Anatolia (B. Spuler, *Die Mongolen in Iran*, Berlin, 1955, p. 133 sqq.).

[93] Presumably I.B.'s rendering of Turkish *chikar*.

[94] The *Ta'rīkh-i Guzīda* (ed. E. G. Browne, Leyden-London, 1910, pp. 636 sqq.) gives a prominent place in the conflicts in Fārs at this time to Shams al-Dīn Ṣa'in, the qāḍī of Simnān (see vol. II, p. 318), but makes no reference to the putsch of Ḥājjī Kāwun.

[95] Presumably of Īg; see n. 87 above.

him hidden in a lavatory, cut off his head and sent it to Sulaimān Khān, and they distributed his members throughout the province in satisfaction of their vendetta against him.

Account of the arrival of the Caliph's son at his court and of what befel him. This was the amīr Ghiyāth al-Dīn Muḥammad son of 'Abd al-Qāhir, son of Yūsuf, son of 'Abd al-'Azīz, son of the 'Abbāsid caliph of Baghdād al-Mustanṣir billāh.[96] He had gone to the court of the Sultan 'Alā al-Dīn Ṭarmashīrīn, king of the lands beyond the Oxus, who had received him honourably and assigned to him the hospice which is built round the tomb of Qutham ibn al-'Abbās[97] (God be pleased with them both). He made his home there for some years, but afterwards, on hearing of the Sultan's affection for the house of al-'Abbās and his support of their cause, he desired to go to him, and despatched to him two envoys, one of whom was | his associate of long standing Muḥammad ibn Abu'l- 259 Sharafī al-Ḥarbāwī, and the other Muḥammad al-Hamadānī al-Ṣūfī. These two persons therefore presented themselves before the Sultan. Now Nāṣir al-Dīn [the preacher] of Tirmidh, of whom we have spoken previously,[98] had met Ghiyāth al-Dīn at Baghdād, and as the men of Baghdād had testified in his presence to the genuineness of his descent, so he now testified to this before the Sultan. Consequently, when his two envoys reached the Sultan he gave them five thousand dinars and sent by them thirty thousand dinars to Ghiyāth al-Dīn to defray the expenses of his journey to join him. At the same time he wrote him a letter with his own hand expressing his veneration for him and inviting him to come to his court.

On receiving this letter Ghiyāth al-Dīn set out to join him. When he reached the province of Sind and the intelligence officials wrote to announce his arrival, the Sultan sent an officer to receive him according to his usual custom. Next, on his arrival at Sarsatī, he sent also Ṣadr | al-Jahān, the 260 Grand Qāḍī Kamāl al-Dīn al-Ghaznawī, with a number of

[96] See vol. I, pp. 225–6 (where the text has 'Abd al-Qādir for 'Abd al-Qāhir). 'Son', of course, is used here in the sense of 'descendant'.

[97] See p. 568 above.

[98] See p. 675 above.

doctors of the law to welcome him. He then sent the amīrs also for the same purpose, and when Ghiyāth al-Dīn halted at Mas'ūd Ābād, outside the capital,[99] the Sultan went out himself to receive him. When they met Ghiyāth al-Dīn dismounted, then the Sultan also dismounted [to show his respect] for him, and he bowed and the Sultan bowed to him. He had brought with him a gift including some robes; the Sultan took one of the robes, placed it on his shoulder, and did homage in the same manner as people do homage to him. Then the horses were brought, and the Sultan took one of them with his hand, led it up to him, adjured him to mount, and himself held his stirrup until he mounted. Then the Sultan mounted also and rode alongside him with the parasol shading the two of them together. He took betel-nut with his own hand and offered it to him; this was the highest mark of the Sultan's consideration for him, for he never does 261 that with anyone. He said to him also 'Had I not | taken the oath of allegiance to the Caliph Abu'l-'Abbās[100] I should have sworn allegiance to you,' whereupon Ghiyāth al-Dīn said to him 'I too am bound by the same oath.' Ghiyāth al-Dīn said to him also 'The Apostle of God (God's blessing and peace upon him) said *Whoso restores dead land to life, it belongs to him*, and you have restored us to life.' The Sultan replied to him in the most courteous and the most affectionate terms, and when they reached the *sarācha* which had been prepared for the Sultan's occupation he assigned it to him as his residence, and another was pitched for the Sultan.

After passing that night outside the city they made their entrance into the capital on the following morning. The Sultan assigned him a residence in the town which is called Sīrī and known also as the 'Abode of the Caliphate',[101] in the castle built by 'Alā al-Dīn al-Khaljī and his son Quṭb al-Dīn. The Sultan ordered all the amīrs to accompany him to the

[99] See p. 617 above.

[100] The date of this episode is difficult to determine. Sultan Muḥammad struck coins in the name of the Cairo caliph al-Mustakfī billāh (Abu'l-Rabī' Sulaimān) from 741 to 743 (1340–43), although the latter had died in February 1340. There is no indication that he had been in communication with the caliph al-Ḥākim II (Abu'l-'Abbās) until the arrival of the presumed 'Abbāsid robes and decree with Shaikh Sa'īd (see vol. I, p. 225), when Ghiyāth al-Dīn was already resident in Delhi.

[101] See p. 619 above.

castle and furnished it for him with all that he might need of gold and silver vessels. Among them there was even a golden bath tub in which to wash himself. He also sent him four hundred | thousand dinars to 'wash his head', according to 262 the usual custom,[102] and a number of pages, servants, and female slaves, and assigned him three hundred dinars a day for his expenses, besides sending him in addition a number of tables with food prepared for his own use. He endowed him further with the whole town of Sīrī as an estate, together with all that it contained of houses and the contiguous gardens and lands belonging to the public treasury, as well as a hundred villages and the government of the eastern territories attached to Dihlī.[103] He gave him also thirty mules with gilded saddles, whose forage would be supplied by the treasury. He ordered him not to descend from his mount when he visited the Sultan's palace except at a particular place where no one might enter on horseback except the Sultan himself, and he ordered the whole population, great and small, to do homage to him in the same way as they do homage to the Sultan. When he entered | the presence of the 263 Sultan the latter would come down from his throne as a mark of respect, and if he were on a chair he would rise to his feet. Each one of them would then make obeisance to one another and he would sit down beside the Sultan on the same carpet. When he rose the Sultan rose also and they made obeisance to one another, and when he went outside the audience hall a carpet was placed for him to sit on as long as he might wish, after which he would return home. He used to do this twice a day.

An anecdote showing the Sultan's respect for him. During his stay at Dihlī the vizier arrived from the land of Bengal, and the Sultan gave orders to all the principal amīrs to go out to meet him. Finally he went out himself to greet him and showed him great honour, and pavilions were set up in the city just as is done for the Sultan's entry. The Caliph's son went out to meet him also, together with the doctors of the

[102] See p. 738 below.

[103] Such assignments in the reign of Sultan Muḥammad were made simply to provide stipends and carried no administrative duties with them: see W. H. Moreland, *The Agrarian System of Muslim India*, Cambridge 1929 pp. 51–2.

law, the qāḍīs and the notables, and when the Sultan re-264 turned | to his palace he said to the vizier 'Go to the residence of *Makhdūm-zāda.*' This was what he used to call him, and it means 'the son of the master'. So the vizier went to visit him and made him a gift of two thousand tangahs of gold and many woven stuffs. The amīr Qabūla and others of the principal amīrs and I myself were present on this occasion.

A similar anecdote. Amongst those who came to visit the Sultan was the king of Ghazna, named Bahrām,[104] between whom and the Caliph's son there was an enmity of long standing. The Sultan gave orders for his lodging in one of the houses of the town of Sīrī, which belonged to the Caliph's son, and ordered that a mansion should be built for him there.[105] The Caliph's son on hearing of this, flew into a rage and, going to the Sultan's palace, sat down on the carpet on which he was accustomed to sit, sent for the vizier and said to him 'Make my salutations to *Khūnd 'Ālam,* and say to him 265 that everything that | he has given to me is still in my residence. I have disposed of none of it, but on the contrary it has increased under my care, and I shall no longer stay with you.' Then he rose and went back. The vizier asked one of his suite the cause of this behaviour and was informed that it was due to the Sultan's orders to build a mansion for the king of Ghazna in the town of Sīrī.

The vizier then went in to the Sultan and informed him of this, whereupon he mounted at once with ten of his household and came to the residence of the Caliph's son. He asked to be announced to him and dismounted from his horse outside the palace, where the general public were accustomed to dismount, then on meeting him made his apologies to him. The Caliph's son accepted his apology, but the Sultan said to him 'By God, I shall not know that you are content with me until you place your foot on my neck.' He replied 'This I can never do, even if I were condemned to death.' The Sultan then said 'I swear by my head that you positively must do this.' Then he placed his head on the ground and the great king Qabūla

[104] Not identified. Since Ghazna was a dependency of Herāt (see *Ta'rīkh-Nāma-i Harāt,* 678) its 'king' was presumably the governor on behalf of Mu'izz al-Dīn Ḥusain.

[105] This reading, adopted by the French editors, appears to be confirmed by what follows. The variant readings are in fact incomprehensible.

took the foot | of the Caliph's son in his hand and set it on the 266 Sultan's neck. Then he rose and said 'Now I know that you are satisfied with me and my heart is at ease.' This is a strange story, the like of which has not been told of any other king.

I was present with this person on a festival day when the great king [Qabūla] brought him three 'open' ceremonial robes[106] from the Sultan; these had in place of the usual silk fastenings pearl buttons of the size of a large hazelnut. The great king stood waiting at the gate of his residence until he came out and then clothed him with them. What the Sultan gave him is beyond reckoning and limit, yet with all that the Caliph's son was the most miserly of God's creatures. On the subject of his miserliness there are told such strange stories and so astonishing to the hearer, that he can be said to have occupied in degree of avarice the position which the Sultan occupied in degree of generosity. We shall now mention some incidents of this kind. |

Stories of the avarice of the Caliph's son. He and I were on 267 terms of friendship. I used to visit him frequently in his house and I even left with him a son of mine, whom I had called Aḥmad, when I left Dihlī. I do not know what God has done with either of them. I said to him one day 'Why do you eat by yourself and never invite your friends to join in your meals?' He replied 'I cannot bear to see them there in large numbers eating my food.' So he used to eat alone and to give his friend Muḥammad ibn Abu'l-Sharafī some of the food for whomsoever he wished, and himself disposed of the rest.

On my visits to him I observed that the vestibule of the palace in which he lived was dark and unlighted. I often saw him picking up little pieces of wood suitable for burning in his garden; indeed he filled whole store houses with them and when I spoke to him about this he said to me 'They may be needed.' He used to employ his attendants, mamlūks, and pages on | work in his garden and on laying it out,[107] and he 268 used to say 'I am not willing that they should eat my food and do no work.' On one occasion I had a debt which I was called upon to pay, and he said to me one day 'Truly I did

[106] For the term *mufarraj* see Dozy, s.v.

[107] The term (*binā'*) perhaps implies masonry or stonework.

intend to pay your debt for you, but I could not find it in my heart to do so or bring myself to it.'

Anecdote. He once told me the following story. 'I went out from Baghdād (he said) with three other persons (one of whom was his friend Muḥammad ibn Abu'l-Sharafī). We were walking on foot and had no provisions with us. We stopped near a water-spring at a certain village and one of us found a dirham in the spring. We discussed what we should do with one dirham and having agreed to buy bread with it sent one of our number to do so. The baker in that village refused to 269 sell bread | by itself but would sell it only along with an equal value of straw,[108] so he brought both bread and straw from him. We threw away the straw since we had no animal with us to eat it, and divided the bread amongst us bite about. Now my fortunes have come to the state in which you see them.' I said to him 'It is your duty to praise God for His favour to you and to give liberally to the poor and the needy and justify your wealth by giving alms.' But he said 'I cannot do it', and in fact I never saw him being liberal with anything or doing a generous action—may God preserve us from meanness!

Anecdote. One day at Baghdād, after my return from India, I was sitting at the gate of the Mustanṣirīya college, which was built by his ancestor, the Commander of the Faithful al-Mustanṣir (God be pleased with him),[109] and I saw a young man in poor circumstances running after a man who was coming out of the college. One of the students said to me 270 'This | youth that you see is the son of the amīr Muḥammad, the grandson of the Caliph al-Mustanṣir, who is in India.' So I called him and said to him 'I have just come from India and can give you news of your father.' But he answered 'I have had news of him recently' and went hurrying off after that man. I asked who the man was and was told that he was the intendant of the endowment, that this youth was imām

[108] Literally 'would sell bread for a *qīrāṭ* and straw for a *qīrāṭ*'. The *qīrāṭ* was both a monetary unit (in 'Irāq, one-twelfth of a silver dirham = 0·247 grammes) and a unit of weight (in 'Irāq, one-fourteenth of a dirham weight = 0·247 grammes) (Hinz, *Islamische Masse*, Leiden, 1955, pp. 2, 27). The phrase therefore means 'one *qīrāṭ* of straw for each *qīrāṭ* of bread', or half a dirham's worth of each (reckoned not by weight but by price).

[109] See vol. II, p. 332.

[prayer-leader] in one of the mosques at a remuneration of one dirham a day, and that he was asking for the pay due to him from this man. My astonishment at this was unbounded —by God, if he had sent him a single pearl of all those pearls which adorned the robes of honour that he received from the Sultan, the boy would have been well-off. May God protect us from such a state of things! |

The Sultan's gift to the amīr Saif al-Dīn Ghadā, son of Hibat Allāh son of Muhannā, the amīr of the Arabs in Syria.[110] When this amīr came to visit the Sultan he received him hospitably and lodged him in the palace of the Sultan Jalāl al-Dīn inside the city of Dihlī.[111] This castle is called *Kushki-la'l*, which means 'the red palace', and it is a huge mansion which includes an exceptionally large audience hall and an immense vestibule. Near the gate there is a pavilion which overlooks this audience hall and also the second audience hall, through which one enters into the palace.[112] The Sultan Jalāl al-Dīn used to sit in this pavilion while they played mall before him in this audience hall. I went into this palace when the amīr took up his residence in it and I found it filled with furniture, beds, carpets, etc., but all of this was tattered and useless; for it is their custom in India to abandon a Sultan's palace | when he dies, with all that is in it, leaving it untouched, and his successor builds a palace for himself. When I entered it I went through it thoroughly and climbed up to the top of it. To see it in this condition served me as a lesson which brought tears to my eyes. With me at the time was the doctor of the law and of medicine, the talented Jamāl al-Dīn al-Maghribī, of Gharnāṭa (Granada) by origin although born at Bijāya and now resident in India, where he had come with his father and now has children. He recited to me as we viewed this scene

271

272

> As for their Sultans, ask the clay of them—
> Those powerful heads are now but empty skulls.[113]

[110] For Muḥanna b. 'Isā, chief of the Āl Faḍl in Syria, see vol. I, p. 107 and n. 152. Nine of his sons are mentioned in the biographical works, but Hibat Allāh is not among them, and Ghadā seems to be otherwise unknown.

[111] See p. 638 above.

[112] This was presumably an open court, the term *mashwar* being used indiscriminately for an open or a roofed-in hall.

[113] The verses offer the typical word-play of later Arabic poetry: 'ask the

It was in this palace that his marriage feast took place, as we shall relate shortly. The Sultan had a great affection for the Arabs and used to show them special favour and speak highly of their virtues. When this amīr visited him he made large 273 gifts to him and treated him with great munificence. | Once when there was brought before him the gift of A'ẓam Malik al-Bāyazīdī from the province of Mānikbūr,[114] he presented the amīr with eleven thoroughbred horses, and on another occasion he gave him ten horses equipped with gilded saddles and with gilded bridles. Then over and above that he married him to his sister Fīrūz Khūnda.

The marriage of the amīr Saif al-Dīn with the Sultan's sister. When the Sultan gave orders for his sister's marriage to the amīr Ghadā he designated the malik Fatḥallāh called *Shawnawīs*[115] to make all arrangements for the marriage feast and its expenses, and he designated me to attend on the amīr Ghadā and to remain with him during those days. The malik Fatḥallāh brought marquees and with them he covered the two audience halls in the Red Palace above-mentioned. 274 In each hall he erected a pavilion of extraordinary size | and furnished it with fine [cushions and] carpets. Shams al-Dīn al-Tabrīzī, the amīr of the musicians, came with the male singers and the female singers and dancers, all of whom are the Sultan's slaves. [The intendant] brought cooks, bakers, roasters, pastry cooks, butlers and betel-servers, and cattle and birds were slaughtered and they continued to supply the people with food for fifteen days. The principal amīrs and distinguished foreigners were present night and day.

Two nights before the night of the wedding procession the khātūns came from the Sultan's palace to this mansion, and having decorated it and furnished it luxuriously, they sent for the amīr Saif al-Dīn (who was an Arab and a stranger and without kinsfolk), put him in the midst of them and made him sit on a cushion which had been placed for him. The Sultan had given orders that his step-mother, the mother

---

clay' (*sali 'ṭṭina*) jibes with 'sultans' (*salāṭīnu*) and 'powerful' ('*iẓāmu*) with 'empty skulls' ('*iẓāma*, lit. 'bones').

[114] Al-Bāyazīdī is mentioned later (p. 731), as a relative by marriage of the Sultan. For Mānikpur see p. 638 above.

[115] Apparently a Persian compound meaning 'marriage-writer'.

of his brother Mubārak Khān, should take the place of the mother of the amīr Ghadā, that another lady among the khātūns should take | the place of his sister, another that of his paternal aunt, and another that of his maternal aunt, so that he might feel himself to be amongst his own people. When they sat him down on the cushion they dyed his hands and his feet with henna,[116] and the rest of them stood before him singing and dancing. After that they withdrew to the mansion in which the wedding was to take place and he stayed behind with his principal companions. 275

The Sultan designated a body of amīrs to be of his party and another body to be of the bride's party. It is their custom that the bride's party stands before the door of the apartment in which the bride will unveil herself to her husband, and the husband comes with his party but they cannot enter until they have overcome the bride's supporters, or given them some thousands of dinars if they cannot get the better of them. After sunset [on the wedding day] there was brought to the amīr Ghadā a ceremonial robe of blue silk embroidered and encrusted with jewels; the jewels covered it so completely | that its colour was not visible because of the quantity of them, and it was the same with his turban. I never saw a more beautiful robe than this one, although I have seen the robes given by the Sultan to his other brothers-in-law, like the son of the malik of maliks 'Imād al-Dīn al-Simnānī,[117] the son of the Malik al-'Ulamā, the son of the Shaikh al-Islām, and the son of Ṣadr Jahān al-Bukhārī,[118] and there was not one of them to match this robe. 276

The amīr Saif al-Dīn then mounted along with his supporters and slaves, each of them carrying in his hand a staff prepared for the occasion. They had made a sort of crown of jasmine, muskrose and *raibūl*,[119] with a veil long enough to cover the head and chest of its wearer; but when they brought it to the amīr to put over his head, he refused to do so. He was [after all] an Arab of the desert, unfamiliar with the ways of kings and settled folk. I tried to persuade him

[116] This practice, universal for brides, seems to be much less commonly applied to bridegrooms.

[117] See p. 676 above.

[118] See p. 569 above.

[119] See p. 622, n. 16 above.

277 and adjured him | until at last he put it on his head and [so] came to the *bāb al-ṣarf*,[120] which they call also by the name of *bāb al-ḥaram*, at which the bride's party was stationed. He led a proper Arab charge upon them with his supporters and unhorsed all those who stood in their way. So the amīr and his men vanquished them, and the bride's party could make no kind of firm resistance. When the Sultan was told of this, he was pleased with his exploit.

When the amīr entered the audience-hall, the bride had already been placed on a high pulpit, adorned with brocade [hangings] and encrusted with jewels. The hall was filled with women, and the female musicians had brought all kinds of musical instruments; all of them were standing on their feet to show him honour and respect. He entered on horseback [and proceeded] until he came up to the pulpit, when he dismounted, and made the gesture of homage on reaching its first step. The bride rose up, standing until he mounted to the top, when she gave him betel with her own hand, and after eating it he sat down below the step on which she had 278 stood. | Gold dinars were thrown over those of his friends who were present,[121] and the women picked them up; at the same time, the singing-girls were singing away, and drums, bugles and fifes were sounded outside the gate. The amīr then rose, took his bride by the hand, and came down, she following him. He mounted his horse on which he rode over the carpets and rugs, and dinars were [again] thrown over him and his companions. The bride was placed in a litter, which was carried by slaves on their shoulders to his palace, conducted by the khātūns riding on horseback in front of her while the rest of the women walked. Every time the procession passed by the residence of an amīr or person of consequence, he came out to [salute] them and scattered over them gold and silver coins, as dictated by his interest or

[120] Apparently meaning 'the gate of repelling' *Bāb al-ḥaram* means only 'gate of the secluded quarters' (i.e. for female relatives). Mahdi Husain notes the close similarity of the ceremony as described by I.B. to Hindu usage (see Mahdi Husain, pp. xlvii–xlviii), particularly the sham fight and the crown of flowers (*sehra*). See also Hughes, *Dictionary of Islam* s.v. Marriage.

[121] This was a traditional Arab custom, so closely associated with a marriage that the term for 'scattering' i.e. of coins (*nithār*), was used as a synonym for it.

concern, until they brought her to the palace of the amīr Saif al-Dīn.

On the next day, the bride sent robes and gold and silver coins to all of her husband's companions. The Sultan also gave to each one of them a horse | with its saddle and bridle 279 and a purse of silver coins, ranging from one thousand to two hundred dinars. The malik Fatḥallāh [the *shawnawīs*] presented the khātūns with silk robes of divers sorts and purses as well, and made similar presents to the musicians. It is the custom in India that no one should give presents to the musicians;[122] only the director of the wedding ceremony may do so. A meal was served to the whole populace that day and [with this] the wedding ceremonies came to an end. The Sultan gave orders that the amīr Ghadā should be given [a grant for] the lands of Mālwa, al-Guzarāt, Kanbāya and Nahrawāla, and he appointed the above-mentioned Fatḥallāh as substitute for him in their government.[123] [In fine] the Sultan showed him immense honour, but he was a raw bedouin, who did not measure up to this standard; the rudeness of the desert folk was his dominant trait, and it brought him to disaster [only] twenty days after his wedding.

The imprisonment of the amīr Ghadā. Twenty days after his wedding | it happened that he came to the Sultan's palace 280 and made to enter. The amīr of the *barddārīya* (who are the high-ranking doorkeepers)[124] stopped him, but the Arab would not listen to him and tried to force his way in. The doorkeeper then seized his *dabbūqa*, that is his braided lock,[125] and pulled him back, whereupon the amīr struck him with a

[122] The text has the masculine plural pronoun, which, however, would seem from the context to include the female musicians.

[123] See n. 103 above. For Mālwa see p. 639 above and for Nahrawāla p. 673 above. 'In their government', literally 'over them', presumably means in collecting the revenues from them.

[124] Apparently Persian *parda-dār*, literally 'doorkeeper of the inner chambers', but this does not seem to fit the situation here; the term *khawāṣṣ*, translated as 'high-ranking', implies that they are in some way distinguished by special functions. Perhaps it is a conflation or confusion with *bārdād* (*amīr al-bār*), described as the officer in charge of admission to the sultan, ap. Bundārī (ed. Houtsma, Leiden 1889) p. 117.

[125] 'Long plaits are the pride of a childishly vain (*jāhil*) Bedouin, and often lead to his undoing. When pursued, he can be easily captured if the enemy catches hold of his plaits' (Alois Musil, *The Manners and Customs of the Rwala Bedouins*, New York, 1928, p. 116).

baton that he found to his hand there, and so violently as to cause him to bleed. Now this person who received the blows was one of the great amīrs; his father was known as 'the qāḍī of Ghazna' and was a descendant of the Sultan Maḥmūd ibn Sabuktagīn.[126] The Sultan used to address him as 'father', and to call this son of his 'brother'. So, when he went into the Sultan's presence with blood on his garments and told him how the amīr had behaved, the Sultan pondered for a moment and then said 'The qāḍī will decide the case between you.' The assault was (in fact) a criminal act, for which the Sultan will not forgive any of his subjects and which is inevitably punished by death, but he showed forbearance to the amīr because he was a foreigner.

281 The qāḍī Kamāl | al-Dīn was present in the audience-hall, and the Sultan ordered the malik Tatar to attend the qāḍī's sitting with them. Tatar had made the pilgrimage to Mecca and sojourned there, and spoke Arabic well. When he came in with the two of them, he said to the amīr [Ghadā] 'You struck him? Rather say "No" ',[127] his intention being to instruct him how to plead. But the amīr Saif al-Dīn was a light-witted and rash person,[128] and he said 'Of course I struck him.' The father of the man who had been beaten came and tried to get the matter settled amicably between them, but Saif al-Dīn would not yield. So the qāḍī ordered him to be imprisoned for that night. And by God, his wife neither sent him bedding to sleep on nor even asked for news of him, out of fear of the Sultan; his associates too were afraid and put their valuables into safekeeping. I had it in mind to visit him in the prison, but then one of the great amīrs happened to meet me, and on gathering from me that I meant to visit him said to me 'Can you have forgotten?' This was to
282 remind me of an incident | that had occurred to me in connection with a visit to the shaikh Shihāb al-Dīn, the son of

[126] The famous sultan of Ghazna (998–1030): see p. 590 n. 203 above.

[127] The malik's Arabic is somewhat loose, but the meaning is clear enough.

[128] *Jāhilan* is precisely the term quoted by Musil (n. 125) above: for the second, the obvious reading is *mughtarran*, the gloss for which in a contemporary dictionary (*al-Miṣbaḥ*, see Lane s.v.) ('thinking himself secure, and therefore not on his guard') fits the context exactly. One cannot imagine I.B. suddenly using an obsolete poetic word like *mughathmiran*.

the shaikh al-Jām,[129] and how the Sultan had intended to kill me for this reason as I shall tell later. So I turned back and did not visit him. The amīr Ghadā was released from his imprisonment about noon; thereafter, the Sultan ostentatiously disregarded him, retracted the orders that he had given for his territorial grant, and had in mind to force him to leave India.

Now the Sultan had a brother-in-law named Mughīth, a son of the 'king of kings',[130] about whose conduct the Sultan's sister used to complain to her brother, until finally she died. Her slave-girls stated that her death was due to the violence with which he treated her; there was, besides, some cause for doubt as to his legitimate descent. So the Sultan wrote [an order] with his own hand 'Let the foundling be expelled,' meaning Mughīth, and then wrote after this 'and let *mūsh khwār* be expelled too'. The meaning of this is 'eater of rats', and by that he meant the amīr Ghadā, because the Arabs of the desert eat the jerboa, which is a kind of rat.[131] On his orders to drive them out the naqībs came to the amīr to expel him; he went into | his house, intending to bid farewell to his wife,[132] but the naqībs made a concerted effort to seek him out and he emerged in tears. 283

At this point I went to the Sultan's palace and spent the night in it. One of the amīrs asked me the reason why I remained overnight, and when I told him that I had come to plead for the amīr Saif al-Dīn, that he might be recalled and not exiled, he said 'It can't be done.' But I said to him 'By God, I shall continue to spend the night in the Sultan's palace, even if I have to stay for a hundred nights until he is recalled'. This was reported to the Sultan, and he did order that he should be recalled and commanded further that he should be attached to the service of the amīr Malik Qabūla al-Lahawrī. He remained for four years in his service, riding when he rode and accompanying him on his journeys, and as

[129] For the story of the shaikh Shihāb al-Dīn see pp. 697–700 below.

[130] I.e. one of the sons of the 'kings', who is called by the Sultan by that name.

[131] This contemptuous phrase was a traditional weapon in the arsenal of Persian polemic against the Arabs.

[132] This is the obvious meaning, although I.B. expresses himself a little confusedly.

a result of this training learned good manners and refinement. The Sultan restored him to his former honours, gave him assignments of land and the command of troops, and elevated him in rank. |

284 *The marriage arranged by the Sultan between the two daughters of his vizier and the two sons of Khudhāwand-Zāda Qiwām al-Dīn, who came to his court along with us.*

When Khudhāwand-Zāda[133] came to the court, the Sultan bestowed on him an immense revenue and lavish benefactions, and went to great lengths in showing him honour. Subsequently he married Khudhāwand-Zāda's two sons to the two daughters of the vizier Khwāja Jahān. The vizier himself was absent at that time, so the Sultan came to his residence by night and attended the ceremony of the marriage contract as though in the capacity of deputy for the vizier. He stood until the Grand Qāḍī read the statement of the dowry,[134] while the qāḍīs, amīrs and shaikhs remained seated. The Sultan took up with his own hands the fabrics and purses [specified in the deeds of dowry] and placed them before the qāḍī and the two sons of Khudhāwand-Zāda. [At this point] the amīrs rose up, protesting that the Sultan should not take upon himself the placing of these gifts before the qāḍī and bridegrooms, but he commanded them to sit down, and after ordering one of the high amīrs to take his place he withdrew. |

285 *Anecdote on the humility of the Sultan and his sense of equity.* One of the Hindu chiefs brought a claim against him that he had killed the chief's brother without just cause, and cited him to appear before the qāḍī. Whereupon he went on foot and unarmed to the qāḍī's tribunal, saluted and made the sign of homage, having previously sent orders to the qāḍī that on his arrival at the tribunal, he (the qāḍī) should not stand up for him nor move from his place. He walked up to the tribunal and remained standing before the qāḍī, who gave judgement against him, [decreeing] that he should give

[133] See pp. 565–6 above.

[134] *Ṣadāq* or *mahr*. The statement of the dowry settled upon the bride and the public consent of the bridegroom to it constitute the legal formality of marriage. The bride is not present in person, but is represented by a *walī* (father or other near male relative), and it was this function which the Sultan took upon himself.

satisfaction to his opponent for his brother's blood, and he did so.

A similar anecdote. An individual, who was a Muslim, once brought a claim against the Sultan that the latter owed him certain moneys. They argued the case before the qāḍī, and judgement was given against the Sultan, enjoining him to pay the sum, which he did. |

A similar anecdote. A young boy, one of the sons of the maliks, brought a claim against the Sultan that the latter had struck him without just cause, and cited him before the qāḍī. Judgement was given against the Sultan, to the effect that he should give the plaintiff monetary compensation, if he would accept that, or alternatively allow him to exercise his right to retaliate in kind. I was present that day when the Sultan returned to his audience-hall, and saw him summon the boy, give him a stick and say to him, 'By my head, you shall strike me just as I struck you.' Whereupon the boy took the stick and gave him twenty-one blows, so that I actually saw his high cap fly off his head. 286

His insistence on the observance of the ritual prayers. The Sultan was strict about the observance of the prayers, making congregational attendance at them obligatory, and punishing any dereliction of them most severely. Indeed, he put to death for neglecting them on one day alone nine persons, | of whom one was a singer. He used to send out men, specially charged with this duty, to the bazaars; any person found in them after the commencement of prayers was punished, and he went so far as to punish the *satā'irīs*,[135] [i.e. the grooms] who hold the riding beasts of the servitors at the gate of the audience-hall, when they disregarded the [hours of] prayer. He gave orders also that the people in general should be required to show a knowledge of the obligations of ablution, prayer, and the binding articles of Islām. They used to be questioned on these matters; if anyone failed to give correct answers he was punished, and they made a practice of studying them with one another in the audience-hall and the bazaars, and setting them down in writing. 287

[135] Dozy (s.v.) derives the word from *sitāra*, 'saddle-cloth'. His references appear to indicate that the term was used chiefly in the Maghrib, but it will be noted that I.B. has to explain its meaning.

His insistence on executing the legal provisions of the Sharī'a.[136] He was strict in upholding the Sharī'a, and set up the following practice. He ordered his brother Mubārak Khān[137] to sit [in the regular judicial sessions] in the audience-hall along with the Grand Qāḍī Kamāl al-Dīn. [The judge 288 sat] in [a chamber] there with a lofty cupola | and furnished with rugs; in it he had a raised divan smothered in cushions, just like the Sultan's divan, and the Sultan's brother would sit to his right. If a claim for debt were laid against any of the great amīrs and he refused to discharge it to his creditor, the men [in the service] of the Sultan's brother would bring him before the qāḍī so that he might execute justice upon him.

His abolition of oppressive dues and impositions, and his sessions for the rendering of justice to the wronged. In the year forty-one[138] the Sultan ordered the abolition of duties on goods and merchandise[139] in his territories, and that nothing should be taken [in taxation] from the people except the alms-tax and the tithe exclusively.[140] He used to sit in person every Tuesday and Thursday in an open space in front of the audience-hall, for the purpose of investigating complaints of oppression.[141] None [of the officers of state] stood in atten- 289 dance on him on these occasions except the Amīr Ḥājib, | the Khāṣṣ Ḥājib, the 'master' of the Chamberlains, and the 'honour' of the Chamberlains,[142] nobody else, and no person who wished to make a complaint might be hindered from presenting himself before him. He designated four of the

[136] I have preferred the more familiar form *sharī'a* to *shar'*. This is the body of legal doctrines and rules derived from the Qur'ān, Prophetic Tradition, and secondary sources; it includes both ritual duties and decisions relating to family, civil, and criminal law.

[137] See p. 664 above.

[138] A.H. 741 = 27 June, 1340 to 16 June, 1341.

[139] *Mukūs*, applied to all market taxes, octroi duties, etc., and commonly translated 'illegal taxes' since they have no basis in Islamic Law: see *E.I.* s.v. *maks*.

[140] See p. 605 above.

[141] This was the traditional tribunal of the ruler in person, for the redressing of abuses (*maẓālim*) committed by high military and administrative officers who were out of reach of the ordinary qāḍī's jurisdiction. See E. Tyan, *Histoire de l'organisation judiciaire au pays d'Islam*, tome II, Beirut 1943, esp. pp. 238 sqq.

[142] See p. 660 above.

principal amīrs to sit at the four gates of the audience-hall to take the petitions from the complainants. The fourth of the amīrs was his uncle's son Malik Fīrūz.[143] If the amīr at the first gate accepted the complainant's petition, well and good; but if he did not, the second or third or fourth [amīr] would accept it. If all of them refused to accept it, he would take it to Ṣadr al-Jahān, the qāḍī of the mamlūks;[144] either he would accept it from him or else the complainant would appeal [directly] to the Sultan. Then, if it was proved to the Sultan that he had taken his petition to one of these persons, and that the latter had not accepted it from him, the Sultan would teach that person a lesson. All the complainants collected on the other days were examined by the Sultan after the last evening prayer. |

His distribution of food during the famine. When the severe drought reigned over the lands of India and Sind and prices rose to such a height that the *mann* of wheat[145] reached six dinars, the Sultan ordered that the whole population of Dihlī should be given six months' supplies from the [royal] granary, at the rate of one and a half *raṭls* (that is to say, Maghribī *raṭls*)[146] per day per person, small or great, free or slave. The jurists and qāḍīs went out to compile the registers with the [names of the] inhabitants of the various quarters);[147] they would [then] present them [to the authorities] and each person would be given enough to provide him with food for six months. 290

This Sultan's murders and reprehensible actions. In spite of all that we have related of his humility, his sense of fairness,

[143] But in the passage cited in the preceding note Malik Fīrūz is identical with the Amīr Ḥājib: see also p. 665 above.

[144] This is presumably not the same person as the Grand Qāḍī, Ṣadr al-Jahān Kamāl al-Dīn [see p. 617 above], but he is not mentioned elsewhere by I.B.

[145] About 15¼ kilograms: see vol. II, p. 312, n. 131.

[146] The *raṭl* of Delhi was half a *mann* i.e. about 16½ lbs. (Thomas, *Pathan Kings*, 223, note *e*). The *raṭl* of Morocco was approximately one English pound avoirdupois (468·75 grammes, according to Hinz, *Islamische Masse*, p. 32). In a later passage (vol. IV, p. 210 Ar.) he evaluates the *raṭl* of Delhi at about 20 *raṭls* of Morocco.

[147] *Ḥārāt*, strictly the enclosed quarters into which the mediaeval Near Eastern city was divided (see Gibb and Bowen, *Islamic Society and the West*, vol. I, part I, London 1950, p. 279), but it is doubtful whether Delhi was similarly divided at this time.

his compassion for the needy, and his extraordinary[148] liberality, the Sultan was far too free in shedding blood. It was but seldom that the entrance to his palace was without a
291 corpse | and I used often to see men being executed at his gate and [their bodies] left to lie there. One day as I arrived my horse shied with me; I saw a white fragment on the ground and said 'What is this?' One of my companions said, 'It is the torso of a man who was cut into three pieces.' The Sultan used to punish small faults and great, without respect of persons, whether men of learning or piety or noble descent. Every day there are brought to the audience-hall hundreds of people, chained, pinioned, and fettered, and those who are for execution are executed, those for torture tortured, and those for beating beaten. It is his custom to have all persons who are in his prison brought to the audience-hall every day except Friday; on this day they are not haled [before him] but it is a day of respite for them, on which they may clear themselves and remain at ease—may God deliver us from misfortune! |

292 *His execution of his brother.*[149] He had a [half] brother named Mas'ūd Khān, whose mother was the daughter of the Sultan 'Alā' al-Dīn, and who was one of the most beautiful persons I have seen on earth. The Sultan accused this brother of rebellion against him and questioned him on the matter. Mas'ūd Khān confessed to the fact through fear of torture, for anyone who denies an accusation of this sort brought against him by the Sultan is put to the torture, and people consider execution a lighter affliction than torture. The Sultan gave orders for his execution and he was beheaded in the midst of the bazaar, and remained exposed there for three days, according to their usage. The mother of the executed prince had been stoned to death in that same place two years before, on her confession of adultery. Her stoning was by [decree of] the qāḍī Kamāl al-Dīn. |

293 *His execution of three hundred and fifty men at one time.* On one occasion he designated a section of the army to proceed with the malik Yūsuf Bughra to engage the infidels in part of

[148] The term *khāriq al-'āda*, 'breaking the natural order of things', is technically employed for 'miraculous'.

[149] I.B. is apparently the sole narrator of this incident.

the hill country bordering on the province of Dihlī. Yūsuf set out, and most of the troops with him, but a number of them stayed behind. Yūsuf wrote to the Sultan to inform him of this, whereupon the Sultan gave orders for the patrolling of the city and the arrest of all who were discovered of those who had remained. This was done, three hundred and fifty of them were arrested, and he ordered the execution of the whole lot of them, so they were executed.

His torture and execution of the shaikh Shihāb al-Dīn. The shaikh Shihāb al-Dīn was the son of the shaikh al-Jām al-Khurāsānī after whose ancestor the city of al-Jām in Khurāsān is named, as we have already related.[150] He was one of the major shaikhs | noted for probity and virtue, and used to fast uninterruptedly for fourteen days. The Sultans Quṭb al-Dīn and Tughluq held him in high esteem and used to visit him and to solicit his blessing. When the Sultan Muḥammad succeeded, he wished to employ the shaikh in some service of his, for it was his practice to assign offices to jurists, shaikhs and devotees, on the argument that the first generation [of the Caliphs] (God be pleased with them) were not in the habit of appointing to office any but men of [religious] learning and probity. The shaikh Shihāb al-Dīn, however, declined to accept office, and when the Sultan raised the point with him in his public audience, he openly refused to yield and give his consent.[151] The Sultan then commanded the venerable shaikh and jurist Ḍiyā' al-Dīn of Simnān to pluck out the hair of his beard. But Ḍiyā' al-Dīn refused to do so, and bluntly rejected his command, whereupon the Sultan gave orders to pluck out the beards of both of them, and plucked out they were. He banished Ḍiyā' al-Dīn to the land of Tiling, and subsequently appointed him as qāḍī | in Warangal, where he died. Shihāb al-Dīn he banished to Dawlat Ābād, where he remained for seven years. He then

294

295

[150] The shaikh Shihāb al-Dīn, a descendant of the shaikh al-Jām (p. 580 above), was deeply honoured by the sultans of India, but was eventually disgraced by Sultan Muḥammad and executed, as the following passage relates. As I.B. had a close relationship with the shaikh, he was deprived of his qāḍī-ship and nearly put to death.

[151] Since the early centuries of Islam, the more scrupulous religious leaders refused all service under or association with the rulers, on the ground that the practice of administration was tainted by illegalities and abuses.

sent for him, received him with great honour and respect and appointed him over the *dīwān al-mustakhraj*,[152] that is to say, the department that deals with the arrears of the revenue officers by 'extracting' them from these officials by beatings and exemplary punishments. Later on, he honoured him still more highly, and issued an order to the amīrs to make their personal salutations to him and to carry out his instructions; indeed, no one in the Sultan's palace was higher than he.

When the Sultan removed [from Dihlī] to take up residence on the river Gang, where he built the palace known as *Sarg Duwār* (which means 'the likeness of Paradise'),[153] and ordered the people[154] to build there as well, the shaikh Shihāb al-Dīn asked his permission to remain in the capital. He was allowed to do so and moved out to some uncultivated land at a distance of six miles from Dihlī, where he excavated for himself an immense cave in the interior of which he fitted 296 up chambers, storerooms, an oven and a bath. | He supplied this land with water from the river Jūn, brought it under cultivation, and gained a considerable fortune from its produce, because these were years of drought. He stayed there for two and a half years, corresponding to the period of the Sultan's absence. His slaves used to work that land during the day, and at night they would go into the cave and close it upon themselves and their cattle for fear of the infidel marauders, since these occupied an inaccessible mountain thereabouts.

When the Sultan returned to his capital, the shaikh went out to welcome him and met him some seven miles from the city. The Sultan showed him high honour and embraced him

[152] Commonly translated 'bureau of extortion', but its functions were precisely as defined by I.B. on the underlying assumption that deficiencies in revenue payments to the central treasury were due to their dilapidation by the officials. The translation of *tankīl* by 'torture' is possible but *ad pensum* rather than *ad verbum*.

[153] In consequence of the severe famine already mentioned (p. 695 above) which began in 1335 and continued for several years, the Sultan in 1338 moved to a temporary capital near Kanauj, on the Ganges, about 200 m. S.E. of Delhi. His palace was called Sargadwārī (i.e. Sarg-dvāra; 'gate of Paradise').

[154] Presumably meaning here the army, court, and administrative officers.

on their meeting. Shihāb al-Dīn returned to his cave; then, some days later, when the Sultan sent for him, he refused to come at his command. Thereupon the Sultan sent Mukhliṣ al-Mulk al-Nadharbārī[155] (who was one of the great maliks) to him; the envoy spoke to him in a tactful way and warned him of the consequences of the Sultan's anger, | but he 297 replied 'never shall I serve an oppressor'. When Mukhliṣ al-Mulk reported this to the Sultan on his return, he received the order to fetch the shaikh, which he did. The Sultan said to him 'Is it you who says that I am an oppressor?' The shaikh replied 'Indeed, you are an oppressor, and such-and-such are instances of your tyrannical conduct,' mentioning a number of things such as his devastation of the city of Dihlī and his expulsion of its population.[156] The Sultan then took his own sword, handed it to [the Grand Qāḍī] Ṣadr al-Jahān, and said 'Establish the fact that I am an oppressor, and cut off my head with this sword'. Shihāb al-Dīn said to him, 'Anyone who is willing to offer evidence of this will be put to death, but you yourself are aware of your tyrannical conduct'. The Sultan ordered him to be handed over to the malik Nukbiya, the chief of the Duwaidārs,[157] who put four irons on his feet and pinioned his hands [to his neck]. He stayed in that condition for fourteen days, fasting continuously, neither eating nor drinking. Every day of the fourteen he was brought to the audience-hall, where the jurists and shaikhs were assembled, and they would say to him, | 'withdraw your 298 statement'. But he would say, 'I shall not withdraw it, and I wish to join the ranks of those who have witnessed to the Faith and suffered martyrdom.' On the fourteenth day, the Sultan sent him food by the hand of Mukhliṣ al-Mulk, but he refused to eat, saying 'My allotted sustenance from the [things of this] earth has come to an end—take your food back to him.' When the Sultan was informed of this, he straightway ordered that the shaikh should be fed with five

[155] I.e. of Nadharbār (see vol. IV, p. 51 Ar.). There seems to be no authority for the suggestion that the word should be read *nudhr-bār*, i.e. admonisher.

[156] See pp. 707–8 below.

[157] *Duwaidār* is not a diminutive but stands for *dawēdār*, a variant of *dawādār*, (*dawātdār*), 'pen-holder', the title of the military officer who was in charge of the chancery; cf. vol. I, p. 54, n. 168, and for Nukbiya pp. 665, 667 above and 713–14 below.

istārs[158] of human excrement—that is, two and a half *raṭls* of the Maghribī standard. Those who are charged with carrying out such punishments, who are a body of Indian infidels, took this stuff, stretched out the shaikh on his back, opened his mouth with forceps, dissolved the ordure in water, and made him drink it. On the following day he was brought to the house of the qāḍī Ṣadr al-Jahān. There the jurists, shaikhs, and leading foreign dignitaries were assembled; they admonished him in homilies, they besought him to withdraw his accusation, but he would have none of it and was beheaded—God Most High have mercy on him. |

299 *His killing of the jurist and professor 'Afīf al-Dīn of Kāsān*[159] *and of two other jurists along with him.* During the years of the famine, the Sultan had given orders to dig wells outside the capital, and have grain crops sown in those parts. He provided the cultivators with the seed, as well as with all that was necessary for cultivation in the way of money and supplies, and required them to cultivate these crops for the [royal] grain-store. When the jurist 'Afīf al-Dīn heard of this, he said 'This crop[160] will not produce what is hoped for.' Some informer told the Sultan what he had said, so the Sultan gaoled him, and said to him 'What reason have you to meddle with the government's business?' Some time later he released him, and as 'Afīf al-Dīn went to his house he was met on the way by two friends of his, also jurists, who said to him 'Praise be to God for your release,' to which our jurist replied 'Praise be to God who has delivered us from the evildoers'.[161] They then separated, but they had not reached their houses before this was reported to the Sultan, and he

300 commanded | all three to be fetched and brought before him. 'Take out this fellow', he said, referring to 'Afīf al-Dīn, 'and cut off his head baldrickwise', that is, the head is cut off along with an arm and part of the chest, 'and behead the other

[158] *Istār* is the Indian *sīr* or *ser*, evaluated at one-fortieth of a *mann* [see p. 695, n. 145 above] ap. Thomas, *Pathan Kings*, p. 222, n.*c.*, i.e. a little less than 400 grammes or about 14 oz. avoirdupois.

[159] A city to the north of Khokand, in Farghāna, on a tributary of the Syr Darya.

[160] From the context one would expect *makhzan* to have here its etymological sense rather than its Moroccan usage as 'public treasury'.

[161] Qur'ān, xxiii, 29.

two.' They said to him 'He deserves punishment, to be sure, for what he said, but in our case for what crime are you killing us?' He replied 'You heard what he said and did not disavow it, so you as good as agreed with it.' So they were all put to death, God Most High have mercy on them.

His killing of two other jurists, men of Sind, who were in his service. The Sultan commanded these two Sindī jurists to accompany an amīr whom he had appointed to a certain province, and said to them 'I have committed the affairs of the province and its population[162] to you two, and this amīr will go with you only to carry out your instructions to him.' They said | to him, 'We should act only as legal witnesses to his administration, and show him the right line of conduct for him to follow,' whereupon he replied 'All that you want is to devour my revenues and squander them, and lay the blame for it on this Turk, who has no experience.' They said 'God forbid, O Master of the World; this was not our intention,' but he replied to them 'You had no other intention. Take them off to the Shaikh-zāda al-Nihāwandī,' that is, the officer in charge of punishment by torture. 301

When they were taken to him, he said to them, 'The Sultan intends to put you to death anyway, so admit what he put it into your mouths to say, and don't expose yourselves to the torture.' But they swore, by God, they had meant nothing more than they had said, so he said to his tormentors[163] 'Give them a taste of something,' meaning of torture. They were laid flat upon their backs and on the chest of each of them there was placed a red-hot iron plate, which was pulled off after | a moment and took with it the flesh of their chests. After that, urine and cinders were brought and put on these wounds, whereupon they confessed that their intention had in fact been no other than as the Sultan had said, and they were criminals and deserving of death, that there was nothing due to them as of right, nor any claim to retaliation for their blood whether by near relatives or others. They wrote all this down in their own handwriting, and testified to it before 302

[162] *ra'īya*, the traditional legal term for the subject of a ruler, generally implying all persons liable to taxation, irrespective of religious or social distinctions.

[163] *zabāniya*, the term applied in Qur. xcvi, 18 to the tormentors of the damned in Hell.

the qāḍī, who then set his seal upon the attestation. It was stated in the document that their confession had been made without compulsion or coercion, for if they had said that they had been forced to make a confession they would have been most severely tortured, and they held that a quick beheading was better for them than to die under painful torture. So they were put to death, God Most High have mercy on them.

His killing of the shaikh Hūd. The shaikh-zāda named Hūd was the grandson of the pious shaikh, the saintly Rukn al-303 Dīn, son of Bahā' al-Dīn ibn Abī Zakarīyā | of Multān,[164] by his daughter. His grandfather, the shaikh Rukn al-Dīn, was held in high honour by the Sultan, as was also the latter's brother 'Imād al-Dīn, who closely resembled the Sultan and was killed during the battle with Kishlū Khān, as we shall relate in due course.[165] When 'Imād al-Dīn was killed, the Sultan gave his brother Rukn al-Dīn a hundred villages, to use their revenues for his own maintenance and to supply food to wayfarers in his hospice [at Multān]. On the death of the shaikh Rukn al-Dīn he had designated his grandson, the shaikh Hūd, as his successor in [control of] the hospice, but his succession was contested by the son of the shaikh Rukn al-Dīn's brother, who claimed that he had a prior right to inherit from his uncle. The two of them came before the Sultan while he was staying in Dawlat Ābād (which is eighty days' journey from Multān), and the Sultan assigned the shaikhly office to Hūd, as the shaikh [Rukn al-Dīn] had specified in his testament. Hūd was full age, whereas the shaikh's nephew was but a young man; and the Sultan honoured him highly and gave orders that he should be treated as a guest in every station at which he should stop, |
304 that the people of every town by which he passed should come out to receive him, and that a banquet should be prepared in it for him.

When this order reached the capital, the jurists, qāḍīs, shaikhs and notables went out to receive him. I was among

[164] Either I.B. or his copyists again get this name wrong; see vol. II, p. 283, n. 47, and for Rukn al-Dīn and Badā' al-Dīn p. 597 above. The French translators reject the phrase 'by his daughter' which follows this word in three MSS, but it no doubt refers to the relationship of Hūd to his grandfather.

[165] P. 712 below.

those who did so. When we met with him he was riding in a *dūla*[166] carried by men [on their shoulders], and his horses were being led. We saluted him, but for my part I resented this way of his of riding in a *dūla* and said, 'The only proper thing for him to do is to mount his horse and ride in alongside the qāḍīs and shaikhs who have come out to receive him.' He was told what I had said and thereupon mounted his horse, making the excuse that his previous behaviour was due to some painful discomfort which had prevented him from riding. On his entry into Dihlī there was given in his honour a banquet which cost a pretty penny of the Sultan's moneys, and was attended by the qāḍīs, shaikhs, jurists and distinguished foreigners. The repast[167] was spread, and the dishes were brought in | as usual, after which gifts of money 305 were made to all of those present, to each according to his worthiness. So the Grand Qāḍī was given five hundred dinars, and I was given two hundred and fifty. This is a regular custom of theirs on the occasion of a royal banquet.

After this the shaikh Hūd set out for his own country, accompanied by the shaikh Nūr al-Dīn al-Shīrāzī, whom the Sultan had sent to seat him on the prayer-mat[168] of his grandfather in his hospice and to arrange a banquet for him there at the Sultan's expense. After he had become established in his hospice and remained there for some years, the governor of Sind, 'Imād al-Mulk, wrote to the Sultan stating that the shaikh and his relatives were devoting themselves to amassing riches and to spending them in the gratification of their carnal appetites, without supplying any food to anyone at the hospice. The Sultan then sent an order to call them to account for the revenues [that had been assigned to Rukn al-Dīn], whereupon 'Imād al-Mulk demanded of them the restitution of the money, jailed some of them, and beat others. | Every day for some length of time he extracted 306 from them twenty thousand dinars, and eventually sequestrated everything that they had. There was found in their possession a great quantity of specie and treasures, including

[166] Hindī *ḍolī*, a covered litter. Cf. vol. IV, p. 73 Ar.

[167] See p. 671, n. 64 above.

[168] The formal symbol of succession to the status and perquisites of a ṣūfī shaikh, whose successor or *khalīfa* is consequently called in Persian *sajjāda-nishīn*, 'he who sits upon the prayer mat.'

two sandals encrusted with jewels and rubies, which were sold for seven thousand dinars. Some said that they belonged to the shaikh Hūd's daughter, others that they belonged to a concubine that he had.

When the shaikh Hūd was reduced to these straits, he fled, making for the land of the Turks, but was seized. This was duly communicated by 'Imād al-Mulk to the Sultan, who ordered him to despatch both the shaikh and his captor [to the capital] manacled like prisoners. On their arrival he released the man who had arrested the Shaikh Hūd, and said to the latter, 'Where were you planning to escape to?' He made various efforts to excuse himself, but the Sultan said to him, 'What you meant to do was to go to the Turks, and then you would say "I am the son of the shaikh Bahā' al-Dīn 307 Zakarīyā, and the Sultan has treated me | in such and such a way," and bring them to fight with us. Cut off his head.' So they beheaded him, God Most High have mercy on him.

His imprisonment of Ibn Tāj al-'Ārifīn and execution of his sons. The pious shaikh Shams al-Dīn, son of Tāj al-'Ārifīn, lived in the city of Kuwil,[169] wholly occupied in religious exercises, and held in high respect. The Sultan, on entering the city of Kuwil [on one occasion] had sent for him, but he refused to come to the Sultan, whereupon the Sultan went to visit him but after approaching his dwelling turned back without seeing him. Some time later, it happened that a certain amīr rebelled against the Sultan in some district or other and received the allegiance of its people. It came to the ears of the Sultan that some mention of that amīr had been made in the shaikh Shams al-Dīn's assembly and that the 308 shaikh had commended him | and said that he possessed the qualities which befit a king. Thereupon the Sultan sent one of the amīrs to [fetch] the shaikh. This officer put fetters on the shaikh and on his sons, as well as on the qāḍī and muḥtasib[170] of Kuwil, because it was reported that both of them had been present at the assembly in which the incident of the shaikh's praise of the rebel amīr had occurred. [The Sultan] gave orders that they should all be gaoled, after first blinding both the qāḍī and the muḥtasib. The shaikh died in

[169] Koil, 75 miles S.S.E. of Delhi, later renamed 'Aligarh.

[170] For the office of the *muḥtasib* see vol. I, p. 219, n. 130.

the prison; the qāḍī and muḥtasib used to be brought out under charge of one of the gaolers and to beg for alms from the townsfolk, and would then be taken back to the prison.

The Sultan had been informed that the shaikh's sons used to be on friendly terms with the Hindu infidels and rebels and to consort with them. When their father died, he released them from the prison and said to them 'Take care not to return to what you used to do.' They replied to him 'And what was it we did?,' upon which he was infuriated and ordered them both to be executed, and executed they were. | He then summoned the qāḍī of whom we have spoken and said, 'Tell me who used to share the views of these men who have been executed and to act in the same way.' The qāḍī dictated the names of numerous persons among the notables of the region,[171] but when the Sultan was presented with his list he said 'This fellow wants the country to go to ruin. Cut off his head.' So he was beheaded, God Most High have mercy on him. 309

The execution of the shaikh al-Ḥaidarī. The shaikh 'Alī al-Ḥaidarī used to live in the city of Kanbāya [Cambay], on the coast of India. He was held in high respect, well spoken of, and of wide reputation. The sea-traders used to vow to give large sums to him, and on arriving [in Cambay] they would go first of all to salute him. He would show them that he knew what was in their minds; often one of them would make a vow and then repent of it, but when he came to salute the shaikh, | the shaikh would tell him first how much he had vowed and order him to fulfil it faithfully. He was successful in this sort of thing many times, and became renowned for it. 310

When the qāḍī Jalāl al-Dīn al-Afghānī and his tribesmen revolted in those parts,[172] it was reported to the Sultan that the shaikh al-Ḥaidarī had prayed for the qāḍī Jalāl and had taken off his own cap and given it to him,[173] and it was alleged that he had even sworn allegiance to him. So the Sultan, when he went out in person to deal with them, and the qāḍī Jalāl had taken flight, appointed as his representative in Kanbāya Sharaf al-Mulk Amīr Bakht, one of those

[171] MS. 2291 reads 'many persons among the infidels of the region'.
[172] See p. 730 below.
[173] Cf. vol. II, p. 297, lines 7–8.

who had come to his court along with us, with orders to search out those involved in the rebellion. He associated also a number of jurists with him, on whose advice he was to pass judgement. The shaikh 'Alī al-Ḥaidarī having been brought for trial before Sharaf al-Mulk, it was established that he had given the rebel his cap and had prayed for him, and they condemned him to death. When the swordsman struck him, 311 however, he produced no effect. | The people marvelled at this, and imagined that he would be granted a pardon because of it; but Sharaf al-Mulk ordered another swordsman to behead him, and he did so—God Most High have mercy on him.

His execution of Ṭūghān and his brother. Ṭūghān al-Farghānī and his brother were of a family of notables in the city of Farghāna.[174] They had come to the Sultan's court, had been generously received by him and given a handsome revenue, and remained with him for some time. When their residence [in Dihlī] lengthened out, they wished to return to their own land and planned to take flight. Their design was denounced to the Sultan by one of their companions; he ordered them to be cut in halves (as was duly done), and gave to the informer who had revealed their plan all of their possessions. Such is their custom in that country—when one person informs against another, and the substance of his accusation is proved, so that the accused person is executed, then he is given the property of the latter. |

312 *His execution of the son of the Malik of the Merchants.*[175] The son of the Malik of the Merchants was a very young man, with no hair as yet on his cheeks. When the rebellion and rising of 'Ain al-Mulk occurred, and [led to] his warfare with the Sultan, as we shall relate,[176] he seized this son of the Malik of the Merchants. The boy was thus included in the rebel forces against his will. Upon the defeat of 'Ain al-Mulk

[174] Strictly the name of the whole province, probably applied at this period to Andigān (Andijān) see G. le Strange, *Lands of the Eastern Caliphate*, 478: and *Tawārikh-i Mu'īnī*, pp. 106 and 296.

[175] The functions of the 'king' of the merchants, *malik al-tujjār*, are not clearly defined; on the analogy of the corresponding Egyptian office, he would appear to be the representative of the merchants engaged in overseas trade in their relations with the government.

[176] See pp. 720–6 below.

and the capture of both him and his supporters, the son of the Malik al-Tujjār and his brother-in-law Ibn Quṭb al-Mulk were amongst the captives, and on the Sultan's orders they were strung up by the hands to a wooden stake and the sons of the maliks shot arrows at them until they died. After their death the chamberlain Khwāja Amīr 'Alī al-Tibrīzī said to the Grand Qāḍī Kamāl al-Dīn 'That youth should not have been killed.' His words were reported to the Sultan, who said, 'Why did you not say so before his death?', and ordered him to be given two hundred or so lashes with the whip and to be cast into prison. All of his possessions were given | to the amīr of the swordsmen. I saw this man on the following day dressed in the garments of the Khwāja Amīr 'Alī, wearing his high bonnet, and riding his horse, and took him to be the Khwāja himself. He meanwhile remained in prison for some months, after which the Sultan released him and restored him to his former post. Later on, he again incurred the Sultan's wrath and was banished to Khurāsān, where he settled in Harāt, and wrote to the Sultan to beg his mercy. The Sultan endorsed the letter in his favour [and returned it to him with the following words written] on its back, *Eger bāz āmadī bāz* [*āy*], which mean 'If you have repented, come back.' So then he returned to his service.

313

His beating to death of the chief Khaṭīb. The Sultan had placed the treasury which contained the jewels during his travels under the guardianship of the chief Khaṭīb of Dihlī. It befel that some infidel thieves came by night, made for this treasury, | and went off with part of its contents. Whereupon the Sultan commanded the Khaṭīb to be beaten until he died[177]—God Most High have mercy on him.

314

His devastation of Dihlī and exile of its population, and killing of the blind man and the cripple. One of the gravest charges against the Sultan is his forcing of the population of Dihlī to evacuate the city. The reason for this is that they used to write missives reviling and insulting him, seal them, and inscribe them, 'By the head of the Master of the World, none but he may read this.' Then they would throw them into the audience-hall by night, and when the Sultan broke the

[177] The Arabic is about as ambiguous as the English, but in strict usage should imply 'so that he died in consequence'.

seal he found them full of insults and abuse of him. So he decided to lay Dihlī in ruins, and having bought from all the inhabitants their houses and dwellings and paid their price to them, he commanded them to move out of the city and go 315 to Dawlat Ābād. They refused, | so his herald was sent to proclaim that no person should remain in it after three nights. The majority of the citizens left, but some of them hid in the houses. The Sultan ordered a search to be made for any persons who had remained in the city, and his slaves found two men in its streets, one of them a cripple and the other blind. They were brought in, and he ordered that the cripple should be flung from a mangonel and the blind man dragged from Dihlī to Dawlat Ābād, a distance of forty days' journey. He fell to pieces on the road, and all of him that reached Dawlat Ābād was his leg. After this action on the part of the Sultan, the whole of the population left the town, abandoning furniture and possessions, and the city was left desolate and disintegrating.[178] A person in whom I have confidence told me that the Sultan mounted one night to the roof of his palace and looked out over Dihlī, where there was neither fire nor smoke nor lamp, and said 'Now my mind is 316 tranquil and my feelings are appeased.' | Afterwards he wrote to the inhabitants of the provinces commanding them to move to Dihlī, in order to repopulate it. The result was that their cities were ruined but Dihlī remained unrestored, because of its extent and immensity, for it is one of the greatest cities in the world. It was in this condition that we found it on our entry into it, empty and unpopulated save for a few inhabitants.[179]

[178] A traditional Qur'ānic phrase (ii, 261, etc.) literally 'fallen down upon its roofs'.

[179] The study of contemporary evidence by Mahdi Husain, *Muḥammad bin Tughluq*, pp. 108–23, suggests that I.B.'s account of the devastation of Dihlī is greatly exaggerated (although supported in large part by some Indian chronicles). The order affected mainly the Muslim notables and shaikhs. The first order was issued in 1327; a second in 1329 may have been more sharply executed. But at this very time, the Sultan was building his new city of Jahānpanāh (see p. 619 above).

CHAPTER XIII

The Reign of Sultan Muhammad Ibn Tughluq

As we have now related many of the generous qualities of this Sultan, as well as the crimes with which he was charged, we shall proceed to give summary accounts of the military and political events which occurred in his time.

His inauguration of his reign by pardoning Bahādūr Būra. When the Sultan took possession of the kingdom after his father's death and the people had taken the oath of allegiance to him, he summoned the sultan Ghiyāth al-Dīn Bahādūr Būra, who had been taken prisoner by the Sultan Tughluq,[1] and having pardoned him and loosed him from his chains, he made him a munificent gift of money, horses and elephants, | and restored him to his kingdom. He sent along with him his brother's son Bahrām Khān[2] and swore him to an agreement that that kingdom should be divided equally between them, both their names should be inscribed on the coinage and mentioned in the *khuṭba*, and that Ghiyāth al-Dīn should send his son Muḥammad, known as Barbāṭ, to be a hostage with the Sultan. Ghiyāth al-Dīn returned to his kingdom and undertook to carry out all these stipulations, but he did not send his son, on the pretext that he refused to go, and he used unseemly expressions in his discourse. The Sultan consequently sent troops to his brother's son Bahrām Khān, under the command of Dulgī[3] the Tatar, and they fought against 317

[1] See pp. 637, 653 above.

[2] So in MSS. 2289 and 2291 and cf. p. 665 above. Mahdi Husain (*Reḥla*, introd. p. xi) corrects the reading further to 'his father's son' on the ground that Sultan Muḥammad had no brother's son. He was, in fact, the adopted son of Tughluq.

[3] Mahdi Husain (*Muḥammad bin Tughluq*) calls him Diljalī Tatāri, better known as Tatār Khān, and dates this expedition in 1330–1.

Ghiyāth al-Dīn, killed him and stripped off his skin and having stuffed it with straw sent it on tour round the provinces. |

318 *The revolt of the son of his father's sister and the events connected with it.* Sultan Tughluq had a sister's son called Bahā al-Dīn Kusht-Asb, whom he appointed governor of one of the provinces. This man, who was brave and warlike, refused to take the oath of allegiance to the son of Tughluq after his uncle's death, and the Sultan sent troops against him, amongst whom were the principal amīrs such as the malik Mujīr, the vizier Khwāja Jahān being in command of the whole expedition. When the horsemen engaged one another a fierce battle ensued, each of the two armies holding its ground, until finally the victory was won by the Sultan's troops and Bahā al-Dīn fled to one of the kings of the infidels called Rāy Kanbīla. *Rāy* is with them, just as it is in the language of the Franks, a word which means Sultan,[4] and Kanbīla is the name of the region where this prince lived.[5] |
319 This Rāy had territories situated in inaccessible mountains and was one of the principal Sultans of the infidels.

When Bahā al-Dīn fled to him he was followed up by the Sultan's armies, who surrounded those territories. The situation became critical for the infidel and all the grain which he had was exhausted. Fearing that he should be taken by force he said to Bahā al-Dīn 'Matters have reached the pass which you see, and I am determined to destroy myself and my family and all those who follow me. Do you go to Sultan so-and-so (mentioning a certain Sultan of the infidels) and remain with him, for he will protect you'. Having sent him with someone to conduct him to the Sultan, Rāy Kanbīla ordered a great fire to be lit, burnt all his possessions in it and said to his wives and daughters 'I intend to kill myself and any of you who wish to follow my example, let her do so.' So every woman amongst them bathed herself, perfumed herself with

[4] A remark that would be unintelligible to an Easterner, since I.B. refers to the Spaniards by the name of *al-Rūm*, and the Spanish *rey*.

[5] Kampila was situated about ten miles north of Vijayanagar. According to Firishta, quoted by Mahdi Husain (*Muḥ. b. Tughluq*, 143–4), Bahā al Dīn had been governor of Sāgar, near Gulbarga, and in the first two battles defeated Khwāja Jahān. These events are probably to be dated about 1327.

yellow sandal-wood,[6] | kissed the ground before him and threw 320 herself into the fire, until they perished to the last one. The same was done by the female relatives of his amīrs and viziers and chief officers; and all other women who wished to follow their example. The Rāy then bathed himself, perfumed himself with sandal and put on his armour except for the breast plate. The same was done by all those of his men who wished to die with him, and they went out to meet the Sultan's army and fought until they were killed to the last man. The city was entered and its population taken prisoner, together with eleven of the sons of Rāy Kanbīla, who were brought before the Sultan. They all accepted Islām and the Sultan made them amīrs and honoured them greatly owing to their noble lineage and their father's action. I saw in his entourage three of these princes, Naṣr, Bakhtiyār, and the *muhurdār*, i.e. the keeper of the seal with which the water which the Sultan drinks[7] is sealed; his name of address is Abū Muslim and he and I | became companions and friends. 321

When Rāy Kanbīla was killed the Sultan's troops made towards the city of the infidel with whom Bahā al-Dīn had taken refuge and surrounded it.[8] This Sultan said 'I cannot do what Rāy Kanbīla did,' so he arrested Bahā al-Dīn and delivered him to the Sultan's troops, who bound him with chains and manacles and brought him to the Sultan. When he was brought before him he ordered him to be taken into the apartments of his female relatives, who showered abuse on him and spat in his face. The Sultan then ordered him to be flayed alive, and when he had been flayed his flesh was cooked with rice and sent to his sons and his family. The remains of him were put in a platter and thrown to the elephants to eat, but they would not eat it. On the Sultan's orders his skin was stuffed with straw and, in conjunction with the skin of Bahādūr Būra, was exhibited in all the provinces in turn. When they arrived in the province of Sind, the ruling amīr there at that time being Kishlū | Khān, the 322 companion of the Sultan Tughluq (he had assisted him to

[6] *Maqāṣarī*: see p. 675, n. 80 above.

[7] I.e. brought from the Ganges; see pp. 594–5 above.

[8] His name is given in the Indian sources as Bilāl Deo, probably to be identified with Vira Ballāla III, Hoysala raja of Dvārasamudra (see *Hobson-Jobson*, s.v. Doorsummund).

seize the kingdom, and Sultan Muḥammad used to show him respect and address him as uncle, and go out to meet him when he came from his territories to visit him), Kishlū Khān gave orders to bury the two skins. When the Sultan learnt of this he was angered by what he had done and determined to put him to death.

The rising and death of Kishlū Khān. When the Sultan learnt of his action in burying the two skins he sent for him, and Kishlū Khān, realising that he intended to punish him, refused to go and rose in revolt.[9] He distributed the revenues and assembled troops; he sent to the Turks, and the Afghāns, and the men of Khurāsān, and was joined by such large numbers of them that his army equalled that of the Sultan or even exceeded it in size. The Sultan went out in person to engage him and when the battle took place at a distance of 323 two days' journey from Multān, in the plain of | Abūhār,[10] he adopted a prudent measure and set in his place beneath the parasol the Shaikh 'Imād al-Dīn, the brother of the Shaikh Rukn al-Dīn of Multān (it was the latter who told me this), since he closely resembled him. When the battle grew hot the Sultan detached himself with 4,000 of his troops, while those of Kishlū Khān made for the parasol in the belief that the Sultan was underneath it and killed 'Imād al-Dīn. The report spread amongst the troops that the Sultan had been killed, whereupon Kishlū Khān's men busied themselves with plundering and became separated from him. When none remained with him but a few, the Sultan attacked him with the troops that had withdrawn with him, killed him and cut off his head. When his army learnt of this they fled and the Sultan entered the city of Multān. He arrested its qāḍī Karīm al-Dīn and ordered him to be flayed, which was done, 324 and ordered Kishlū Khān's head to be set | over its gate, and I myself saw it there when I arrived at Multān.

The Sultan gave to the Shaikh Rukn al-Dīn, the brother of 'Imād al-Dīn, and to 'Imād al-Dīn's son Ṣadr al-Dīn a hundred villages, as a gift to them for their own consumption

[9] The cause assigned by I.B. is obviously derived from popular rumour, since the rising took place at least two years before the expedition to Bengal (see n. 3 above). Its real causes are obscure.

[10] See p. 609 above.

and to supply food [to travellers] in their hospice, which is called by the name of their grandfather Bahā al-Dīn Zakarīyā.[11] The Sultan commanded his vizier Khwāja Jahān to go to the city of Kamālpūr,[12] which is a large city on the sea coast, whose inhabitants had revolted. A certain doctor of the law told me that he was present when the vizier entered the city. He said 'He had brought before him the qāḍī there and the khaṭīb and gave orders that they should be flayed. They said to him "Put us to death without this." He said to them "For what reason have you deserved to be put to death?" They replied "For our disobedience to the Sultan's commands." Whereupon he said to them "Then why should I disobey his command when he has ordered me to put you to death this way?" Then he said | to those responsible for flaying them 325 "Dig out hollows for them under their faces so that they may breathe,"' because when men are flayed (God preserve us) they are laid down on their faces. After all this was done the province of Sind was pacified and the Sultan returned to his capital.

Account of the defeat suffered by the Sultan's army in the mountain of Qarāchīl. This is a great range of mountains extending for a distance of three months' journey, and ten days' journey from Dihlī,[13] and its Sultan is one of the most powerful sultans of the infidels. The Sultan [Muḥammad] had sent Malik Nukbiya, the chief of the dawīdārs, to war against these mountains, with an army of 100,000 horsemen and many infantry in addition. He occupied the town of Jidya,

[11] See p. 702 above for the ultimate fate of Rukn al-Dīn.

[12] The identification of this place is uncertain. There is a Kamālpur near Karachi, but no city of this description is known to have existed at this time.

[13] Evidently the Himalayas, but the name itself and its source are dubious. Yule (*Cathay*, IV, 17–18 note) regards it as a corruption of *Kuverachal*, the Sanskrit name of Mount Kailas (from Sanskrit *achala* 'mountain'). For the numerous other forms of the name, see Mahdi Husain, *Muḥ. b. Tughluq*, 126, n. 2. He also (p. 129) suggests that it stands here for Kurmachal, the old name of Kumaun, and the placing of the expedition at ten days' journey from Delhi would confirm that it was directed towards the Kumaun-Garhwal region, ruled at this time by the Rajputs of the Chand dynasty. The purpose and date of the expedition are both uncertain; but since it almost certainly preceded the rebellions in the south described in the following sections, and is distinct from the expedition led by the Sultan in person to Nagarkot (in Kangra district, about 80 miles north of Simla) in 1338 it may be dated between 1330 and 1333.

326 which lies at the foot of the mountain, and seized | the neighbouring regions, taking prisoners, destroying and burning. The infidels fled to the upper part of the mountain, abandoning their lands and possessions and the treasuries of their king. There is only one road to this mountain; below it there is a valley and above it the mountain itself and it cannot be used except by single horsemen in file. The Muslim troops climbed up along this road and took possession of the town of Warangal, which is on the upper part of the mountain, and seized all that it contained.[14] On their informing the Sultan of their victory by letter, he sent a qāḍī and a khaṭīb to them, together with orders to them to remain there. But when the rainy season began there was an epidemic in the army; the troops were enfeebled, the horses died, and the bows became slack. Thereupon the amīrs wrote to the Sultan asking his permission to leave the mountain and to descend 327 to the foot of it until the end of the rainy | season, when they would go back again. On receiving his permission to do that, the amīr Nukbiya took the goods which he had captured from the treasuries and the precious metals and distributed them amongst the troops to carry them and bring them down to the bottom of the mountain. As soon as the infidels learnt of their withdrawal they lay in wait for them at those precipitous places and held the defile against them. They cut great[15] trees into sections and rolled them down from above, so that all who were in their way were thrown to destruction. In this way the greater part of the troops perished, and the rest of them were taken captive. The infidels seized the treasures, goods, horses and weapons, and out of the army only three of the amīrs escaped, their commander Nukbiya, Badr al-Dīn the malik Dawlat-Shāh, and a third whose name I do not recall. This defeat seriously affected the army of India and weakened it in a manifest degree. Afterwards the Sultan made 328 peace with | the inhabitants of the mountain on condition of payment of tribute to him, because they possess the lands at the bottom of the mountain but they are unable to cultivate them except with his permission.

[14] The town is given the name of the chief city in Telingana.

[15] The word translating 'great' is corrected in the French translation to the reading *'ādīya*.

The revolt of the sharīf Jalāl al-Dīn in the province of al-Maʿbar and the death of the vizier's nephew which was connected with that event. The Sultan had appointed the sharīf Jalāl al-Dīn Aḥsan-Shāh as governor over the province of al-Maʿbar, which is at a distance of six months' journey from Dihlī. He revolted, claimed the kingship for himself, killed the Sultan's military and civil officers, and struck dinars and dirhams with his own name. He had inscribed on one side of the dinar 'The offspring of Ṭā Hā and Yā Sīn, the father of the poor and the humble, Jalāl al-Dunyā wa'd-Dīn' and on the other side 'He who puts his trust | in the support of the Merciful One, Aḥsan-Shāh, the Sultan.' 329

On learning of his revolt the Sultan went out with the object of engaging him in battle and encamped at a place called *Kushki Zar* (which means Castle of Gold) and remained there for eight days for the provisioning of his troops. During this stay there was brought before him the sister's son of the vizier Khwāja Jahān, with three or four of the amīrs, all of them chained and manacled. The Sultan had sent his vizier with the vanguard of the troops; on reaching the city of Dhihār, which is a distance of twenty-four days' journey from Dihlī he had stayed there for some days. His sister's son was a brave and distinguished warrior and he came to an arrangement with those amīrs who were arrested [with him] to kill his uncle and to flee to the sharīf who had risen in the province of al-Maʿbar with the treasures and moneys which were in the vizier's possession. They decided to assassinate the vizier as he came out to attend the Friday prayer, but | one of those whom they had admitted into their plot—he was called the malik Nuṣra, the chamberlain—denounced them to the vizier and told him that the proof of their intention was their wearing breastplates under their outer garments. The vizier sent for them and on finding them so dressed sent them to the Sultan. I was in the Sultan's suite when they were brought in and I saw one of them, he was a tall bearded man, trembling and reciting the sūra of Yā Sīn. On the Sultan's orders they were thrown to the elephants which are trained to kill men, and the vizier's sister's son was sent back to his uncle to put him to death, which he did as we shall relate later. 330

These elephants which kill men have their tusks fitted with

pointed blades of iron resembling ploughshares, with edges like knives. The mahout mounts on the elephant and when a man is thrown before it it winds its trunk round him, 331 throws him in the air, then catches him with its tusks | and throws him after that at its feet, places one foot upon his chest and does with him what the mahout orders him to do in accordance with the Sultan's command to him. If he orders him to cut the victim in pieces the elephant cuts him in pieces with those blades; if he orders him to be left alone it leaves him lying on the ground and he is then flayed. It was this punishment which was inflicted on those amīrs, and when I came out of the Sultan's encampment at sunset I saw the dogs eating their flesh, their skins having been stuffed with straw—God preserve us.

When the Sultan made his preparations for this expedition he ordered me to remain at the capital, as we shall relate, and set out on his march until he reached Dawlat Ābād. At this point the amīr Halājūn rose in rebellion in his province,[16] although the vizier Khwāja Jahān had stayed behind in the capital to collect forces and to enlist mounted troops. |

332 *The revolt of Halājūn.* When the Sultan had reached Dawlat Ābād and was thus at a great distance from his province, the amīr Halājūn revolted in the city of Allāhūr and laid claim to the kingship. He was assisted in this enterprise by the amīr Quljund,[17] whom he appointed as vizier to himself. On learning of this the vizier Khwāja Jahān, being then in Dihlī, collected his forces and assembled the mounted troops and Khurāsānians; he took the men of all the officials who were residing in Dihlī and amongst them were taken my men, because I was staying there. The Sultan gave him the assistance of two high amīrs, one being Qīrān Malik Ṣaffadār (which means who orders the line of troops) and the other the king Tamūr the shurbadār (that is to say the cupbearer).[18] Halājūn came out with his troops and the battle was fought on the bank of one of the great rivers. Halājūn was defeated

[16] The amir Halājūn was governor of Lahore.

[17] I.e. Gul Chand, a Hindu amīr. See Mahdi Husain, *Muḥammad bin Tughluq*, 161.

[18] Compare p. 652. MS. 2287 reads al-Samantī.

and fled and a large part of his army was drowned in the river. The vizier entered | the city, flayed some of its inhabitants 333 and put others to death in various other ways. The person who carried out their executions was Muḥammad ibn al-Najīb, the vizier's lieutenant, who was known by the name of *Ajdar malik*, and was also called Ṣag al-Sulṭān, *ṣag* being the word for 'dog' in their language. He was a violent and brutal man, and the Sultan used to call him 'the lion of the bazaars'. He used often to bite persons who were guilty of crimes with his own teeth out of an uncontrollable desire to inflict violence on them. The vizier sent about three hundred of the female relatives of the rebels to the fortress of Gāliyūr where they were imprisoned, and I have myself seen some of them there. One of the doctors of the law had a wife amongst them whom he used to visit, and she even bore a child to him in the prison.

The outbreak of plague in the Sultan's army. When the Sultan reached | the land of Tiling on his way to engage the 334 Sharīf in the province of Ma'bar, he halted at the city of Badrakūt, capital of the province of Tiling, which is at a distance of three months' march from the land of Ma'bar. At that moment a pestilence broke out in his army and the greater part of them perished; there died black slaves, the mamlūk troopers, and great amīrs such as malik Dawlat-Shāh, whom the Sultan used to address by the name of uncle, and such as the amīr 'Abdallāh al-Harawī, whose story has been related in the first voyage.[19] It was he whom the Sultan ordered to carry away from his treasury all the money that he could manage to lift, and who attached thirteen money-bags to his arms and carried them off. When the Sultan saw what had befallen the army he returned to Dawlat Ābād. | The provinces withdrew their allegiance and the outer regions 335 broke away, and the sovereignty was on the point of slipping out of his hand had it not been for the prior decree of Providence to reaffirm his good fortune.

The false report of his death and the flight of king Hūshanj. While on his way back to Dawlat Ābād the Sultan fell ill, the rumour of his death was bruited amongst the people and being carried far and wide gave rise to several widespread

[19] See vol. II, p. 311.

revolts. The malik Hūshanj son of the malik Kamāl al-Dīn Gurg was at Dawlat Ābād and he had given his solemn oath to the Sultan that he would never take the oath of allegiance to any other person either during the Sultan's lifetime or after his death. When the rumour of the Sultan's death was circulated, he fled to an infidel Sultan called Burabra who lived in some inaccessible mountains between Dawlat Ābād and Kūkan Tānah. On learning of his flight, and fearing the outbreak of revolt, the Sultan made a forced march to Dawlat Ābād, following the trail of Hūshanj and surrounded him | 336 with cavalry. He invited the infidel by letter to surrender him, but the latter refused saying, 'I shall never surrender my protégé even if I am forced to the same extreme as Rāy Kanbīla.' Hūshanj, however, fearing for his own safety, entered into correspondence with the Sultan and made an agreement with him that the Sultan should return to Dawlat Ābād and leave at that place his preceptor Quṭlū Khān, in order that Hūshanj should receive guarantees from him and go down to him upon promise of safety. The Sultan withdrew accordingly, and Hūshanj went down to Quṭlū Khān and took a guarantee from him that the Sultan would not put him to death nor lower his rank. He then came out with his possessions, his household and his followers, and presented himself before the Sultan, who was rejoiced at his coming and gave him satisfaction and invested him with a robe of honour. Quṭlū Khān was a man of his word, in whom men placed implicit confidence and on whose loyalty they relied. His position with the Sultan was very high; the respect which the latter showed to him was immense, and whenever he came before him he would rise up in honour of him. For this 337 reason therefore | Quṭlū Khān never used to come into the Sultan's presence unless he himself should have invited him, so that he might not weary him by rising to greet him. He was a man who loved to give alms, of great liberality, and eager to do good to poor brethren and the indigent.

The project of revolt of the sharīf Ibrāhīm and the end of this affair. The sharīf Ibrāhīm, who was known as *Kharīṭa-dār*, that is to say keeper of the paper and the pens in the Sultan's household, was governor of the province of Ḥānsī and Sarsatī when the Sultan set out for the land of Ma'bar. His father was the governor who was in rebellion in the land of Maʿbar, the sharīf Aḥsan-Shāh. When the rumour of the Sultan's death spread abroad, Ibrāhīm, who was brave and generous and had a fine figure, became ambitious of the sultanate. I was married to his sister Ḥūrnasab; she was a pious woman, who used to spend part of the night in prayers and to compose *wirds* for | the recollection of God (High and Mighty is He) and she bore a daughter by me. I do not know what God has done with them both. She used to read but not to write. 338

When Ibrāhīm proposed to revolt there passed his way one of the amīrs of Sind with revenue moneys which he was carrying to Dihlī. Ibrāhīm said to him 'The road is dangerous and infested by robbers; stay with me until the road is in order and I can convey you to safety,' but his real purpose was to get authentic news of the death of the Sultan so that he might take possession of those moneys. When he was assured of his life he released that amīr whose name was Ḍiyā' al-Mulk son of Shams al-Mulk.

On the Sultan's return to the capital after an absence of two and a half years the sharīf Ibrāhīm came to his court, but one of his dependents denounced him and told the Sultan of his former intention. The Sultan intended to order his immediate execution but procrastinated because of his affection for him. It happened that | one day there was brought to the Sultan a slaughtered gazelle, and he looked at the manner of its slaughtering and said 'It is not properly cut, throw it away.' Ibrāhīm on seeing it said 'It has been properly slaughtered and I shall eat it,' which was told to the Sultan and displeased him and furnished him with an excuse to seize him. On his orders Ibrāhīm was chained and manacled, then the Sultan forced him to confess to that of which he had been accused, namely that he intended to seize the moneys which Ḍiyā' al-Mulk was carrying through. Ibrāhīm realized that the Sultan really wished to put him to death because of his father and that no exculpation would serve him, so, fearing that he would be put to the torture and seeing death to be preferable for him, he acknowledged the charge and on the Sultan's orders was cut in two and left there. 339

It is their custom that when the Sultan puts anyone to

death he is left lying at the place of his execution for three days, and after the third night a corps of infidels who are 340 charged | with that duty take him away and carry him to a trench outside the town into which they throw him. They themselves live round about the trench to prevent the family of the executed man from coming and taking him away, but sometimes one of them will give money to these infidels and they give up to him his executed relative so that he may bury him. This was done in the case of the sharīf Ibrāhīm, God have mercy on him.

The rebellion of the Sultan's lieutenant in the province of Tiling. When the Sultan returned from Tiling and the report of his death spread abroad, it reached the ears of Tāj al-Mulk Nuṣra Khān, whom he had left as his deputy in the province of Tiling and who was one of his intimates of long standing. This man having performed and carried out the memorial services for the Sultan, proclaimed his own sovereignty and the people took the oath of allegiance to him in the capital city of Badrakūt. When the news of this reached the Sultan he sent his preceptor Quṭlū Khān with an immense body of 341 troops, | who besieged him after a violent battle in which whole tribes of men perished. The siege pressed heavily upon the people of Badrakūt, although it was difficult of approach, and when Quṭlū Khān began to undermine it Nuṣra Khān went out to him with a safe-conduct. Quṭlū Khān gave him a promise of safety and sent him to the Sultan, and also pardoned the inhabitants of the city and the troops.

The Sultan's removal to the river Gang and the rising of 'Ain al-Mulk. When the land was in the grip of famine the Sultan removed with his troops to the river Gang, to which the Indians go on pilgrimage, at a distance of ten days from Dihlī. He gave orders to his men to erect buildings; before this they had made tents of grasses, which used frequently to catch fire and cause losses to the people, until they adopted the habit of making caves under the earth and when a fire 342 occurred they threw their goods | into them and covered them over with earth. I myself arrived about that time at the Sultan's camp. The districts which were west of the river, where the Sultan was, were suffering from severe famine, while the districts to the east of it were abundantly provisioned. The governor of the latter was 'Ain al-Mulk ibn Māhir,[20] and they included the city of 'Awḍ and the city of Ẓafar Ābād and the city of Al-Laknaw, with others. The amīr 'Ain al-Mulk used to furnish 50,000 maunds daily, partly in wheat, rice, and chickpeas as fodder for the animals. The Sultan gave orders that the elephants and most of the horses and mules should be transported to the eastern district where there was abundance, to pasture there, and he instructed 'Ain al-Mulk to guard them. 'Ain al-Mulk had four brothers named Shahrallāh, Naṣrallāh, Faḍlallāh, and I do not remember the name of the fourth; they made an agreement with their brother 'Ain al-Mulk to seize the Sultan's elephants and riding beasts, to acknowledge 'Ain al-Mulk as their king and to rise against the Sultan. | 'Ain al-Mulk fled to join them 343 by night and their plan very nearly succeeded.

It is the custom of the King of India to set alongside every amīr, great or small, a mamlūk of his, to spy upon him and keep him informed of everything to do with him. He also places slave girls in their houses, who act as spies for him upon his amīrs, as well as women whom they call sweepers, who come into the houses without asking permission. The slave girls pass on their information to those women and the sweepers in turn pass that on to the 'king' of the intelligencers, who then informs the Sultan of it. They tell a story that a certain amīr was in bed with his wife and wished to have intercourse with her; she adjured him by the head of the Sultan not to do so but he would not listen to her, and in the morning the Sultan sent for him and told him the whole story, and that brought him to his death. |

The Sultan had a mamlūk named Ibn Malik-Shāh who was 344 a spy upon this 'Ain al-Mulk. When he informed the Sultan of his flight and crossing of the river, the Sultan bitterly repented of his action and thought that this was the decisive blow for himself, because horses, elephants, grain, all of them, were with 'Ain al-Mulk, and his own troops were widely scattered. He proposed therefore to go to the capital, collect mounted troops, and then come back to engage him in battle, and consulted the chief officers of the kingdom on this plan. The amīrs of Khurāsān and the foreigners were in the greatest

[20] For Ibn Māhir MS. 2287 reads Ibn Māhrū.

fear of this rebel, because he was an Indian, and the people of India hold the foreigners in hatred because of the Sultan's favouritism for them. They were in consequence opposed to his idea and said 'O Master of the World, if you do this, he will learn of it and his position will be strengthened; he will enrol troopers and will become a leader to whom all evil-345 seeking men | and fermenters of rebellions will flock, so the best plan is to get a blow in quickly[21] before his power is established.' The first man to speak in this sense was Nāṣir al-Dīn Muṭahhar al-Awharī, and all of them supported him. The Sultan accordingly acted on their advice; he wrote that same night to those of the amīrs and regular troops who were in his neighbourhood and they came forthwith. In this connection he adopted an excellent ruse; whenever a hundred horsemen for example arrived at his camp he sent out some thousands of those who were with him to meet them by night and these came in with them to the camp as though the whole body of them were reinforcements for him. The Sultan marched out along the bank of the river in order to place the city of Qinnawj behind his back and to use it as a fortress because of its strength and fortifications. It lay at a distance of three days' march from the position which he occupied. When he set off on the first stage he disposed his army in battle order, and on their halting he formed them in a single 346 line, | each man of them having his weapons in front of him and his horse by his side. He had with him a small tent in which he used to eat and make his ablutions and then return to his post; the main *maḥalla* was at some distance from them and during those three days the Sultan never entered a tent nor shaded himself with any cover.

On one of these days I was in my tent when one of my eunuchs named Sunbul called out my name and urged me to make haste. I had with me my slavegirls, and when I went out to him he said 'The Sultan has this hour given orders that every person who has with him his wife or his slave girl shall be put to death.' After the amīrs had interceded with him, however, he commanded that there should not remain a single woman in the *maḥalla* forthwith and that they should be transported to a castle thereabouts, at a distance of three

[21] MS. 2287 reads *mu'ajalatihi* in contrast to the other MSS.

miles, called Kanbīl,[22] so no woman was left in the *maḥalla*, not even with the Sultan.

We passed that night in battle order and on the following morning the Sultan organised his army | in troops, each troop 347 being given mailed elephants carrying towers filled with fighting men. The soldiers having put on their armour and made ready for battle passed that night under arms. On the third day word was brought that the rebel 'Ain al-Mulk had crossed the river. The Sultan was alarmed at this news and suspected that he would not have taken this action without first corresponding with the other amīrs who were still on his side, so he gave an immediate order to distribute the thoroughbred horses [from his private stable] to his personal suite and he sent me a proportion of them. I had a companion called Amīr-amīrān al-Kirmānī, one of the bravest of men, to whom I gave one of these horses, a grey, but when he set it in motion it ran off with him and as he was unable to hold it in, it threw him off its back, and he died, God have mercy on him.

That day the Sultan made a forced march and reached the city of Qinnawj[23] in the late afternoon, for he was afraid that | the rebel might reach it before him. He spent that night 348 attending to the organisation of the troops in person and he came to inspect us as we were in the vanguard with his uncle's son Malik Fīrūz, having with us the amīr Ghadā ibn Muhannā, the saiyid Nāṣir al-Dīn Muṭahhar and the amīrs of Khurāsān. He added us to the circle of his personal attendants and said to us 'You are dear to me and must never leave me'. In the upshot it all turned out well, for the rebel made an assault towards the end of the night upon the vanguard, in which was the vizier Khwāja Jahān; a great hubbub broke out amongst the troops, whereupon the Sultan gave orders that no man should break ranks nor engage the enemy except by the sword. The troops then, drawing their swords, advanced towards their adversaries and a hot battle ensued. The Sultan gave orders that his army's password should be 'Dihlī' and 'Ghazna'; each one of them therefore on meeting a horseman said to him 'Dihlī' and if he received the

[22] Kanbīl, 28 miles north of Fatehgarh, was erected as a fortress by Balban.

[23] In modern spelling Kannauj, situated 180 miles S.E. of Delhi.

answer 'Ghazna' he knew that he was one of his side and if 349 not he engaged him. The aim of the rebel had been to | attack only the place where the Sultan was but the guide led him astray and he attacked the place of the vizier instead and consequently cut off the guide's head. In the vizier's regiment there were Persians, Turks and Khurāsānians; these, being enemies of the Indians, put up a vigorous fight and though the rebel's army contained about 50,000 men they were put to flight at the rising of the day.

The malik Ibrāhīm, known as al-Banjī the Tatar, to whom the Sultan had given in fief the lands of Sundīla, which is a village in the province of 'Ain al-Mulk, had joined in the revolt with him and been appointed his deputy. Dāwud, son of Quṭb al-Mulk, and the son of the 'king of the merchants', who had been in charge of the Sultan's elephants and horses, also combined with him and he appointed Dāwud his chamberlain. This Dāwud, at the moment when they made the assault on the vizier's *maḥalla,* shouted out abuse of the 350 Sultan, reviling him in the foulest | terms, and the Sultan himself heard it and recognised his voice. When the rout began 'Ain al-Mulk said to his deputy Ibrāhīm the Tatar 'What is your opinion, malik Ibrāhīm? Most of the army is in flight, including the best fighters amongst them, so shall we try to make our escape?' Ibrāhīm said to his friends in their language 'When 'Ain al-Mulk is about to flee I shall seize him by his *dabbūqa,*[24] and when I do that do you strike his horse so that he will fall to the ground. Then we shall seize him and take him to the Sultan so that that may be an expiation of our crime in joining in his rebellion and a way of escape for me.' When 'Ain al-Mulk made ready to flee Ibrāhīm said to him 'Where to, O Sultan 'Alā al-Dīn?' (for he used to be called by that name), and seized his *dabbūqa* while his companions struck his horse. So he fell to the ground and Ibrāhīm threw himself on top of him and seized him. The 351 vizier's officers came to take possession of him | but he held them off, saying 'I shall not let him go until I bring him before the vizier or die in the attempt,' so they left him alone and he brought him to the vizier.

That morning I was watching the elephants and standards

[24] I.e. mache of hair at the back of his head.

being brought to the Sultan when one of the 'Irāqīs came to me and said ' 'Ain al-Mulk has been seized and taken to the vizier.' I did not believe him, but a little later the malik Tamūr the *shurbadār* came up to me and taking me by the hand said 'Good news, for 'Ain al-Mulk has been taken and is now with the vizier.' At that moment the Sultan set out, and we in his company, for the *maḥalla* of 'Ain al-Mulk on the river Gang, and the troops plundered its contents. Many of the soldiers of 'Ain al-Mulk rushed into the river and were drowned. Dāwud ibn Quṭb al-Mulk and the son of the 'king of the merchants' were seized along with many others, and the treasures, horses, and goods were plundered. The Sultan alighted at the crossing-place and the vizier brought 'Ain al-Mulk, who was placed on the back of an ox, naked | except 352 for a rag over his loins tied with a rope, the end of which was round his neck. He halted at the gate of the enclosure, and the vizier went on to the Sultan who gave him the *shurba* as a special mark of attention.[25] The 'sons of the kings' came to 'Ain al-Mulk and set about reviling him and spitting in his face and slapping his companions, and the Sultan sent to him the 'great king' [Qabūla], who said 'What is this that you have done?' but he found no answer. On the Sultan's orders he was dressed in a muleteer's cloak, had four chains attached to his feet and his hands manacled to his neck, and was delivered to the vizier to be kept under guard.

His brothers crossed the river in flight and reached the town of 'Awḍ[26] where they took their wives and children and all the wealth that they could, and said to the wife of their brother 'Ain al-Mulk 'Save yourself | and your sons by 353 escaping with us.' She replied 'Shall I not do as the wives of the infidels do who burn themselves with their husbands? I too shall die for my husband's death and live for his life.' Thereupon they left her, but this was reported to the Sultan and became the cause of her good fortune, for he was overtaken by compassion for her. The eunuch Suhail overtook Naṣrallāh, one of those brothers, killed him and brought the Sultan his head. He brought also the mother, sister, and wife of 'Ain al-Mulk, who were delivered over to the vizier and

[25] The Sultan offers him the *shurba*, that is the ceremonial drink.

[26] The 'town of 'Awḍ' is the capital of the future Oudh.

placed in a tent near the tent of 'Ain al-Mulk, who used to go to visit them and sit with them and then return to his prison.

In the afternoon of the day of the rout the Sultan gave orders to release the lower orders of those who were with 'Ain al-Mulk, such as muleteers, pedlars, slaves and persons of no importance. The 'king' Ibrāhīm al-Banjī, whom we have 354 mentioned, was brought in, and the 'king of the army', | the malik Nuwā, said 'O Master of the World, kill this man for he is one of the rebels.' The vizier replied 'He has ransomed himself by the leader of the rising,' so the Sultan pardoned him and set him free to go back to his own country. After the sunset prayer the Sultan took his seat in the wooden tower and sixty-two of the principal associates of the rebel were brought in. Then the elephants were brought and these men were thrown down in front of them, and they started cutting them in pieces with the blades placed on their tusks and throwing some of them in the air and catching them, and all the time the bugles and fifes and drums were being sounded. 'Ain al-Mulk too was standing watching their slaughter, and parts of them were thrown at him, then he was taken back to his prison.

The Sultan remained near the river-crossing for some days owing to the multitude of the troops and the small number of boats. He sent over his personal effects and his treasures upon the elephants, and distributed elephants to his chief courtiers 355 to send over their effects. | He sent me one of those elephants on which I sent over my baggage.

The Sultan then went, taking us with him, to the city of Bahrāyij,[27] a fine town on the bank of the river Sarū, which is a great stream with a strong current. The Sultan crossed it in order to visit the tomb of the pious shaikh, the warrior Sālār 'Ūd [Mas'ūd][28] who made the conquest of most of these territories. There are wonderful stories told of him and celebrated expeditions.

There was such a crowding and scrambling of people for the crossing that a large vessel sank with about 300 souls, not

[27] Bahrāyij was a town on the river Ganges.

[28] The title of Sālār 'Ūd is the name of Mas'ūd al-Ghāzī who died in 557 (1162) in the war with the Hindus. Another account is that he was born in 1013 and was killed at Bahrāyij in 1033.

one of whom escaped except one Arab of the party of Amīr Ghadā. We ourselves had embarked in a small boat and God Most High delivered us. The Arab who escaped from drowning was called Sālim ['safe'] which is a strange coincidence. He had intended to mount with us into our boat but he found that we had already | started to cross the river so he took his 356 place in the boat which was sunk. When he came out the people thought that he was with us and there was great alarm amongst our companions and the rest of the people, imagining that we were drowned, and then when they saw us afterwards they rejoiced at our safety.

We visited the tomb of the saint whom I have mentioned, situated in a pavilion which we were unable to enter because of the multitude of the press. It was on that journey that we entered a thicket of canes and a rhinoceros came out of them against us. It was killed and the man brought its head, and though it is smaller in size than an elephant yet its head is many times bigger than an elephant's head. We have mentioned this animal in a previous passage.[29]

Account of the Sultan's return to his capital and the rebellion of ʿAlī Shāh Kar. When the Sultan was victorious over ʿAin al-Mulk, as we have related, he returned to his capital after an absence | of two and a half years. He pardoned ʿAin al- 357 Mulk, and pardoned also Nuṣra Khān, who had revolted in the province of Tiling, and set them both to a common task, namely the supervision of the Sultan's gardens, and furnished them with robes and horses and fixed for them a daily allowance of flour and meat.

News was received after that that one of the associates of Quṭlū Khān namely ʿAlī Shāh Kar (Kar means 'deaf'), had revolted against the Sultan. He was a gallant man of fine figure and character, and having taken possession of Badrakūt he made it the capital of his kingdom. The troops went out against him and on the Sultan's orders his preceptor [Quṭlū Khān] went out to engage him in battle with large forces. He besieged him in Badrakūt, and when its towers were mined and the rebel's position became desperate he requested a promise of security and Quṭlū Khān gave it to him and sent him to the Sultan in chains. The Sultan pardoned him | and 358

[29] See p. 596.

exiled him to the city of Ghazna in the border of Khurāsān. He stayed there for some time but subsequently he pined for his native land and determined to return to it in accordance with God's decree for his destruction. He was arrested in the land of Sind and brought to the Sultan, who said to him 'You have come solely to stir up disorder again' and gave orders for his execution.

Account of the flight and capture of Amīr Bakht. The Sultan had a grievance against Amīr Bakht, who was entitled Sharaf al-Mulk, one of those who had come to him along with us, and in consequence reduced his stipend from 40,000 to one thousand and sent him to Dihlī in the service of the vizier. It happened that Amīr 'Abdallāh al-Harawī died in the plague at Tiling; his property was in the hands of his associates in Dihlī and they arranged with Amīr Bakht to take flight. When the vizier went out from Dihlī to meet the 359 Sultan | they fled with Amīr Bakht and his associates and reached the land of Sind in seven days, though it is a journey of forty days, for they had with them led horses. They determined that they would cross the river of Sind swimming and that Amīr Bakht and his son, with those who could not swim, would cross on a raft of reeds which they would make, and they had already prepared ropes of silk with this object. When they reached the river they were afraid to cross it by swimming and so sent two of their party to Jalāl al-Dīn, the governor of the city of Ūcha,[30] who said to him that there were merchants here who wished to cross the river and sent him this saddle in order that he might permit them to pass over. The amīr was suspicious that merchants should give him such a gift as this saddle and ordered the arrest of the two men. One of them escaped, rejoined Sharaf al-Mulk and his companions, who were sleeping in consequence of the 360 fatigue that had overtaken them | and the sequence of wakeful nights, and told them what had happened, whereupon they mounted in panic and fled. Jalāl al-Dīn gave orders to beat the man who had been seized and he confessed the whole story of Sharaf al-Mulk. On Jalāl al-Dīn's orders his lieutenant rode out with the troops in pursuit of them and finding that they had already ridden off followed up their

[30] The governor of Ucha is mentioned on p. 604 as governor of Ūja (Uch).

track and overtook them. They attacked the troops with arrows and Ṭāhir, the son of Sharaf al-Mulk, struck the lieutenant of the amīr Jalāl al-Dīn with an arrow which lodged in his forearm, but they were overpowered and taken to Jalāl al-Dīn. He put chains on them and manacled their hands and wrote to the vizier about them. The vizier ordered him to send them to the capital which he did. They were imprisoned there and Ṭāhir died in prison, and the Sultan gave orders that Sharaf al-Mulk should be beaten a hundred lashes every day.

He continued to suffer this punishment for some time but eventually the Sultan pardoned him and sent him | with the 361 amīr Niẓām al-Dīn Mīr Najla to the province of Chandīrī, where he was reduced to the extreme of riding oxen, having no horse to ride. He remained in this condition for a time but later on that amīr [Najla] visited the Sultan with Sharaf al-Mulk in his company, and the Sultan appointed him *shāshankīr*, that is the person who cuts up the meat in front of the Sultan and walks round with the food. Later on he raised him in honour and dignity and he reached such a height that when he fell ill the Sultan visited him, ordered him to be weighed with gold, and gave him the amount as a present. We have already told this story in the first journey.[31] Afterwards the Sultan married him to his sister and gave him the very province of Chandīrī in which he used to ride oxen in the service of the amīr Niẓām al-Dīn—Glorified be the Turner of hearts and the Changer of conditions! |

Account of the rebellion of Shāh Afghān in the land of Sind.[32] 362 Shāh Afghān had rebelled against the Sultan in the land of Multān in the province of Sind, had killed the governor there, who was called Bihzād, and claimed the Sultanate for himself. When the Sultan made preparations to engage him he realized that he could not resist him and so fled to join his own people, the Afghāns, who inhabit forbidding mountains impossible of access. The Sultan was filled with anger at his action and wrote to his governors to seize all those of the Afghāns whom they found in his territories. This was one cause of the rebellion of the qāḍī Jalāl.

[31] See vol. II, p. 312.
[32] Shāh Afghān stands for Shāhū Afghan.

Account of the rebellion of the qāḍī Jalāl. The qāḍī Jalāl and a body of Afghāns were living in the vicinity of the city of Kanbāya and the city of Bulūdhra.[33] When the Sultan sent written orders to his governors to arrest the Afghāns, he 363 instructed | the malik Muqbil, the lieutenant of the vizier in the provinces of Juzarāt and Nahrawāla, to find some means or other to arrest the qāḍī Jalāl and those with him. The region of Bulūdhra had been given as a fief to the 'king of the physicians', and the 'king of the physicians' was married to the Sultan's step-mother, the wife of his father Tughluq, and she had a daughter by Tughluq, the one whom the amīr Ghadā married. The 'king of the physicians' was at that time in the company of Muqbil because his estates were under the supervision of the latter, and when they reached the provinces of Juzarāt, Muqbil ordered the 'king of the physicians' to fetch the qāḍī Jalāl and his associates. When the 'king of the physicians' arrived in his lands he secretly warned them, because they were of the people of his country, and said 'Muqbil has sent for you in order to arrest you, so do not enter his presence without your arms.' They mounted accordingly to the number of about three hundred mailed men, and came to him and said, 'We shall not enter except in 364 a body.' As it was evident to him that he could not | seize them while they were united, he became afraid of them, ordered them to return home and made an appearance of guaranteeing their security. But they rose against him, entered the city of Kanbāya and plundered the Sultan's treasury there and the goods of the inhabitants. Amongst them they plundered the goods of the merchant Ibn al-Kawlamī, the person who founded the fine college at Alexandria; we shall speak of him later on. The malik Muqbil came to engage them but they drove him in headlong rout; then the malik 'Azīz, the vintner, and the malik Jahān Bunbul (?) came to engage them with 7,000 horsemen and they routed them also. They became notorious amongst the turbulent and criminal classes, who flocked to join them. The qāḍī Jalāl claimed the Sultanate and received the oath from his followers, and when the Sultan sent troops against him they defeated them. At Dawlat Ābād

[33] Bulūdhra is I.B.'s word for Broach which is called in al-Idrīsī Broch.

too there was a company of Afghāns and they also rose in rebellion. |

Account of the rebellion of the son of the malik Mall. The son 365 of the malik Mall was residing in Dawlat Ābād with a body of Afghāns. The Sultan sent written orders to his lieutenant there, who was Niẓām al-Dīn, the brother of his preceptor Quṭlū Khān, to arrest them, sending him at the same time many loads of shackles and chains and also the winter robes. It is the custom of the King of India to send to every amīr in command of a city and to the principal officers of his troops two robes of honour every year, a winter robe and a summer robe. When the robes arrive the amīr and the troops go out to receive them, and on reaching the person who has brought them they alight from their horses and each one takes his robe, lays it on his shoulder, and does homage in the direction of the Sultan. The Sultan wrote to Niẓām al-Dīn that when the Afghāns came out and dismounted to receive their robes he should arrest | them at that moment, but one of the 366 horsemen who had brought the robes came to the Afghāns and told them what was planned for them. The result was that Niẓām al-Dīn became one of those who made a plan and it turned against him. He rode out and the Afghāns rode out with him, but when they met the robes and Niẓām al-Dīn dismounted from his horse the Afghāns attacked him and his companions, seized him, killed many of his companions, entered the city and seized the treasuries. They appointed as their chief Nāṣir al-Dīn the son of the malik Mall, and the disturbers of the peace flocked to join them so that they became very powerful.

Account of the Sultan's expedition in person to Kanbāya. The Sultan, on learning of the action of the Afghāns at Kanbāya and Dawlat Ābād, went out in person, and decided to begin with Kanbāya and then return to Dawlat Ābād. He sent out his relative by marriage A'ẓam malik | al-Bāyazīdī with 4,000 367 troops in advance, but they were met by the troops of the qāḍī Jalāl, who defeated them, surrounded them in Bulūdhra and fought with them there. There was in the army of the qāḍī Jalāl an old man named Jalūl, a man of great bravery, who was continually attacking the troopers and killing them, and inviting them to single combat, but no one was bold enough to engage him singly. It happened one day that he spurred on his horse and it stumbled with him in a ditch so that he fell off it and was killed. They found on him two breastplates. They sent his head to the Sultan, crucified his body on the wall of Bulūdhra and sent his hands and feet round the provinces.

After that the Sultan came up with his troops. It was impossible for the qāḍī Jalāl to resist and he fled with his associates, abandoning their property and their children, and all that was plundered. The city was entered and the Sultan 368 remained there for some days, then set out from it | leaving in it his brother-in-law Sharaf al-Mulk Amīr Bakht, whom we mentioned above, relating the story of his flight, capture in Sind, imprisonment and all that happened to him first in the way of humiliation and then in the way of honour. The Sultan ordered him to seek out those who had given their allegiance to Jalāl al-Dīn and left with him some doctors of the law so that he might decide according to their judgements, and this brought about the killing of the shaikh ʿAlī al-Ḥaidarī, as we have already related.[34]

After his flight the qāḍī Jalāl joined Nāṣir al-Dīn the son of the malik Mall at Dawlat Ābād and enrolled amongst his partisans. When the Sultan came to meet them in person they assembled, about 40,000 in all, consisting of Afghāns, Turks, Indians, and black slaves, and swore together that they would never flee but would fight against the Sultan. Then the Sultan came to engage them but without raising the parasol which is an emblem of his, and when the battle grew hot the parasol was displayed. The rebels on seeing it were struck with 369 astonishment and were driven | in ignominious flight. The son of the malik Mall and the qāḍī Jalāl with about 400 of their chief officers took refuge in the fortress of al-Duwaiqīr, which we shall describe later on and which is one of the strongest natural fortresses in the world.[35] The Sultan took up his residence in the city of Dawlat Ābād (of which Duwaiqīr is the citadel) and sent messages to them to surrender at his discretion, but they refused to surrender except on guarantee of safety. The Sultan, however, refused to give them any guarantee but sent them foodstuffs as a sign of contempt for

[34] See pp. 705–6 above. [35] See vol. IV, pp. 46–51 Ar.

them and continued to stay there, and that is the last of my information about them.

Account of the battle between Muqbil and Ibn al-Kawlamī. This took place before the rising and rebellion of the qāḍī Jalāl. Tāj al-Dīn ibn al-Kawlamī was one of the principal merchants, who had come to the Sultan from the land of the Turks with magnificent gifts, including | mamlūks, camels, 370 merchandise, weapons and woven stuffs. The Sultan was highly delighted with his action and gave him twelve laks, though it is said that the value of his gift was no more than one lak, and appointed him to the government of the city of Kanbāya, which was under the supervision of the 'king' al-Muqbil, the lieutenant of the vizier.

On reaching the city he sent vessels to the towns of Mulaibār, the island of Sailān and elsewhere, and valuable articles and gifts came to him in these vessels and he became enormously wealthy. When the time came[36] to send the revenues of those parts to the capital, the malik Muqbil instructed Ibn al-Kawlamī to send what he had received in the way of gifts and moneys along with the gifts from those parts, according to the usual custom. Ibn al-Kawlamī, presuming upon the honour and the generous gift which the Sultan had bestowed on him, refused to do so and said 'I shall transport them myself or send them by my own servants, for neither the vizier's lieutenant nor the vizier has any authority over me.' | Thereupon Muqbil wrote to the vizier 371 and the vizier endorsed his letter with the words 'If you are incapable of maintaining order in our lands, leave them and return to us.' On receiving this reply Muqbil set out with his troops and mamlūks and the two of them met outside Kanbāya; Ibn al-Kawlamī was defeated, a number on both sides were killed, and Ibn al-Kawlamī sought concealment in the house of the *nākhūda* Ilyās, one of the leading merchants.

Muqbil on entering the town executed the commanders of Ibn al-Kawlamī's army but sent a guarantee of safety to him on condition that he should retain his own private possessions, and release the Sultan's property and the gifts due to him and the revenues of the town. Muqbil despatched all of this by his own servants to the Sultan along with a letter of

[36] The word *āna* is omitted.

complaint against Ibn al-Kawlamī, who also wrote complaining of Muqbil. The Sultan then sent the 'king of the physicians' to mediate between them but immediately afterwards | 372 the rising of the qāḍī Jalāl al-Dīn took place and Ibn al-Kawlamī's property was plundered and he himself fled with some of his mamlūks and rejoined the Sultan.

Account of the dearth which occurred in the land of India. During the Sultan's absence from his capital, he having set out towards the province of al-Ma'bar, the dearth broke out and became severe. The maund [of corn] reached sixty dirhams and afterwards rose even higher; there was general distress and severe hardship. One day when I went out to meet the vizier I saw three women cutting pieces from the hide of a horse which had died some months before and eating it. Skins were cooked and sold in the bazaars and when cattle were slaughtered people used to collect the blood and eat that. Some of the law-students from Khurāsān told me that 373 they went into a township called Akrūha between Ḥānsī | and Sarsatī, and finding it abandoned they went to one of its dwellings in order to pass the night, and found in a room in the house a man who had lit a fire and had in his hand a human foot which he was roasting in the fire and eating—God preserve us.

When conditions became serious the Sultan gave orders that all the inhabitants of Dihlī should be supplied with six months' sustenance. The qāḍīs, secretaries and amīrs, therefore, went round all the streets and quarters, writing down their inhabitants and giving each one of them six months' provision at the rate of one and a half pounds (Barbary weight) a day for each person. During this time I used to provide food for the people out of the provisions which I prepared in the mausoleum of the Sultan Quṭb al-Dīn, as will be related in due course, and the people were sustained[37] in this way—may God Most High reward according to the purpose of that action!

[37] *Yata'ayyashūna* 'were fed'.

CHAPTER XIV

Ibn Baṭṭūṭa's Stay in Dihlī

Now since we have related enough stories about the Sultan and of the events concerning him which took place in his days, | let us return to what concerns 374 ourselves in all this, and relate the circumstances of our arrival in the first place at his court and our changes of fortune until we left his service, and our subsequent departure from the Sultan on a mission to China and our return therefrom to our own land, if God Most High will.

Account of our coming to the Sultan's palace on our arrival during his absence. When we entered the capital of Dihlī we proceeded directly to the Sultan's court. We passed through the first door, then the second and the third, finding at each the naqībs, of whom a description has already been given, and when we came to them the chief naqīb introduced us into a great and spacious audience-hall. Here we found the vizier Khwāja Jahān awaiting us. The first to go forward was Ḍiyā al-Dīn Khudhāwand-Zāda, followed by his brother Qiwām al-Dīn, then by their brother | 'Imād al-Dīn; I came next 375 and was followed by their brother Burhān al-Dīn, then the amīr Mubārak of Samarqand, then the Turk Arun Bughā, then Malik-Zāda, the sister's son of Khudhāwand-Zāda, and finally Badr al-Dīn al-Faṣṣāl.

On entering from the third door the vast hall called *Hazār Ustūn,* which means 'thousand pillars', met our eyes. Here the Sultan sits in public audience. On entering, the vizier made obeisance until his head nearly touched the ground, and we too made obeisance by inclining the body and touched the ground with our fingers, our obeisance being in the direction of the Sultan's throne. All who were with us made obeisance also and when we finished this ceremony the naqībs cried in a loud voice *Bismillāh* and we all retired. |

376 *Account of our visit to the palace of the Sultan's mother and of her virtuous qualities.* The Sultan's mother is called Makhdūma Jahān ['Mistress of the World']. She is one of the most virtuous of women and munificent in charity, and has founded many hospices and endowed them to supply food to all travellers. She is blind, and the reason for this is that when her son came to the throne she was visited by all the princesses and daughters of the 'kings' and the amīrs wearing their finest apparel. As she was sitting on a golden couch encrusted with jewels and they all made obeisance before her, her sight went suddenly and although she has been treated in all kinds of ways it has done no good. Her son is of all men the most filial in his respect for her, and here is an example. Once when she went on a journey with him the Sultan returned some time before her, and on her arrival he went out to meet her, alighted from his horse, and kissed her foot as she was in her litter[1] in the sight of all the people.

377 To return to | our subject. When we withdrew from the Sultan's palace the vizier went out, taking us in his company, to the *Bāb al-Ṣarf,* which they call also by the name of *Bāb al-Ḥaram,* where the Makhdūma Jahān has her residence. When we reached her gate we alighted from our mounts, each of us having brought a gift proportioned to his quality. The chief judge of the mamlūks,[2] Kamāl al-Dīn ibn al-Burhān, went in with us; both he and the vizier did homage at her gate and we did homage in the same manner. The clerk at her gate made a list of our presents and then a company of eunuchs came out, the chief of whom presented themselves to the vizier and spoke with him privately. They then went back into the palace, then came out again to the vizier, then went back to the palace while we stood waiting. At length we were commanded to sit down in an arcade at that place, after which they served us with food, bringing golden vessels 378 which they call *suyun,* | resembling our pitchers, with golden saucers on which they stand called *subuk,*[3] as well as drinking

[1] The edition translated by M. Gayangos has *juḥfat* in place of *maḥaffat.* The term is used for palanquins for ladies.

[2] This represents the reading in one manuscript *quḍāt al-mamālīk* in place of the other reading which is *quḍāt al-mamālikī,* that is chief judge of the state.

[3] The reading *subuk* is apparently *subīka.*

vessels, plates and jugs all in gold. They set out the food in two tables, with two rows [of guests] at each table, and at the head of each row was the principal of the persons present. When we went forward to the tables the chamberlains and naqībs did homage and we did homage likewise, after which they brought a sherbet and we drank and the chamberlain said *Bismillāh.* We then ate, and after they had brought the barley-water followed by the betel the chamberlains said *Bismillāh* and we all did homage. We were then invited to go to a certain place there and were invested with silk robes of honour embroidered in gold. Next we were taken to the gate of the palace where we did homage and the chamberlains said *Bismillāh.* The vizier remained standing and we with him until there was brought out from inside the palace a chest containing unsewn fabrics | of silk, linen and cotton, 379 and each one of us was given his share of them. Then they brought a golden platter containing dried fruits, a similar platter with juleps, and a third with betel. It is their custom that the person to whom this is brought out takes the platter in his hand, places it on his shoulder and then does homage with his other hand touching the ground. The vizier took the platter in his hand with the purpose of showing me what I should do, out of kindly condescension on his part and courteous solicitude, may God reward him with good, and I did as he had done. We then withdrew to the mansion which had been prepared for our occupation in the city of Dihlī and in the neighbourhood of the *darwāza* of Pālam, and the hospitality gift was sent to us.

Account of the hospitality. On arrival at the mansion which had been prepared for my occupation I found in it everything that was required in the way of furniture, carpets, mats, vessels, | and bed. Their beds in India are light and one of 380 them can be carried by a single man; every person when travelling has to transport his own bed, which his slave-boy carries on his head. It consists of four conical legs with four crosspieces of wood on which braids of silk or cotton are woven.[4] When one lies down on it, there is no need for anything to make it pliable, for it is pliable of itself. Along with the bed they brought two mattresses and pillows and a

[4] This is apparently the Hindī *chārpāy.*

coverlet, all made of silk. Their custom is to use white slips made of linen or cotton as cover for the mattresses and coverlets, so that when they become dirty they wash the slips, while the bedding inside is kept clean. That night they came with two men, one of them the miller, whom they call the *kharrāṣ*, and the other the butcher, whom they call the 381 *qaṣṣāb*.[5] They told us to take from the one so much | flour and from the other so much meat—the exact weights I do not remember now. It is their custom that the meat which they give is equal to the weight of the flour, and this which we have described was the hospitality gift of the Sultan's mother. Later on there was delivered to us the hospitality gift of the Sultan, which we shall describe in due course.

Next day we rode to the Sultan's palace and saluted the vizier, who gave me two purses, each containing a thousand silver dinars, saying 'This is *sarshushtī*' which means 'for washing your head',[6] and in addition gave me a robe of fine goathair. A list was made of all my companions, servants, and slave boys, and they were divided into four categories; those in the first category were each given two hundred dinars, in the second a hundred and fifty, the third a hundred, 382 and the fourth sixty-five. | There were about forty of them, and the total sum given to them was four thousand odd dinars. After that the Sultan's hospitality gift was fixed. This consisted of a thousand Indian pounds of flour, one third of it in *mīrā*, that is fine flour, and two-thirds in *khushkār*, that is coarsely-ground flour,[7] a thousand pounds of flesh-meat, and I cannot say how many pounds of sugar, ghee, *salīf*,[8] and areca-nuts, with a thousand betel leaves. The Indian pound equals twenty of our Moroccan pounds and twenty-five Egyptian pounds. The hospitality gift to Khudhāwand-Zāda was four thousand pounds of flour and the same of meat, together with similar quantities of the other things we have mentioned.

Account of the death of my daughter and their action on that

[5] *Qaṣṣāb* is the usual term for butcher.

[6] Cf. p. 663 above.

[7] *Mīrā* and *khushkār* are the Indian equivalents.

[8] The reading *salīf* is not given in any dictionary. It is probably from the Indian *saleb*, which is a restorative made from the tubers of various species of orchis (*Hobson-Jobson*, s.v. Saleb).

occasion. One and a half months after our arrival a daughter of mine died, aged less than a year. When the report of her death reached | the vizier he gave orders that she should be 383 buried in a hospice which he had built outside the *darwāza* of Pālam, close to a tomb there of our Shaikh Ibrāhīm al-Qūnawī.[9] After we had buried her there he wrote to the Sultan about her and the reply reached him in the evening of the next day, although the distance between the Sultan's hunting-field and the capital was ten days' journey.

It is their custom to go to visit the grave of the dead person in the morning of the third day after burial. They spread carpets and silk fabrics on all sides of the tomb and place on it flowers, of which there is a never-ending supply there in all seasons of the year, such as jasmine, and *gul shabah*[10] which has yellow flowers, *raibūl* which is white, and *nisrīn*, which is of two kinds, white and yellow. They also set up branches of orange and lemon trees with their fruits, and if there should be no fruit on them they attach some to them with threads, and they heap upon the tomb dried fruits and coconuts.[11] Then the people assemble | and copies of the 384 scriptures are brought and they recite the Korān. When they have completed the recitation servants bring julep and give it to the people to drink, then rose-water is sprinkled over them profusely and they are given betel and retire.

On the morning of the third day after the burial of this daughter I went out at dawn according to the custom, having made ready what I could of all this. Then I found that the vizier had already commanded everything to be put in order for the ceremony and that a *sarācha* had been erected over the tomb on his order. Among those present were the chamberlain Shams al-Dīn al-Fūshanjī, who had welcomed us in Sind, the qāḍī Niẓām al-Dīn al-Karwānī, and a number of the principal men of the city. I did not enter until all these persons had taken their seats with the chamberlain in front of them, and all reciting the Korān, then I sat down with my companions in the vicinity of the tomb. When they finished

[9] Shaikh Ibrāhīm al-Qūnawī was buried at Konia. His tomb at Pālam is unknown.

[10] See p. 622 nn. 15, 16 and 17.

[11] Mahdi Husain takes the meaning of *nārjīl* to be copra.

their recital the professional Korān-readers gave a recitation 385 | with beautiful voices, after which the qāḍī rose and recited an elegy on the dead girl and a panegyric on the Sultan. As his name was mentioned the whole assembly rose to their feet and did homage, then sat down again and the qāḍī pronounced a beautiful invocation. After this the chamberlain and his companions took barrels of rose-water and sprinkled it over those present. They then went round with cups of sherbet made of candy, after which they distributed betel to them, then eleven robes of honour were brought for me and my companions.

The chamberlain then mounted and we rode with him to the Sultan's palace, where we did homage to the throne, according to the custom, and I returned to my house. I had scarcely arrived when there came from the palace of the Makhdūma Jahān so much food as filled my house and my companions' houses. After they had all eaten and the poor had eaten also, there were left over quantities of bread-cakes and sweetmeats and candy, the remains of which lasted for 386 several days. All this was done | by the Sultan's orders.

Some days later the eunuchs from the palace of the Makhdūma Jahān brought a *dūla*, that is a litter in which women are carried, though men also use it for journeys, resembling a couch.[12] The roof of the litter is made of braids of silk or cotton and on top of these there is a curved piece of wood like that on the top of parasols in our country, made of curved Indian bamboo.[13] It is carried by eight men in two lots of four, who rest and carry in turn. These *dūlas* in India are like the donkeys in Egypt, it is on them that most people go about on business; if a man has slaves of his own they carry him, and if he has no slaves he hires men to carry him. In the town there are always a number of these men standing in the bazaars and at the Sultan's gate and at the gates of other persons for hire. The *dūlas* of women are covered with 387 silk curtains, and it was a *dūla* of this kind | which the eunuchs brought from the palace of the Sultan's mother and in which they carried my slave-girl, who was the mother of

[12] The *dūla* is apparently the Indian *ḍolī* resembling a small palanquin. See p. 703, n. 166.

[13] This is the explanation of the Indian cane.

the daughter that died. I for my part sent with her a Turkish slave-girl as a gift. The girl that was the mother of the daughter stayed with them for a night and came back the next day after they had given her a thousand silver dinars, and bracelets of gold set with jewels and a crescent of gold also set with jewels, and a linen chemise embroidered with gold and a silk robe gilded and a chest full of clothing. When she brought all of this I gave it to my companions and to the merchants to whom I was indebted, in order to protect myself and to guard my honour, because the intelligencers were sending reports to the Sultan about everything that concerned me. |

Account of the generosity shown to me by the Sultan and the vizier during the Sultan's absence from the capital. While I was waiting, the Sultan gave orders to assign to me such a number of villages as would produce a revenue of 5,000 dinars a year. The vizier and the officers of the administration assigned them to me accordingly, and I went out to visit them. One was a village called Badalī, another a village called Basahī, and half of a village called Balara.[14] These villages were at a distance of sixteen *kurūhs* that is to say miles, in a *ṣadī* known as the *ṣadī* of Hind-But, the *ṣadī* being in their usage a group of a hundred villages. The territories of the city [also] are divided into hundreds, each hundred of which has a *jawṭarī*,[15] that is to say a shaikh, from among the infidels of those lands, and a *mutaṣarrif*, who is the person who collects the revenues. 388

There had arrived at that | time some captives taken from the infidels and the vizier sent me ten girls from among them. I gave the man who brought them one of them—he was not at all pleased with that—and my companions took three young ones amongst them; as for the rest I do not know what happened to them. Female captives there are very cheap because they are dirty and do not know civilized ways. Even the educated ones are cheap, so that no one there needs to buy captives. The infidels in the land of India inhabit a territory which is not geographically separated from that of 389

[14] These villages are about sixteen miles north of Delhi in the hundred of Hind But. The *ṣadī* is written as *hindīyat* by error.

[15] *Al-Jawṭarī* is the Hindī *chowdhrī*.

the Muslims, and their lands are contiguous, but though the Muslims have the upper hand over them yet the infidels maintain themselves in inaccessible mountains and rugged places, and they have forests of reeds, and as their reeds are not hollow but of large growth and are interlaced with one another, fire makes no impression on them and they are of great strength. The infidels live in these forests which are for them as good as city walls, and inside them they have their cattle and grain and supplies of water collected from the rains, so that they cannot be overcome except by strong
390 armies | of men who go into those forests and cut down those reeds with instruments made for the purpose.

Account of the festival which I attended during the Sultan's absence. The feast of the fast-breaking now approached, and the Sultan had not yet returned to the capital. On the day of the festival the khaṭīb mounted an elephant, on whose back there had been constructed for him a kind of divan, with four banners planted at its four corners. The khaṭīb was dressed in livery of black. The muezzins also rode on elephants, chanting *Allāhu akbar* in front of him, and the jurists and judges of the town were mounted, each one of them carrying with him an alms to bestow as he came out of the city to go to the *muṣallā*. Over the *muṣallā* there was spread a marquee of cotton, and it was furnished with carpets. The people assembled there reciting the praises of God the Most High,
391 and when the khaṭīb had led them in prayer | and delivered the address, they returned to their dwellings. We returned to the Sultan's palace where food was served, attended by the 'kings', the amīrs, and the 'honourables' (that is to say, the foreigners) and after they had eaten they withdrew.

Account of the Sultan's arrival and our meeting with him. On the fourth of Shawwāl [8th June 1334] the Sultan alighted at a castle called Tilbat, seven miles from the capital, and the vizier ordered us to go out to him. We set out, each man with his present of horses, camels, fruits of Khurāsān, Egyptian swords, mamlūks, and sheep brought from the land of the Turks, and came to the gate of the castle where all the newcomers were assembled. They were then introduced before the Sultan in order of precedence and were given robes of
392 linen, embroidered | in gold. When my turn came I entered

and found the Sultan seated on a chair. At first I took him to be one of the chamberlains until I saw him with the 'king' of the royal intimates, Nāṣir al-Dīn al-Kāfī of Harāt, whom I had come to know during the Sultan's absence. The chamberlain made obeisance and I did so too, then the amīr Ḥājib, who was the son of the Sultan's uncle named Fīrūz, came forward to meet me and I made obeisance a second time along with him. After this the 'king' of the intimate courtiers said to me '*Bismillāh,* Mawlānā Badr al-Dīn', for in India they used to call me Badr al-Dīn, and *mawlānā* [Our Master] is a title given to all scholars. I approached the Sultan, who took my hand and shook it, and continuing to hold it addressed me most affably, saying in Persian 'This is a blessing; your arrival is blessed; be at ease, I shall be compassionate to you and give you such favours that your fellow-countrymen will hear of it | and come to join you.' Then he asked me where I came from and I said to him 'From the land of the Maghrib'. He said to me 'The land of 'Abd al-Mu'min?' and I said 'Yes'. Every time he said any encouraging word to me I kissed his hand, until I had kissed it seven times, and after he had given me a robe of honour I withdrew. 393

All the persons present then assembled and a meal was served to them. At the head of them were placed the Grand Qāḍī Ṣadr al-Jahān Nāṣir al-Dīn of Khwārizm, who was one of the most eminent of jurists, the grand qāḍī of the mamlūks Ṣadr al-Jahān Kamāl al-Dīn al-Ghaznawī, 'Imad al-Mulk, the inspector of mamlūks, the malik Jalāl al-Dīn al-Kījī, and a number of the chamberlains and amīrs. Present also was Khudhāwand-Zāda Ghiyāth al-Dīn, the son of the paternal uncle of Khudhāwand-Zāda Qiwām al-Dīn the qāḍī of Tirmidh, who had arrived in our party. The Sultan used to hold him in high esteem and address him by the title of 'brother', and he in turn frequently made the journey from | his own country to visit the Sultan. 394

The new arrivals upon whom the robes of honour were bestowed on this occasion were: Khudhāwand-Zāda Qiwām al-Dīn and his three brothers, Ḍiyā al-Dīn, 'Imād al-Dīn and Burhān al-Dīn, as well as his sister's son Amīr Bakht, the son of the Sayyid Tāj al-Dīn (his grandfather, Wajīh al-Dīn, was the vizier of Khurāsān and his maternal uncle 'Alā al-Dīn

Amīr Hind was a vizier too), the amīr Hibatallāh son of al-Falakī al-Tabrīzī (his father was the deputy of the vizier in al-'Irāq and it was he who built the Falakīya College in Tabrīz),[16] Malik Karāy, one of the descendants of Bahrām Jūr,[17] the associate of Kisrā—he was an inhabitant of the mountain of Badhakhshān, from which the *balaksh* ruby and lapis lazuli are obtained—the amīr Mubārak-Shāh of 395 Samarqand; Arun Bughā of Bukhārā; Malik-Zāda | of Tirmidh; and Shihāb al-Dīn of Kāzarūn, the merchant who came from Tabrīz with the present for the Sultan and was robbed of it on the way.

Account of the Sultan's entry into his capital and the mounts which he ordered for us. On the day following that on which we went out to the Sultan each one of us was given a horse from the Sultan's stables, with a richly ornamented saddle and bridle, and when the Sultan mounted for the entry into his capital we rode in the front part of the procession together with [the Grand Qāḍī] Ṣadr al-Jahān. The elephants were decorated [and paraded] in front of the Sultan, with standards fixed on them and sixteen parasols, some of them gilded and some set with precious stones. Over the Sultan's head there was displayed a parasol of the same kind and in front of him was carried the *ghāshiya*, which is a saddlecloth studded with gems.[18] On some of the elephants there were mounted small military catapults, and when the Sultan 396 came | near the city parcels of gold and silver coins mixed together were thrown from these machines. The men on foot in front of the Sultan and the other persons present scrambled for the money, and they kept on scattering it until the procession reached the palace. There marched before him thousands of foot-soldiers, and wooden pavilions covered with silk fabrics were constructed with singing-girls in them, as we have already related.

Our entry into his presence and the gifts and offices which he conferred on us. On the Friday, the day after the entry of the Sultan, we came to the gate of the audience-hall and sat down in the galleries of the third door, since permission for us to

[16] See vol. II, p. 310.
[17] Bahrām Gūr is one of the heroes of the Persian epic.
[18] See p. 664 n. 33.

enter had not yet been given. After the chamberlain Shams al-Dīn al-Fūshanjī had come out and instructed | the clerks 397 to make a list of our names, he authorized them to allow us to enter together with some of our companions, and fixed the number to enter with me at eight, so we went in and they came with us. They then brought bags of money and *qabbān*, that is to say the balance, and after the Grand Qāḍī and the clerks had taken their seats they summoned those of the 'honourables' (that is to say foreigners) who were at the door, and assigned to each man his share of those moneybags, of which I got 5,000 dinars. The total amount of the money was 100,000 dinars, which the Sultan's mother had distributed as alms on the arrival of her son, and we retired for that day.

Afterwards the Sultan used to summon us to eat in his presence and would enquire how we fared and address us most affably. He said to us one day 'You have honoured us by your coming and we cannot sufficiently reward you. The elder amongst you is in the place of my father, the man of mature age is my brother, | and the young man like my son. 398 There is in my kingdom nothing greater than this city of mine and I give it to you,' whereupon we thanked him and invoked blessings upon him. Later on he assigned us stipends giving me twelve thousand dinars a year, and added two villages to the three he had already commanded for me, one of them the village of Jawza, and the other the village of Malikpūr.[19]

One day he sent Khudhāwand-Zāda Ghiyāth al-Dīn and Quṭb al-Mulk, the governor of Sind, to us to say, 'The Master of the World says to you "Whoever amongst you is capable of undertaking the function of vizier or secretary or commander or judge or professor or shaikh, I shall appoint to that office" '. Everyone was silent at first, for what they were wanting was to gain riches and return to their countries. Amīr Bakht, son of the sayyid Tāj al-Dīn, of whom mention has been made above, spoke up and said 'As for | the office of vizier, it is my 399 inheritance, and the duty of secretary is my occupation, but I know nothing of the other functions'. Hibatallāh ibn al-Falakī said the same. Then Khudhāwand-Zāda said to me in Arabic 'What do you say, *yā sayyidī*?' (The people of that

[19] Two villages in the vicinity of Delhi.

country never address an Arab except by the title of *sayyid*, and it is by this title that the Sultan himself addresses him, out of respect for the Arabs.) I replied 'Vizierships and secretaryships are not my business, but as to qāḍīs and shaikhs, that is my occupation, and the occupation of my fathers before me. And as for military commands, you know that the non-Arabs were converted to Islam only at the point of the sword of the Arabs'. The Sultan was pleased when he heard what I had said.

He was at the time in the Thousand Columns eating a meal, and he sent for us and we ate in his presence as he was eating. We then withdrew to the outside of the Thousand Columns and my companions sat down, while I retired on account of a boil which prevented me from sitting. When the 400 Sultan summoned us | a second time my companions presented themselves and made excuses to him on my behalf. I came back after the *'aṣr* prayer and I performed the sunset and night prayers in the audience-hall.

The chamberlain then came out and summoned us. Khudhāwand-Zāda Ḍiyā' al-Dīn, the eldest of the brothers whom we have mentioned, went in and the Sultan appointed him *amīr-dād*, who is one of the great amīrs. He had a seat in the qāḍī's tribunal, and if anyone had a claim against an amīr or man of rank he summoned him before him. The Sultan fixed his stipend for this office at 50,000 dinars a year and assigned to him a number of manors[20] whose revenues came to that amount. He also ordered him to be given 50,000 dinars forthwith and placed on him a silk robe of honour with gold embroidery of the kind called *ṣūrat al-shīr*, which means 'picture of a lion' because it has on its breast and its back the 401 figure of a lion. Inside the robe there was sewn a tag | showing the amount of gold used in its embroidering. He also ordered him to be given a horse of the first class, for the horses with them are of four classes, and their saddles are like those of the Egyptians, and they cover the greater part of them with silver-gilt.

The next to enter was Amīr Bakht, and the Sultan ordered him to sit alongside the vizier on his couch and to examine the accounts of the government departments. He fixed for

[20] The word for manors is *majāshir* which is used in N. Africa for villages.

him a stipend of 40,000 dinars a year, assigning him villages which yielded that amount of revenue, and gave him 40,000 [dinars] on the spot and a horse with full equipment, and bestowed on him a robe of honour like the one described above, and he was given the title of Sharaf al-Mulk. The next to enter was Hibatallāh ibn al-Falakī. The Sultan appointed him *rasūldār*, which means the chamberlain[21] for missions, and assigned him a stipend of 24,000 dinars a year, giving him villages whose revenues would produce that sum, along with 24,000 | dinars on the spot, a horse with full equipment 402 and a robe of honour, and he assigned as his title Bahā al-Mulk.

Then I went in and found the Sultan on the terrace of the palace with his back leaning on the [royal] couch, the vizier Khwāja Jahān before him, and the 'great king' Qabūla standing there upright. When I saluted him the 'great king' said to me 'Do homage, for the Master of the World has appointed you qāḍī of the royal city of Dihlī and has fixed your stipend at 12,000 dinars a year, and assigned to you villages to that amount, and commanded for you 12,000 dinars in cash, which you shall draw from the treasury tomorrow (if God will), and has given you a horse with its saddle and bridle and has ordered you to be invested with a *maḥārībī* robe of honour,' that is, a robe which has on its breast and on its back the figure of a mihrāb. So I did homage and when he had taken me by the hand and presented me before the Sultan, the Sultan said to me | 'Do not think that 403 the office of qāḍī of Dihlī is one of the minor functions; it is the highest of functions in our estimation.' I understood what he said though I could not speak [in Persian] fluently, but the Sultan understood Arabic although he could not speak it fluently, so I said to him 'O Master, I belong to the school of Mālik and these people are Ḥanafīs, and I do not know the language.' He replied 'I have appointed Bahā al-Dīn al-Multānī and Kamāl al-Dīn al-Bijanawrī to be your substitutes; they will be guided by your advice and you will be the one who signs all the documents, for you are in the place of a son to us,' to which I replied 'Nay, but your slave and your

[21] One manuscript reads *ṣāḥib* which means the officer responsible for receiving messages.

servant.' He said to me in Arabic with humility and friendly kindness 'No, but you are our lord and master,' then he said to Sharaf al-Mulk Amīr Bakht 'If the stipend which I have fixed for him is not enough for him, for he is very prodigal in spending, I shall give him a hospice, if he is able to look after | 404 the poor brethren.' Then he said 'Say this to him in Arabic' for he thought that he [Amīr Bakht] spoke Arabic well, but it was not the case, and when the Sultan realised that he said to him *Biraw wa-yakjā bikhuṣbī wa-ān ḥikāyah bar ū bigū'ī wa-tafhīm kunī tā fardā in shā'allāh pīsh man biyā'ī jawābi ū bigū'ī*, which means 'Go away for tonight and sleep in the same room; tell him the meaning of what I said just now and come to me in the morning, if God will, and tell me his answer.'

Thereupon we retired, and as this was in the first third of the night, after the beating of retreat (it being the custom with them that when it is beaten no person goes out), we waited for the vizier until he came out and went out in his company. We found the gates of Dihlī closed and therefore spent the night at the house of the sayyid Abu'l-Ḥasan al-'Ibādī of 'Irāq in the lane called Sarāpūr-Khān. This 405 shaikh used | to trade with the Sultan's money and to buy weapons and goods for him in 'Irāq and Khurāsān. On the following day the Sultan sent for us and we took possession of the moneys, horses and robes of honour. Each one of us took the sack containing the money, put it on his shoulder, and we came like this into the Sultan's presence and did homage. When the horses were brought we kissed their hoofs after some rags of cloth had been put over them, and then led them ourselves to the gate of the Sultan's palace, where we mounted them. All this ceremony is customary with them, and after it we withdrew. The Sultan commanded for my companions 2,000 dinars and ten robes of honour, but he gave nothing to the companions of any of the others, for my companions made a good impression on the Sultan by their appearance and won his admiration and they did homage before him and he thanked them.|

406 *Account of a second gift which he ordered to be given to me and of its suspension for some time.* One day I was in the audience-hall some time after my appointment as a qāḍī and the

Sultan's gift to me. As I was sitting under a tree there with Mawlānā Nāṣir al-Dīn of Tirmidh, the learned preacher, beside me, one of the chamberlains came up and summoned Mawlānā Nāṣir al-Dīn. He went into the presence of the Sultan, who bestowed a robe of honour upon him and gave him a Korān with a jewelled binding. Afterwards one of the chamberlains came to me and said 'Give me something, and I shall get for you a *khaṭṭi-khurd* for 12,000 dinars which the Master of the World has ordered to be paid to you.' I did not believe him, thinking that he was playing a trick on me, but when he insisted on what he said one of my companions said 'I shall give him something.' So he gave him two or three dinars, and he came back with a *khaṭṭi-khurd,* that is the minor certificate, inscribed with the chamberlain's notification to the effect that 'The Master of the World has given orders that there shall be given from the abounding treasury | so much to so-and-so on the notification of such and such a person,' that is to say on his certification of it. 407

After the certifying official has written his name this authority for payment is signed by three of the amīrs, namely the Great Khān Quṭlū-Khān, the Sultan's preceptor, the *kharīṭadār,* who is the keeper of the portfolio of paper and pens, and the amīr Nukbiya the *dawādār,* i.e. keeper of the inkhorn. When each one of these has appended his signature, the document is taken to the dīwān of the vizier, where the clerks of the dīwān make a copy of it for their records, then it is registered in the dīwān of the inspector of finances, and after that registered again in the dīwān of supervision, then there is written the *parwāna,* that is the order from the vizier to the treasurer to make payment, after which the treasurer registers it in his dīwān, and he writes every day a summary report showing the amount of money the Sultan has ordered to be paid that day and presents it to him. If the Sultan wishes payment to be expedited to anyone he gives orders to that effect, | and those in whose cases he wishes payment to be delayed he suspends, but payment of that sum is always made even if a long time after. These twelve thousand dinars were in fact suspended for six months, after which I received them along with other moneys, as will be related. It is their custom that when the Sultan gives orders for a grant of 408 money to any person a tenth is deducted from it, so that a person in whose favour an order has been made, for instance, for 100,000 is given 90,000, or for 10,000 is given 9,000.

Account of my creditors' demand for payment of my debt to them, of my panegyric addressed to the Sultan, of his order for the acquittal of my debt, and the suspension of that for some time. As I have already mentioned, I had borrowed from the merchants a sum of money for my expenses on my journey, for the present which I had furnished to the Sultan, and what I spent in staying [at Dihlī]. When they were about to set 409 out for | their own lands they pressed me for payment of their loans, so I wrote a long ode in praise of the Sultan, beginning as follows:

Commander of the Faithful, lord revered,
  To thee we come, through deserts toward thee hasting.
A pilgrim I, thy glory's shrine to visit,
  A refuge meet for sanctuary thy dwelling.
Had majesty a rank above the sun,
  Fit pattern wert thou for its most excelling.
Thou art the Imam, unique and glorious, ever
  Thy words infallibly with deeds investing.
I am in need, thy bounty's overflow
  My hope, and by thy greatness eased my questing.
Shall I declare it—or thy blush suffice?
  —To say 'thy bounty's plash' were seemlier punning. |
410 Make speed to aid the votary to thy shrine,
  And pay his debt—the creditors are dunning.

I then presented it to him in person as he was sitting upon a chair; he placed it upon his knee and held one end of it in his hand, with the other end in my hand. Whenever I finished one line of it I said to the Grand Qāḍī Kamāl al-Dīn of Ghazna 'Explain its meaning to Khūnd-'Ālam' and he did so, to the Sultan's delight, for they are fond of Arabic poetry. When I came to the verse 'Make speed to aid the votary to thy shrine' he said '*Marḥama*' which means 'I have compassion upon you,' whereupon the chamberlains took me by the hand to conduct me to their ranks [in the audience hall] and that I should do homage, according to the custom. But the Sultan said 'Leave him until he finishes it,' so I finished it and did homage. Those present congratulated me on this; then I waited for a few days and wrote | a petition, which 411 they call *'arḍ-dāsht* and delivered it to Quṭb al-Mulk, the governor of Sind. He delivered it to the Sultan, who said to him 'Go to Khwāja Jahān and tell him that the man's debt is to be acquitted.' Quṭb al-Mulk therefore went to him and informed him of this, to which he replied 'Certainly', but this dragged on for some days, during which the Sultan ordered him to set out for Dawlat Ābād, and in the meantime the Sultan himself went on a hunting expedition. The vizier set out, and so I received none of this money until much later.

The reason for which the payment of this sum was suspended I shall now relate in detail. When my creditors were ready to travel I said to them 'When I go to the palace of the Sultan, "assail" me for your debt according to the custom of this country,' for I knew that when the Sultan learned of that he would pay them. Their custom is this; when anyone has lent money to a person under the Sultan's protection and is unable | to obtain payment of it, the creditor awaits the 412 debtor at the door of the palace, and when the debtor is on the point of entering he says to him '*Darūhai as-Sulṭān*[22] ["O enemy of the Sultan"], by the head of the Sultan you shall not enter until you have paid me what you owe.' The debtor may not leave his place after this until he pays him or obtains a delay from him.

It happened one day that the Sultan went out to visit his father's grave and alighted at a palace there. I said to my creditors 'This is your moment,' so when I was about to enter they waited for me at the gate of the palace and said to me '*Darūhai as-Sulṭān,* you shall not enter until you pay us what you owe.' The clerks at the gate sent a written report of this to the Sultan, whereupon the *ḥājib qiṣṣa,* Shams al-Dīn, who was one of the principal doctors of the law, came out and asked them why they had assailed me. When they replied that I was in debt to them, he returned to the Sultan with this information, and on receiving the Sultan's orders to ask

[22] The phrase 'Darūhai as-Sulṭān' is an exclamation uttered by a petitioner calling for redress by the Sultan. The term is commonly 'Dohāī', meaning 'justice' (*Hobson-Jobson*, s.v. Doai).

the merchants the size of the debt he asked them and they
413 said to him | 'Fifty-five thousand dinars'. The chamberlain returned to the Sultan and informed him of this, whereupon he ordered him to return to them and to say to them, 'The Master of the World says to you "The money is in my possession, and I shall give you justice; do not demand it of him".' He then commanded 'Imād al-Dīn al-Simnānī and Khudhāwand-Zāda Ghiyāth al-Dīn to sit in the Hall of the Thousand Columns to examine and verify the creditors' documents. They did so, the creditors brought their documents, and they went in to the Sultan and informed him that the accounts were in order, whereupon he laughed and said jestingly 'I know he is a qāḍī and has seen to his business with them.' He then commanded Khudhāwand-Zāda to issue that sum to me from the treasury, but he greedily demanded a bribe to do so and refused to write the *khaṭṭi-khurd*. I sent him two hundred tangas, but he returned them and would not accept that amount. One of his servants told me from
414 him that he demanded | five hundred tangas, but I refused to pay it and informed 'Amīd al-Mulk, the son of 'Imād al-Dīn al-Simnānī, about this and he informed his father of it. It came to the ears of the vizier, between whom and Khudhāwand-Zāda there was a feud, and he informed the Sultan of the matter, telling him at the same time many of the doings of Khudhāwand-Zāda. The Sultan, displeased with the latter, ordered him to be detained in the city saying 'Why has so-and-so given him this money? Suspend this order until it is known whether Khudhāwand-Zāda pays out anything when I have given it[23] or refuses to pay when I give it.' So it was for this reason that the payment of my debt was suspended.

Account of the Sultan's leaving for the hunt, of my going out with him, and of what I did on that occasion. When the Sultan went out to hunt I went out along with him without any delay, as I had already made ready all that was required, and
415 in accordance with the practice | of the people of India I had bought a *sarācha*, that is to say an *āfrāj*. Anyone there is at liberty to pitch a *sarācha*, and it is indispensable for all men of high rank. The Sultan's *sarācha* is distinguished by its red

[23] The reading is 'given it' although one manuscript reads 'forbidden it'.

colour, while the others are white embroidered with blue. I bought also the *ṣīwān*, which is the tent under which one shelters inside the *sarācha*; it is supported upon two stout poles, and the whole thing is carried on their shoulders by men called *kaiwānīya*.[24] It is the custom there for the traveller to hire the *kaiwānīya*, whom we have spoken of already, and also to hire men who furnish him with green fodder for the animals, because the Indians do not feed them with hay. He hires also *kahārs*,[25] that is those men who carry cooking utensils, as well as men to carry him in a *dūla*, the palanquin which we have already described, and to carry the palanquin itself when it is empty, and *farrāshes* whose business it is to erect the *sarācha* and to furnish it with carpets and to load up | the camels, and also *dawādawīya*, whose business it 416 is to walk ahead of him carrying torches at night. So I too hired all of these servants that I needed, and showed such vigour and energy that I left the city on the same day as the Sultan while the rest remained for two or three days after him.

After the *'aṣr* prayer on the day of his departure the Sultan mounted his elephant with the object of investigating how matters stood with regard to his officers, and of finding out who had been quick in leaving and who had delayed. He [first] took his seat outside the *sarācha* on a chair, and when I came up and saluted and took up my place on the right he sent to me the 'great king' Qabūla, the *sar-jāmadār* (it is he who whisks the flies away from him),[26] and commanded me to sit as a special mark of attention. Nobody sat down that day except me. After that | the elephant was brought and he 417 mounted it by a ladder placed against it, and the parasol was raised over his head. The principal officers rode along with him and he spent some time making a tour of inspection and then returned to the *sarācha*.

It is his custom when he rides that the amīrs also ride in squadrons, each amīr with his squadron, his standards, his drums, bugles and flutes, and this they call the *marātib* [ceremonial honours]. No one rides in front of the Sultan

[24] See p. 563 above.

[25] Hindi *kahār*, 'scullion', 'water-carrier'.

[26] *Sar-jāmadār* is the supervisor of the wardrobe (of the Sultan).

except the chamberlains, the musicians, the drummers, who carry small drums slung round their necks, and the men who play the flutes. On the Sultan's right there are about fifteen men and on his left the same number; amongst these are the Grand Qāḍī, the vizier, some of the principal amīrs and some of the 'honourables'. I myself was one of the group on his right. In front of the Sultan there are the foot-soldiers and guides, and behind him his standards, which are of silk with 418 gold embroidery, and drums upon camels; behind | these again are his mamlūks and his household familiars, and behind them the amīrs and the general body of troops, and no one knows where the halt will be made. When the Sultan passes by a place where he would like to encamp, he gives the order to halt and no one's *sarācha* is set up before his. After that, those persons who are responsible for the camping arrangements come and assign his place to each person. Meanwhile the Sultan encamps on the bank of a river or among trees and there is brought before him flesh of sheep, fattened fowls, cranes, and other kinds of game. The 'sons of the kings' present themselves, each of them carrying a spit in his hand, and they light a fire and roast these meats. A small *sarācha* is brought and set up for the Sultan; he takes his seat outside of it with those who are present of his intimate courtiers, and when the food is brought he invites anyone whom he wishes to eat with him.

One day when the Sultan was in his *sarācha* he enquired 419 who were outside. The sayyid Nāṣir | al-Dīn Muṭahhar al-Awharī, one of his familiars, said 'So-and-so, the Moroccan, who is very upset.' 'Why so?' asked the Sultan, and he replied 'Because of his debt, since his creditors are pressing for payment. The Master of the World had commanded the vizier to pay it, but he left before doing so. Would not the Master of the World order the creditors to wait until the vizier returns or else give orders for their claims to be met?' The 'king' Dawlat-Shāh, whom the Sultan used to address as 'Uncle', was present at this conversation and added 'O Master of the World, every day this man talks to us in Arabic, and I do not know what he is saying. Do you know, Sayyid Nāṣir al-Dīn?' He said this so that Nāṣir al-Dīn might repeat what he had said. Nāṣir al-Dīn answered 'He talks about the debt which he has contracted.' The Sultan said 'When we return to the capital, go yourself, O *Ūmār*[27] (that is, O Uncle), to the treasury and give him this money.' Khudhāwand-Zāda also was present | and said 'O Master of the World, he is very extravagant. I have seen him before, in our own land, at the court of the Sultan Ṭarmashīrīn.' After this conversation the Sultan invited me to his meal, I being in total ignorance of what had taken place. As I went out the sayyid Nāṣir al-Dīn said 'Thank the king Dawlat-Shāh,' and Dawlat-Shāh said to me 'Thank Khudhāwand-Zāda.' 420

On one of these days when we were out hunting with the Sultan, he mounted in the camp and took a road which led past my encampment, I myself being with him on the right and my companions in the escort. There were some tents belonging to me beside the *sarācha* and my companions halted at them and saluted the Sultan. He sent 'Imād al-Mulk and malik Dawlat-Shāh to ask who owned these tents and *sarācha*: they were told that they belonged to so-and-so and when they informed the Sultan of this he smiled. On the following day an order was issued that I should return to town | along with Nāṣir al-Dīn Muṭahhar al-Awharī and the son of the Qāḍī of Egypt and Malik Ṣabīḥ, and we were given robes of honour and returned to the capital. 421

Account of the camel which I presented to the Sultan.[28] In the course of these days the Sultan had asked me whether al-Malik al-Nāṣir rode camels. I replied 'Yes, he rides *mahārī* camels at the pilgrimage season, and they make the journey to Mecca from Cairo in ten days, but these camels are not like the camels in this country.' I told him that I had with me one of the *mahārī* camels and when I returned to the capital I sent for one of the Arabs of Egypt, who made for me a model in wax of the saddle used for riding on *mahārī* camels.[29] I showed this to a carpenter, who made the saddle very skilfully, and I covered it with blanket cloth and furnished it with stirrups. I placed on the camel a fine striped cloak and

[27] O Ūmār, translated by 'oh uncle', is not known. Mahdi Husain is inclined to read it as *audar*, which means father's brother. All the readings in the manuscripts are confused.

[28] See the reference in Chauvin, *Bibliographie*, VII, p. 19.

[29] The *mahārī* camels (plural of *mahrī*) are noted for their excellence for riding.

made for it a bridle of silk. I had with me a man from Yemen 422 who was very skilful in making | sweetmeats, and he prepared some which resembled dates and other objects. I sent the camel and the sweets to the Sultan and ordered the bearer to deliver them into the hand of malik Dawlat-Shāh, to whom I sent also a horse and two camels. When this reached him he went in to the Sultan and said 'O Master of the World, I have seen a wonder' and on the Sultan asking him what it was, said 'So-and-so has sent a camel carrying a saddle.' The Sultan said 'Bring it in', so the camel was led into the *sarācha*. The Sultan was delighted with it and said to my man 'Mount it'. So he mounted it and walked it about in front of him, and the Sultan ordered him to be given two hundred silver dinars and a robe of honour. When the man came back and told me about it I was full of joy, and I sent him two more camels after his return to the capital. |

423 *Account of the two camels which I presented to the Sultan, and of the sweetmeats, and of his order for the settlement of my debt and matters relating thereto.* When my man whom I had sent to conduct the camel came back to me and told me how it had been received, I had two camel-saddles made. The front and the back of each I had covered with silver-gilt plates and both of them covered with blanket cloth, and I made a head-rope ornamented with plaques of silver; for both of them also I made horse-cloths of *zardkhāna* lined with *kamkhā*, and for both camels I made anklets of silver. I prepared also eleven platters and filled them with sweetmeats, and covered each platter with a silk napkin.

When the Sultan came back from the hunt and took his seat, on the day after his arrival, in his place of public audience, I put in an early appearance and presented the camels to him, and on his orders they were exercised in front of him. As they were trotting the anklet of one of them flew 424 off, | and he said to Bahā al-Dīn ibn al-Falakī *Pāyal wardārī*, which means 'Pick up the anklet,' and he did so. Then the Sultan looked at the platters and said *Che dārī dar ān ṭabaqhā ḥalwā ast*, which means 'What have you got in those plates? Surely it is sweetmeats,' and I said to him 'Yes.' He then said to the doctor of the law and preacher Nāṣir al-Dīn of Tirmidh,

'I have never eaten nor ever seen such sweetmeats as those which he sent to us when we were in the camp.' After this he ordered that the platters should be taken to his private sittingroom, which was done, and when he rose to go to his sittingroom, he summoned me and ordered food to be brought and I ate.

He then asked me about a particular kind of the sweetmeats which I had sent him previously. I said to him 'O Master of the World, those sweetmeats were of many kinds and I do not know which kind you are asking about.' He said 'Bring those plates' (for they call a platter | a plate), and 425 when they brought them and laid them before him and removed their covers, he said 'It was about this one that I asked' and took the dish in which it was. I said to him 'This kind is called *al-muqarraṣa*,' then he took another kind and said 'What is the name of this?' and I said to him 'These are the "judge's sweet-mouthfuls" '. Now there was present a merchant, one of the shaikhs of Baghdād, called al-Sāmarrī, who claimed to be descended from the house of al-'Abbās (God be pleased with him) and a wealthy man, whom the Sultan used to address as 'My father'. This man was jealous of me, and wishing to humiliate me said 'These are not the "judge's sweet-mouthfuls." but those are,' and he took a piece of the kind which is called *jild al-faras*. There was opposite him the 'king' of the intimate courtiers Nāṣir al-Dīn al-Kāfī of Harāt, who used often to jest with this shaikh in the Sultan's presence, and he said to him 'O khōja, you lie and it is the qāḍī who speaks the truth.' | The Sultan said to him 426 'How so?' He replied 'O Master of the World, he is the qāḍī and these are his sweet mouthfuls, for he brought them' and the Sultan laughed and said 'You are right.'

At the end of the meal the sweetmeats were eaten; after that the barley-water was drunk and we took betel and withdrew. A few moments later the treasurer came to me and said 'Send your friends to receive the money,' so I sent them, and on returning to my house after the sunset prayer found the money there in three sacks, containing 6,233 tangas, this being the balance of the fifty-five thousand which was the amount of my debt, together with the twelve thousand which the Sultan had previously commanded to be paid to me, less one-tenth according to their custom. The exchange value of the tanga is two and a half dinars in the gold coinage of the Maghrib. |

427 *The Sultan's departure and command to me to remain in the capital.* On the 9th of First Jumādā[30] the Sultan went out with the design of proceeding to al-Ma'bar and engaging the rebel leader in that province. I had settled with my creditors and was all prepared to accompany the expedition, having paid nine months' wages to the kahārs, the farrāshes, the kaiwāns and the dawādīs, of whom I have already spoken. At that moment a command was issued that I should remain behind with some others, and the chamberlain took written acknowledgements of the order from us as proof that he had communicated it. This is their custom as a precaution against the denial of receipt by the person so notified. The Sultan ordered that I should be given 6,000 dinars and that the son of the Qāḍī of Cairo should receive 10,000 and similar amounts should be paid to all of the 'honourables' who remained behind; as for the natives they were not given anything. The 428 Sultan also commanded me to take charge of | the mausoleum of Sultan Quṭb al-Dīn, whose history has been related above. The Sultan used to hold his tomb in great respect because he had been one of his servitors. I have seen him on coming to his grave take Quṭb al-Dīn's sandal, kiss it and place it on his head, for it is their custom to put the sandals of the dead man on a cushion beside his grave. Whenever he came to the grave he would do homage to it, as he used to do homage in Quṭb al-Dīn's lifetime, and he held Quṭb al-Dīn's wife in great respect and used to address her as his sister. He gave her a place amongst the women of his own household and married her later on to the son of the Qāḍī of Cairo and on her account he showed him special favour; he used also to go to visit her every Friday.

When the Sultan went out he sent for us to bid us farewell. The son of the Qāḍī of Cairo stood up and said 'I shall not bid farewell to nor be separated from the Master of the World.' This brought him good fortune and the Sultan said to him 'Go and make ready for the journey.' I came forward after to 429 say farewell, | and I was pleased to be staying behind, although

[30] Equivalent to 21 October 1341.

the consequences were not happy. He said 'What requests have you?' so I took out a piece of paper with six petitions, but he said to me 'Speak with your own tongue.' I said to him 'The Master of the World has commanded me to act as a qāḍī but I have not yet sat for that purpose; and I do not desire to have nothing but the honour of the qāḍīship,' whereupon he commanded me to sit as a judge and that two substitutes should sit with me. Then he said to me 'Well?' and I said 'The Mausoleum of Sultan Quṭb al-Dīn, what shall I do about it, for I have already given appointments in connection with it to four hundred and sixty persons, and the income from its endowments does not cover their wages and their food?' He said to the vizier *Panjāh Hazār*, which means '50,000', and then added 'You must have an anticipatory crop.' This means 'Give him a hundred thousand maunds of the corn produce (that is to say wheat and rice) to be expended during | this year until the crops of the endowment for the tomb come in.' The maund is twenty pounds Barbary weight. 430

He then said to me 'And what more'? so I replied 'My friends have been imprisoned on account of the villages which you gave me, for I have exchanged them for other revenues; but the officials of the dīwān have demanded from me either to pay what I have received from them or to present the order of the Master of the World to be dispensed from that.' He said 'How much did you receive from them?' I replied 'Five thousand dinars'. He said 'They are a gift to you.' I then said to him 'And my house which you have ordered for me as my residence is in need of repairs.' He said to the vizier *'Imārat kunīd*, that is to say 'Have it repaired,' and went on to say to me *Dīgar namānad*, which means 'Have you anything more to say?' and I said to him 'No'. He then said to me *Waṣīyat dīgar hast*, which means 'There is another recommendation, and that is that you incur no debts and so avoid being pressed for payment, for you will not find anyone | to bring me news of them. Regulate your expenses according to what I have given you, as God has said [in the Korān] *Keep not thy hand bound to thy neck, neither open it to fullest extent*, and again *Eat and drink, and be not prodigal*, and again *And those who, when they spend, neither incline to excess nor fall short through niggardliness, but between these* 431 *there is an upright mean.*'[31] I desired to kiss his foot, but he prevented me and held back my head with his hand, so I kissed that and retired.

I returned to the capital and busied myself with repairing my house; on this I spent four thousand dinars, of which I received from the dīwān six hundred and paid the rest myself. I also built a mosque opposite my house, and occupied myself with the dispositions for the mausoleum of the Sultan Quṭb al-Dīn. The Sultan had ordered that a dome should be built 432 over it to the height of 100 cubits, exceeding by | 20 cubits the height of the dome built over [the tomb of] Qāzān, the king of al-'Irāq. He had given orders also that thirty villages were to be purchased to constitute an endowment for it, and he placed them in my hands on the understanding that I should enjoy the tenth part of their revenue according to custom.

Account of the ceremonial which I established for the mausoleum. It is the custom for the people of India to observe in regard to their dead a ceremonial similar to that observed in their lifetime. Elephants fully caparisoned are brought and picketed at the gate of the tomb chamber. I organised everything in this tomb-chamber in accordance with that custom and enrolled of reciters of the Korān, whom they call *khatmīyūn*, a hundred and fifty, of theological students eighty, of assistant teachers, whom they call *mukarrirūn*, eight, one professor, of the ṣūfīs eighty, and the imām, the muezzins, reciters who possessed fine voices, rhapsodists, | 433 and clerks to note the name of absentees, and announcers of names. All these people are known in that country by the designation of *arbāb*.

I appointed also another category of persons known as the *ḥāshiya*: these are the *farrāshes*, cooks, *dawādīs*, *ābdārīs* (who are water carriers), *shurbadārīs* (who serve the drink called shurba), *tanbūldārīs* (who present the betel), *silaḥdārīs*, *naizadārīs*, *shaṭradārīs*, *ṭishtdārīs*, chamberlains and *naqībs*. The total number of these was four hundred and sixty. The Sultan had fixed the daily issue of food there at twelve maunds of flour and a like quantity of meat. I saw that this amount was too small, and that the produce which the

[31] Qur'ān, xvii, 31; vii, 29, xxv, 67.

Sultan had put at my disposal was plentiful, and consequently I dispensed every day thirty-five maunds of flour and thirty-five of meat, together with the usual subsidiaries of sugar, candy, ghee and betel, | in feeding not only the salaried 434 employees but also visitors and travellers. The famine at that time was severe, but the population was relieved by this food, and the news of it spread far and wide. The 'king' Ṣabīḥ, having gone to join the Sultan at Dawlat Ābād, was asked by him for news of the doings of the people [in Dihlī] and answered 'If there were in Dihlī two such men as so-and-so there would be no complaints of famine.' The Sultan was pleased at this and sent me a robe of honour from his own wardrobe.

I used to prepare on the occasion of the major festivals, namely the two feasts [of the fast-breaking and of the pilgrimage], the noble birthday [of the Prophet Muḥammad], the day of *'Āshūrā*, the night of mid-Sha'bān, and the anniversary of the death of Sultan Quṭb al-Dīn, a hundred maunds of flour and the same of meat. This was eaten by the poor brethren and the destitute; as for the dignitaries there is placed before each one of them a portion for his own use and we shall now describe their custom in this matter. |

Description of their custom in serving food at banquets. In the 435 land of India and in the land of Sarā[32] it is their custom at a feast, when the guests finish eating, to place in front of each of the sharīfs, doctors of the law, shaikhs, and qāḍīs a container shaped like a cradle, with four legs and the upper part woven of palm-fibre. On this table are set thin cakes of bread, a roasted sheep, four bread-cakes kneaded with ghee and filled with marzipan then covered with four pieces of sweetmeats in the shape of bricks, also two small saucers made of leather containing sweetmeats and *samūsak*. The whole container is covered over with a piece of new cotton. Those who are of a rank below those whom we have mentioned have set before them the half of a sheep, which they call *zallah*, and half the amounts | of the other dishes that we 436 have mentioned. Those who are of lower rank than these again have set before them the equivalent of a quarter of all this. Each person's servants remove and take away what is

[32] Referring to the land of Sarā, i.e. the capital of the Khan of Qipchaq.

set before him. The first time that I saw them practising this custom was in the city of Sarā, the capital of Sultan Ūzbak, when I prevented my men from taking it away since I was unfamiliar with the custom. In the same way also they send some of the meats of the banquets to the houses of the chief personages.

Account of my excursion to Hazār Amrūhā. The vizier had delivered to me 10,000 maunds of the grain which had been commanded for me and had given me an assignation for the rest on Hazār Amrūhā. The controller of revenues in this place was 'Azīz al-Khammār, and its commandant was Shams al-Dīn of Badhakhshān. I sent my men, who collected 437 part of the assignation but complained of | the fraudulence of 'Azīz al-Khammār, so I went out myself in order to obtain the balance. From Dihlī to this region it is a three days' journey and this happened during the period of the rains. I took out with me about thirty of my companions and added to my company two brothers, accomplished singers, who used to sing to me on the way. When we reached the town of Bijnaur, I found there three other brothers, singers also, so I took them with me as well and they and the first two used to sing to me in turn.

We then came to Amrūhā, which is a small and pretty town, and its officials came out to meet me, followed by its qāḍī, the sharīf Amīr 'Alī and the shaikh of its hospice, who gave me jointly a fine banquet. 'Azīz al-Khammār was at a place called Afghān-pūr on the river Sarū; the river was between us and him and there was no ferry, but we took our 438 baggage on a raft | which we constructed of planks and vegetable matter, and crossed on the following day. Najīb, the brother of 'Azīz, came with a number of his companions and pitched a *sarācha* for us, and later on his brother the tax-collector came to visit me. He had made a name for oppressiveness; the villages which were in his district were 1,500 in number and their revenue amounted to sixty laks in a year,[33] of which he enjoyed one twentieth.

A surprising thing about the river beside which we encamped is that no person drinks from it during the rainy season and no animal is watered at it. We stayed on its banks

[33] The revenue amounted to sixty lakhs of silver tankas in the year.

for three nights and not one of us took a cupful of water from it, indeed we scarcely approached it.[34] The reason is that it comes down from the mountains of Qarāchīl, in which there are gold mines, and passes over poisonous grasses,[35] so that whoever drinks from it dies. These mountains form a continuous chain for a distance of three | months' journey, and 439 from them one descends to the land of Tubbat, where the muskdeer are found. We have previously related the disaster that befel the army of the Muslims in these mountains. It was in this place that I was visited by a company of Ḥaidarī brethren who held a musical recital and lit fires and walked through them without any injury to themselves. We have already given an account of this.[36]

A dispute had arisen between Shams al-Dīn of Badhakhshān, the commander of this district, and its finance director 'Azīz al-Khammār, and Shams al-Dīn had brought up troops to engage the latter, who defended himself against him in his house. When the complaint of one of the parties reached the vizier in Dihlī he sent word to me and to the malik Shāh, commander of the mamlūks at Amrūhā (who were about 4,000 mamlūks belonging to the Sultan), and to Shihāb al-Dīn al-Rūmī to look into their affair and to send the one of them who was | in the wrong to the capital in chains. They 440 all assembled in my camp, when 'Azīz formulated a number of charges against Shams al-Dīn, amongst them that a subordinate of his called al-Riḍā al-Multānī had alighted at the house of the treasurer of the aforesaid 'Azīz, had drunk wine in it, and stolen 5,000 dinars of the moneys which were held by the treasurer. I interrogated al-Riḍā on this subject and he said to me 'I have never drunk wine since I left Multān, which is eight years ago.' I said to him 'Then you did drink it in Multān?,' and when he said 'Yes' I ordered him to be given eighty lashes and imprisoned him on the charge preferred, because of the presumptive evidence against him.

I returned from Amrūhā after an absence from Dihlī of

[34] The three manuscripts all read 'we scarcely knew of it' but the correct reading is evidently 'approached it'.

[35] There are no gold mines in the Himalayas and if there are poisonous grasses they must be due to another cause.

[36] See vol. II, pp. 274–5.

about two months. Every day I used to kill an ox for my companions, and I left them behind to bring the grain which had been assigned to me upon 'Azīz and for the transport of which he was responsible. Consequently he distributed among the population of the villages which were under his jurisdic-
441 tion 30,000 maunds to be transported by them on | 3,000 oxen. The people of India use no animals but oxen as beasts of burden and it is on them that they load their baggage on journeys. To ride asses is regarded by them as a terrible disgrace; their asses are small in body and called *lāsha*[37] and when they wish to expose anyone after he has been beaten they mount him on an ass.

Account of a generous action by one of my friends. The Sayyid Nāṣir al-Dīn al-Awharī had left 1,060 tangas with me when he left, and I had spent them. When I returned to Dihlī I found that he had given a credit on this sum to Khudhāwand-Zāda Qiwām al-Dīn, who had arrived as deputy for the vizier. I was ashamed to tell him that I had spent the money and after giving him about a third of it I stayed in my house for some days and it was given out that I was ill. Nāṣir al-Dīn al-Khwārizmī, Ṣadr al-Jahān, came to
442 visit me and on | seeing me said 'You do not seem to me to be ill.' I said to him 'I am ill at heart,' and when he asked me to explain what I meant I said to him 'Send your deputy, the Shaikh al-Islām, to me and I shall tell him the whole story.' He did so and when I told the Shaikh and he returned to the Ṣadr with the story, he sent me a thousand silver dinars, although I already owed him another thousand. I was then asked for the balance of the money and I said to myself 'No one can get me out of this but Ṣadr al-Jahān' (that is, the same person), because he is very wealthy. So I sent him a saddled horse whose value together with the value of its saddle was 1,600 dinars, a second horse whose value with that of its saddle was 800 dinars, two mules worth 1,200 dinars, a silver quiver and two swords with scabbards veneered with silver, and I said to him 'Estimate the value of all this and send me the money.' He took it all and fixed for
443 the whole of it a value of 3,000 | dinars and sent me a thousand, deducting the 2,000 which I owed him. I felt sore

[37] A Persian term for a carcase.

at this and fell ill of a fever, but I said to myself 'If I complain of this to the vizier I shall disgrace myself'; so I took five horses, two slave girls and two mamlūks, and sent them all to the king Mughīth al-Dīn Muḥammad, son of the 'king of kings' 'Imād al-Dīn al-Simnānī, who was a young man. He returned them to me at the same time, sending me two hundred tangas 'with his excuses',[38] and I was able to get clear of that debt—what a difference between the action of one Muḥammad and the other!

My departure for the maḥalla of the Sultan. The Sultan, after setting out on the expedition to the land of al-Ma'bar, had reached Tiling when a epidemic broke out among his troops. Accordingly he returned to Dawlat Ābād and then marched to the river Gang, where he encamped and ordered his men to put up buildings. I went out during this time to join his *maḥalla*. It was at this time also that the events which we have related of the revolt | of 'Ain al-Mulk occurred 444 and I remained constantly with the Sultan during this period. He gave me some thoroughbred horses on distributing them to his courtiers and included me in the number of the latter. I was present with him at the battle against 'Ain al-Mulk and at his capture, and I crossed with him the river Gang and the river Sarū to visit the tomb of the warrior saint Sālār 'Ūd, all of which I have already related in detail, and I returned with him to Dihlī when he returned to it.

Account of the Sultan's intention to punish me and of my escape from this by the mercy of God. The cause of this was that I went one day to visit Shaikh Shihāb al-Dīn son of Shaikh al-Jām in the cave which he had dug for himself outside Dihlī.[39] My object was to see that cave, but when the Sultan seized him and asked his sons about those who used to visit him, they mentioned my name amongst those of others. Thereupon the Sultan gave orders that four of | his slaves 445 should remain constantly beside me in the audience-hall, and customarily when he takes this action with anyone it rarely happens that that person escapes. The day on which they began to guard me was a Friday and God Most High inspired me to recite His words *Sufficient for us is God and*

[38] For *aghzara* read *a'dhara* 'he excused himself'.
[39] See above p. 698.

excellent the Protector.[40] I recited them that day 33,000 times and passed the night in the audience-hall. I fasted five days on end, reciting the Korān from cover to cover each day, and tasting nothing but water. After five days I broke my fast and then continued to fast for another four days on end, and I was released after the execution of the Shaikh, praise be to God Most High.

Account of my withdrawal from the Sultan's service and leaving of the world. Sometime later I withdrew from the Sultan's service and attached myself to the shaikh and imām, the learned, devout, ascetic, humble-minded, pious Kamāl al-Dīn 'Abdallāh al-Ghārī, the unique and unequalled

446 personality of his age. | He was one of the saints and had performed many miracles, some of which that I saw with my own eyes I have already related on speaking of him previously.[41] I devoted myself to the service of this shaikh and gave my possessions to the poor brethren and the needy. The shaikh used to fast for ten days on end, and sometimes for twenty days, but when I wished to fast continuously he would check me and bid me not to overstrain myself in devotional exercise, saying to me 'He who breaks down from exhaustion has neither covered ground nor spared a mount.'[42] There seemed to me to be a certain sluggishness in me because of something which remained in my possession, so I rid myself of everything that I had, little or much, and I gave the clothes off my back to a mendicant and put on his clothes. I remained with this shaikh as a disciple for five months, the Sultan being at that time absent in the land of Sind. |

447 *Account of the Sultan's sending for me and my refusal to return to his service and my zeal in devotional exercises.* When the Sultan was informed of my leaving the world he summoned me, being at that time in Sīwasitān. I entered his presence dressed as a mendicant, and he spoke to me with the greatest kindness and solicitude, desiring me to return to his service. But I refused and asked him for permission to travel to the Ḥijāz, which he granted. I withdrew from him and lodged in a hospice known by the name of the malik Bashīr. This was in the last days of Second Jumādā of the year

[40] Qur'ān, iii, 167.
[41] See p. 627 above.
[42] From a saying of the Prophets.

forty-two.[43] I remained there engaged in devotional exercises during the month of Rajab and ten days of Sha'bān and at length was able to fast for five days in succession, after which I tasted a little rice without any seasoning. I used to recite the Korān every day and to keep vigils by night as God willed. Whenever | I ate food it was disagreeable to me and 448 when I discarded it I found relief. I remained in this state for forty days and then the Sultan sent for me again.

Account of his command to me to proceed to China on embassy. When I had completed forty days the Sultan sent me saddled horses, slave girls and boys, robes and a sum of money, so I put on the robes and went to him. I had a quilted tunic of blue cotton which I wore during my retreat, and as I put it off and dressed in the Sultan's robes I upbraided myself. Ever after, when I looked at that tunic, I felt a light within me, and it remained in my possession until the infidels despoiled me of it on the sea. When I presented myself before the Sultan, he showed me greater favour than before, and said to me 'I have expressly sent for you to go as my ambassador to | the king of China, for I know your love of 449 travel and sightseeing'. He then provided me with everything I required, and appointed certain other persons to accompany me, as I shall relate presently.

[43] June 1341.

BIBLIOGRAPHY

Oriental texts and translations

'Anonym of Iskandar' (*Muntakhab al-Tawārīkh-i Mu'īnī*). Ed. J. Aubin. Tehran, 1336 Sh.

Athār al-Islām al-ta'rīkhīya fi 'l-Ittiḥād al-Sūfīyitī. Tashkent, undated.

BADAKHSHĪ, NŪR AL-DĪN JA'FAR. *Eine Lebensbeschreibung des Scheichs 'Alī-i Hamadānī*. Trans. J. K. Teufel. Leiden, 1962.

CHAO JU-KUA. *Chau Ju-Kua: or the Chinese and Arab Trade*. Trans. F. Hirth and W. W. Rockhill. St. Petersburg, 1912.

COMBE, E. *et al.* (edd.) *Répertoire chronologique d'épigraphie arabe*. Cairo, 1931–. In progress.

Ḥudūd al-'Ālam. Ed. and trans. V. Minorsky. London, 1937.

IBN AL-ATHĪR. *Ibn-el-Athiri Chronicon, quod perfectissimum inscribitur* (*Al-Kāmil*). Ed. C. J. Tornberg. Leiden, 1851–76. 14 vols.

IBN BAṬṬŪṬA. *Voyages*. Ed. and trans. C. Defrémery and B. R. Sanguinetti. *Paris*, 1853–8. 4 vols.

—*Travels in Asia and Africa*. Trans. and selected by H. A. R. Gibb. London. 1929.

—*Die Reise des Arabers Ibn Baṭūṭa durch Indien und China*. Ed. H. von Mžik. Hamburg, 1911.

—*The Reḥla of Ibn Baṭṭūṭa*. Trans. Mahdi Husain. Baroda, 1953.

IBN KHALDŪN. *Muqaddima*. Trans. F. Rosenthal. New York, 1958. 3 vols.

IBN QUTAIBA. *Kitāb al-Ma'ārif*. Göttingen, 1850.

IBN SA'D. *Kitāb al-Ṭabaqāt al-kabīr*. Leiden, 1905–28. 9 vols.

IBN TAGHRĪBIRDĪ. *Al-Nujūm al-Zāhira*. Cairo, 1929–50. 11 vols.

AL-IṢFAHĀNĪ, ABŪ NU'AIM. *Ḥilyat al-Awliyā'*. Cairo, 1936. 12 vols.

AL-JĀḤIẒ. *Kitāb al-Bukhalā'*. Ed. I. Hajirī. Cairo, 1948.

JĀMĪ. *Nafaḥāt al-Uns*. Tehran, 1957.

JUWAINĪ, 'AṬA-MALIK. *Ta'rīkh-i Jahāngushā*. Leiden and London, 1912–37. 3 vols.

—*History of the World-Conqueror*. Trans. J. A. Boyle, Manchester, 1958. 2 vols.

AL-KHAṬĪB AL-BAGHDĀDĪ. *Ta'rīkh Baghdād*. Cairo, 1931. 14 vols.

MUSTAWFĪ. *Nuzhat al-Qulūb*. Ed. and trans. G. Le Strange. London, 1919. 2 vols.

NAJM AL-DĪN AL-KUBRĀ. *Fawā'iḥ al-Jamal*. Ed. F. Meier. Wiesbaden, 1957.

AL-NASAWĪ. *Histoire du Sultan Djelāl ed-Din*. Tr. O. Houdas. Paris, 1895.

AL-SAM'ĀNĪ. *Kitāb al-Ansāb*. Leyden, London. 1912.

AL-SULAMĪ. *Ṭabaqāt al-Ṣūfīya*. Leiden, 1960.

Ta'rīkh-i Guzīda. Ed. E. G. Browne. Leiden and London, 1910. 2 vols.

Ta'rīkh Nāma-i Harāt. Calcutta, 1944.

The Thousand and One Nights. Trans. E. W. Lane. London, 1839–41. 3 vols.

YĀQŪT AL-RŪMĪ. *Mu'jam al-Buldān*. Ed. F. Wüstenfeld. Leipzig, 1866–73. 6 vols.

Books and articles in western languages

AHMAD, M. A. *The Early Turkish Empire of Delhi*. Lahore, 1949.

BARTHOLD, W. *Turkestan down to the Mongol Invasions*. London, 1928.

—*Histoire des Turcs d'Asie Centrale*. Paris, 1945.

BAYUR, HIKMET. 'Sultan Iletmiş'in adĭ hakkĭnda'. *Türk Tarih Kurumu, Belleten* (Ankara, 1950), XIV.

BRETSCHNEIDER, E. *Mediaeval Researches from Eastern Asiatic Sources*. London, 1910.

CAHEN, C. 'Un Traité d'Armurerie composé pour Saladin'. *Bulletin d'Etudes Orientales* (Beyrouth, 1948), XII.

—'Mouvements populaires et autonomisme urbain dans l'Asie musulmane du Moyen Age'. *Arabica* (Paris, 1959), VI.

CAILLÉ, J. *La Mosquée de Hassan à Rabāt*. Paris, 1954. 2 vols.

CHAUVIN, V. *Bibliographie des ouvrages arabes ou relatifs aux arabes*. Liége, 1892–1922. 12 parts.

DIEZ, E. *Kunst der islamischen Völker*. Berlin, 1917.

DOZY, R. *Supplément aux dictionnaires arabes*. Leiden, 1881. 2 vols.

—*Dictionnaire détaillé des noms des vêtements chez les arabes*. Amsterdam, 1945.

ENCYCLOPAEDIA OF ISLAM. Ed. M. Th. Houtsma (*et al.*) Leiden, 1913–38, 4 vols and Supplement. (Cited as *E.I.*).

—New Edition, ed. H. A. R. Gibb (*et al.*). Leiden, 1954–. (Cited as *E.I.*[2])

FANSHAWE, N. C. *Delhi: Past and Present*. London, 1902.

GIBB, H. A. R. and BOWEN, H. *Islamic Society and the West*, vol. I, part i, London, 1950.

HAIG, M. R. 'Ibn Baṭūṭa in Sindh'. *Journal of the Royal Asiatic Society* (London, 1887), new series, XIX.

HEARN, Sir GORDON. *The Seven Cities of Delhi*, second edition, Calcutta, 1928.

HINZ, W. *Islamische Masse und Gewichte*. Leiden, 1955.

HUGHES, T. P. *Dictionary of Islam*. London, 1885 (reprint, 1935).

HUMLUM, J. *La Géographie de l'Afghanistan*. Copenhagen, 1959.

HUSAIN, MAHDI. *The Rise and Fall of Muḥammad bin Tughluq*. London, 1938.

IMPERIAL GAZETTEER OF INDIA. Oxford, 1907–09. 26 vols.

KINDERMANN, H. *'Schiff' in Arabischen*. Zwickau, 1934.

KOMROFF, M. *Contemporaries of Marco Polo*. London, 1928.

LAL, K. S. *History of the Khaljis*. Allahabad, 1950.

LANE, E. W. *An Arabic-English Lexicon*. London, Edinburgh, 1863–1893. 8 parts.

LE STRANGE, G. *Lands of the Eastern Caliphate*. Cambridge, 1905.

MARÇAIS, G. *L'Architecture musulmane d'Occident*. Paris, 1954.

MARICQ, A. and WIET, G. *Le Minaret de Djam*. Paris, 1959.

MARQUART, J. *The Provincial Capitals of Ērānšahr*. Berlin, 1901.

MASSIGNON, L. *Lexique technique de la mystique musulmane*. Paris, 1922.

MORELAND, W. H. *The Agrarian System of Moslem India.* Cambridge, 1929.

MUSIL, ALOIS. *The Manners and Customs of the Rwala Bedouins.* New York, 1928.

NAZIM, M. *The Life and Times of Sultan Mahmud of Ghazna.* Cambridge, 1931.

PELLIOT, P. *Notes sur l'histoire de la Horde d'Or.* Paris, 1950.

PRASAD, ISHWARI. *History of the Qaraunah Turks.* vol. I. Allahabad, 1936.

PUGACHENKOVA, G. A. and REMPEL, L. E. *Vydayushchiyesya Pamyatniki Uzbekistana.* Tashkent, 1958.

RADLOFF, W. *Versuch eines Wörterbuches der Türkdialecte,* second ed., ed. O. Pritsak. The Hague, 1960. 4 vols.

RAVERTY, H. G. *Afghanistan and Part of Baluchistan.* London, 1880.

SACY, S. DE, *Chrestomathie arabe.* Paris, 1806.

SCHWARZ, P. *Iran im Mittelalter.* Leipzig–Berlin, 1896–1936. 9 parts.

SPULER, B. *Die Mongolen in Iran,* second edition. Berlin, 1955.

THOMAS, EDWARD. *Chronicles of the Pathan Kings of Delhi.* London, 1871.

TYAN, E. *Histoire de l'organisation judiciaire au pays d'Islam.* Beirut, 1943.

VERNADSKY, G. 'The Scope and Contents of Chingis Khan's Yasa'. *Harvard Journal of Asiatic Studies* (Cambridge, Mass., 1938), III.

WOLFE, N. H., in collaboration with Ahmad Ali Kohzad. *An Historical Guide to Kabul.* Kabul, 1965.

YULE, H. (ed.). *Cathay and the Way Thither.* London, Hakluyt Society, 1913–16. 4 vols.

—and BURNELL, A. C. *Hobson-Jobson.* London, 1886.

The Indian chronicles have been omitted from this bibliography; they criticise or eulogise Sultan Muḥammad Shāh and thereby change the picture of him given by Ibn Baṭṭūṭa.